Effective

PUBLICATIONS

Management

11   10   09   08   07   5   4   3   2   1

Published by Allworth Press
An imprint of Allworth Communications, Inc.
10 East 23rd Street, New York, NY 10010

Cover design by Derek Bacchus
Interior design and typography by SR Desktop Services, Ridge, NY

ISBN-13: 978-1-58115-486-3
ISBN-10: 1-58115-486-0

Library of Congress Cataloging-in-Publication Data
    Lips, Cathy Connor.
    Effective publications management : keeping print communications on time, on budget, on message / Cathy Connor Lips.
        p.   cm.
    Includes index.
    ISBN-13: 978-1-58115-486-3
    ISBN-10: 1-58115-486-0
    1. Business communication.   2. Publications—Management.   I. Title.

HF5718.L564   2007
659.2—dc22

                                    2007006844

Effective

PUBLICATIONS

Management

KEEPING PRINT COMMUNICATIONS ON TIME, ON BUDGET, ON MESSAGE

Cathy Connor Lips

ALLWORTH PRESS
NEW YORK

Contents

Foreword

Like most designers my age (I'm in my 70s), after graduating from art school I began my design career as a "mechanical artist." That means that I spent most of my time surrounded by jars of rubber cement, type spec'ing tools, and X-Acto knives. It was quite a while before I would be allowed to venture into the forbidden territory of actual design, not to mention concept development and, eventually, client contact. There were plenty of books about the art of graphic design and the craft of printing but almost none about the way the two work together. Whatever I learned about this came about mostly by hanging around printers and talking with other designers.

After many of these conversations, I finally resolved my issues with the conflicting goals of "art" and "commerce" with which I had wrestled in school. I realized that a designer cannot engage in one of these categories to the exclusion of the other. Only then did I begin to make a reasonable living so that I could support my family in the style they wanted to become accustomed. At the same time, I found myself indulging my inner child by spending my days playing in the sandbox of creativity.

Through error, blind faith, and sometimes just dumb luck, I found the right path in designing. Or, at least, *my* right path. But the book you are holding—Cathy Connor Lips's *Effective Publications Management*—could have helped me when I was starting out. Indeed, it could have helped me during the entire length of my career. In sensible, clear language, it explains a process that is often confusing and always complex. In these pages, experienced designers will find solid, new, useful information; at minimum, they'll find validation of their own methods and judgments. And newcomers to design will find that their path to understanding what makes for a successful publication has been made a bit smoother.

The thirty design firms whose publications strategies are featured here offer some of the clearest, most intelligent descriptions that I have read anywhere of what they do and how they do it. That's a boon to all of us. In today's constantly changing world of publications, one thing is certain—to determine what direction to go in, we need a good roadmap. This book is a darn good map. I just wish it existed when I graduated from college. It would have made my professional life so much easier.

When producing a design, a final result that is less than perfect will most likely be a failure. That is an absolute truth, no matter how creative the initial idea or how exquisite the eventual design. It's a truth because the journey from idea to design, from concept to image, is fraught with dangers that we should avoid like the plague or deal with as matters of absolute necessity. Most of the time, a designer is doing a major juggling act, trying to keep everything under control while still moving forward. Thankfully, the public only sees our finished products. The hundreds of decisions we make—large and small—are invisible to them, and that's as it should be. There's no reason the public should be privy to what goes on behind the curtain of the creative process. By hiding the sweat and the confusion and the dead-ends that frustrate and confound designers, nondesigners are freed to be amazed, delighted, and thrilled. Now, with the deft help of Cathy Connor Lips, we can thrill them even more.

■ ■ ■

EDWIN GOLD is a professor; director, M.F.A. in Integrated Design program; and director, Ampersand Institute for Words & Images at the School of Communications Design, University of Baltimore. A seasoned, international award-winning creative director and educator, Ed has been, and continues to be, a strong advocate for the design community and a valuable mentor to countless graphic designers. His book, *The Business of Graphic Design,* was cited by *Critique* magazine as one of the eighty-two greatest books on design ever written and is considered the definitive guide and a requisite text for any creative department's library.

Acknowledgments

I can no other answer make, but, thanks, and thanks.
—WILLIAM SHAKESPEARE

Time and thought. Dozens of contributors—those featured on the following pages and others who acted behind the scenes—offered their valuable hours and expertise to this book.

Thanks to the busy graphic designers and consultants who agreed to share their industry insights and provide samples of their exemplary work: Rodney Abbot, Jim Ales, Christina Arbini, Reid Armbruster, Giorgio Baravalle, Megan Berryman, Richard Boynton, Bill Cahan, Aimee Churchill, Emily Ruth Cohen, Dominik D'Angelo, Barbara Dobbins, Julia Evins, Dirk Fowler, Matt Greenwell, Bob Hambly, Kathleen Hatfield, Hayes Henderson, Mike Hillsinger, Mick Hodgson, Jill Howry, Kevin Kennedy, Yang Kim, Steve Kirwan, Deanna Kuhlmann-Leavitt, Clark Malcolm, Sally Morrow, Barry Nelson, Sarah Nelson, Todd Richards, Paul Rustand, Tony Rutka, Karen Salsgiver, Pat Samata, David Schimmel, James Sholly, Jon Sholly, Yuri Shvets, Jack Sichterman, Angela Sinickas, DJ Stout, Beth Swanson, Mejra Ticic, Michael Vanderbyl, Michael Warchol, Sharon Werner, and Tracy West. Their participation has brought the real world into these chapters.

Thanks to Allworth Press for its interest in publishing the book. Special thanks to senior editor Nicole Potter-Talling and editorial assistant Allison Caplin for leading me through the process.

Thanks to Susan Ramundo for her extraordinary dedication to artfully designing a book with evolving needs.

Thanks to friend and photographer Michael Swaby-Rowe for his generosity.

Thanks to the past and present faculty and students of the University of Baltimore's Publications Design master's program. My professors provided me an education in the field, and my students inspired me to write about what I have learned. I am especially grateful to Ed Gold, teacher, colleague, and friend.

Thanks to dear friends and relatives who expressed their encouragement throughout the writing and rewriting of this project.

And most important, thanks to my husband, George, for hours of listening and reading, for hundreds of insightful suggestions, and for infinite patience and calm.

Introduction

Coordinating a publication from concept to delivery may seem an overwhelming task—but someone needs to manage it. As a publications manager, you're charged with ensuring each contributor and client understands his responsibilities, and the impact his work and schedule have on others involved in the process—not to mention moving the project to the finish line.

Managing the process effectively can be rewarding. Well-considered communications can not only provide valuable information, support sales efforts, and launch new products and programs successfully; they can also enhance customer satisfaction and call your audience to action. The reward comes when your publications go beyond their initial objectives to satisfy new objectives with even greater impact.

A successful publication can have a very public face that reflects well on the client and gets you the recognition you deserve. You'll begin to see each new assignment as an opportunity.

The problem, though, is that many design, communications, and marketing pros are tasked with publications management duties but are untrained and inexperienced in some of the fundamentals of the process. This book will guide you, step by step, through the entire publications process.

Effective Publications Management will help you avoid pitfalls that can cost quality, time, and money—and your reputation. This book provides questions to ask in advance and the answers that will help you make smart decisions during each phase of the job. Just as important, you'll learn how to educate your internal and external clients on the process, avoiding surprises for anyone involved as the project goes forward.

The process doesn't have to be complicated. This isn't neurosurgery, after all. Publications managers simply need to understand each step and its effect on subsequent steps. How do you know the concept is going to work, for example? How do you gather and motivate the creative resources who will execute the piece? How do you plan a schedule and make sure it sticks? What do you need to know to create a budget you can work within?

In *Effective Publications Management,* you'll learn how to work the process to your advantage and to the project's success. You'll discover that you can create your own methods and smart shortcuts that will personalize your process for future publications. Creativity—the ability to be imaginative—and management are not mutually exclusive. When you're handling publications effectively, creativity and management work hand in hand.

IT'S ABOUT DEFINING NEEDS, *ALL* OF THE NEEDS

Imagine you're a designer at an association, and you were assigned the president's pet project. This is a great opportunity for you to shine. You created an invitation to donors to support his favorite charity.

Thousands will be distributed, mailed nationally to all of your company's members and vendors. And everyone just loves the design, especially the unusual size and accordion fold. It's sure to stand out amid prospective donors' piles of other mail. Great start, now on to the envelopes.

You order the size of envelope you need from your printer, only to discover that the solicitation's dimensions require a custom gusseted envelope that puts you over budget. Postage for the nonstandard piece will be more expensive, too. And worse, the heavy card stock you used and the multiple folded panels add even more to the mailing cost.

Result? Dissatisfied management, balking at the additional cost, plus the loss of some of your valuable credibility. If you had understood the full publications process, you could have avoided these mistakes by knowing what questions to ask before you made your design decisions.

IT'S ABOUT SMART PLANNING

Let's say you're the communications coordinator at a financial services corporation. Work is demanding because you don't have the internal staff to readily add their creative expertise to publications projects.

It was your job to research and write the copy for a large new family of product pamphlets, and you had to manage the design and production. Well, that didn't seem so difficult. You hired the graphic artist and a printer, and the suite of brochures seemed to be progressing well.

When three more brochures, not budgeted, were added at the last minute, you saw the red flag that signaled rush charges. Your boss suggested that you give the late arrivals to a quickie printer who could deliver them in time. It might have worked. The new printer recommended using a color-build for the background instead of the PMS (Pantone Color Matching System) color. In this way he would be able to keep the cost low enough to offset the rush charges, and he'd meet your deadline painlessly.

Result? The background color of the new pieces doesn't match that of the original set, and the publication family already looks like it has a few stepchildren. You didn't know that using another vendor might alter the production integrity of the entire bunch of brochures. Knowing what questions to ask before veering off in a new production direction can save more than just rush charges.

IT'S ABOUT UNDERSTANDING RIGHTS AND RESPONSIBILITIES

You might be a corporate marketing manager newly charged with publishing the annual report. It's a big responsibility and also a terrific opportunity. Say the company was doing great, and you budgeted to add extra colors and lots of beautiful photography to the book. Because you had excellent recommendations for external resources—writer, designer, photographer, and printer—the job went smoothly and the report showed it. Kudos.

Now the corporation wants to create a full-color investor piece using several of those striking photos you commissioned for the annual report. You call the photographer to obtain the shots you need, only to discover that you don't own the rights to publish them again—you didn't negotiate a multiple-use agreement or a photo buyout.

Result? Doling out money to use each of the annual report's pictures again. Understanding usage rights before contracting with a photographer or an illustrator can save your company or client money, your time, and the embarrassment of having to explain unwelcome surprises.

EVEN A SEASONED MANAGER CAN MAKE MISTAKES

Take the experienced design-firm account executive who followed every project-management step to a *T*—well, except who was responsible for final proofreading—before his project, a student viewbook, went to press. Apparently he didn't pay much attention to the back cover, which only contained the university's name and address. And although he considered final proofing to be the client's job, that detail hadn't been discussed.

The otherwise successful product had one obvious and easily avoidable error: The school was located in Philadelphia, not *Philadelephia*. Did it matter that the account executive didn't think the error rested with him? No.

Result? The client demanded reprinting of the 20,000 books, and the design firm ate the cost.

GET HELP

Each of these situations could have been avoided. In this book you'll read about dozens of other problems that won't occur when you have a thorough understanding of how to manage all of the phases of creating publications.

Effective Publications Management explores the critical steps involved in developing and delivering a wide variety of publications.

Taken a step at a time, the publications process is highly manageable and satisfying. Planning ahead and knowing the right questions to ask upfront will ensure the successful, timely, and on-budget delivery of your publication. And you'll gain a firm foundation for creating future, cohesive communications that work. Following these steps also will enable you to build systems and checkpoints that make the process flow smoothly for future publications.

By using *Effective Publications Management* as your guide, you'll learn from real-world problems and solutions. The book delivers expert advice from nationally recognized designers and communications pros. You'll see examples of publications that work, plus sample schedules, budgets, contracts, and other documents that will help you manage your own publications effectively.

Students in my Publications Management class often take the course simply to fulfill a business requirement. *Management*, what an off-putting word for many. *Business* sounds so boring to a lot of people.

I believe that managing a publication can require as much creativity as the hands-on writing, designing, or other credited responsibilities. Publications management is a specialized skill that allows creative teams to succeed by giving them a solid footing in the process, from concept through delivery. Mastery of these skills can alleviate a lot of the panic surrounding an unexpected project with a nearly impossible deadline. You can learn to approach and manage the process calmly, creatively, and professionally.

The Role of the Publications Manager

The most efficient way to produce anything is to bring together under one management as many as possible of the activities needed to turn out the product.
—PETER DRUCKER

Expansive. It's one of the first words that come to my mind when I think about publications management. It encompasses far-reaching responsibilities. It requires extensive skills. And it relies on expertise in diverse areas. It's a sizable challenge for a single person to be proficient in all of the wide-ranging tasks of publications management. Yet coordinating all aspects of a publication project under one management can make for the most effective outcome—and prove rewarding for the publications manager.

Until fairly recently, the duties of coordinating communications were divided among several people: account executive, project manager, production manager, and business manager. But increasingly, as job descriptions trend toward generalists, the responsibilities of these various individuals fall to one person who is tasked with producing a publication from its inception through delivery to the audience. "You might have someone who is actually the head of the whole communications program managing publications himself," says Barry Nelson, president of the Story Board, LLC, an international network of business journalists and graphic artists. This requires not only an understanding of all publications-process stages and their interdependencies but also the management of both immediate details and the long-range plan. Beth Swanson, the editor of *Wendy's Magazine* (by and about the Wendy's International restaurant chain) for five years, had a small support staff. She was the epitome of a true publications manager. From budgeting, scheduling, and editorial planning to overseeing the creative development, production, and distribution of the magazine, "I did everything," she says.

A prime reason the position of publications manager has grown in scope is economy. When companies shrink their internal resources, they either load more responsibilities on employees they retain or turn to freelancers to manage many of the steps of the publications process. So, frequently the publications manager actually goes by a different title. From the graphic designer to the public relations officer, from the corporate communications manager to the editorial assistant who knows a little bit about how to lay out a newsletter, the unprepared are often charged with coordinating the entire publishing process. Most are not trained in every facet of publications management. They may, by default, have to take on creating a publication without prior experience.

Taking the Lead:
Herman Miller's *SEE* Magazine
CAHAN & ASSOCIATES, SAN FRANCISCO, CA

"It's true, I carry many roles at *SEE*," says Todd Richards, Cahan & Associates designer and art director, and designer of client Herman Miller's groundbreaking *SEE* magazine, "from management, project coordination, and art direction to design, art coordinator and buyer, prop stylist, etcetera. Herman Miller has its own army of people, from editor to managing editor, from art director to production manager. They all play key roles in the production of the publication. I just gather all the bits and pieces, and make it all up from there."

Clark Malcolm, senior writer/editor at Herman Miller and editor of the biannual, explains that "the business objective for *SEE* magazine is to make a very important connection between readers and the company, its traditional position as a thought leader in the contract furniture industry ever since the fifties. Herman Miller has really led the way in research around ergonomics, time, and materials. Over the years the company has done various things to promote research. *SEE* is another example."

"They were looking to do a thought leadership magazine for designers, architects, and anybody else involved in the design industry," says Cahan & Associates principal Bill Cahan and *SEE*'s creative director, "and for a way of getting Herman Miller's name out there without being so obvious about it. Most journals talk about all the great things that they've done for their client, and talk at them instead of to them. I think that creating a communication tool that is a very gentle nod to Herman Miller but primarily is about other brilliant people doing brilliant things is just smart and at the same time more believable."

"We needed to appeal to a very visually oriented audience" to achieve that connection with the design industry, Malcolm says. "And we wanted to teach them something that they didn't already know, so the subjects of the articles we hope they don't find in other kinds of magazines. The intellectual level of the articles, we wanted to raise above the usual contract furniture marketing material. That was my job. Todd and I work very closely together to link the content of the pieces with his images."

"We manage ten to fifteen photography/illustration commissions each issue," Richards says. "Most everything is original artwork.

"This is where the importance of scheduling can really factor in," he says. "When we have a clear idea of the content early on, we in turn have a better handle on the artists we would like to commission and what dollar amount we have to put aside for each. On the opposite side, when you don't have a tight manuscript and can't commit to an artist until much later in the process, you can easily end up short on money for unforeseen production costs, thus going over budget.

"Keeping people on schedule can greatly impact your performance in managing the budget.

Photography: Hans Gissinger

Editor: Clark Malcolm
Design: Todd Richards, Erik Adams, Cahan & Associates
Managing Editor: Gay Strobel
Contributing Writers: Marcia Davis, Dick Holm, Carol Lecocq, Julie Ridl
Production: Marlene Capotosto, Clare Rhinelander
Editorial Board: Bill Cahan, Steve Frykholm, Lois Maassen, Kris Manos
Printing: The Hennegan Company
Client: Herman Miller

The budget for *SEE* is a set number for the year—that's for two issues. If we go over budget on the first issue of the year, this affects the second issue, which has to then be produced under budget. And it's very easy to go over budget when you have so many moving parts."

Richards says that to process those components smoothly, "Clark and I work like this: He supplies us with a loose table of contents that changes around as things crystallize with the whole team. Once we have the rough drafts, we spend a couple of weeks reading and rough-storyboarding a few ideas for each of the articles; these storyboards are mainly written ideas. We circulate our compiled ideas via e-mail. We usually attach photography and illustrator links to each of our ideas.

"Everyone conferences about three weeks after we began. We decide then, collectively, what ideas resonate," Richards says. "So basically, Clark and his team supply us with the writing and we take it from there. It's about a two-month process of design, reviews, revisions—a lot of back-and-forth PDFs. Then we finish up with final production of the layouts during the last two weeks of the process. We all get together for four days of editing and fine-tuning one week before we go to press. We sequence the articles and it all finally comes together."

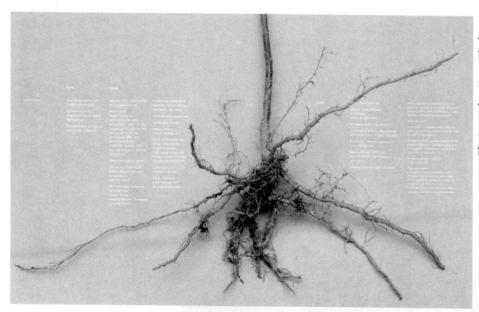

Photography: Hans Gissinger

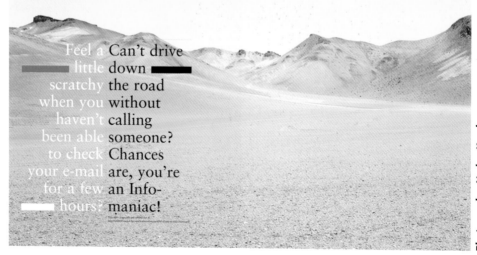

Feel a little scratchy when you haven't been able to check your e-mail for a few hours? Can't drive down the road without calling someone? Chances are, you're an Info-maniac!

Photography: Nadav Kander

As Drucker asserts, coordination of all the components of a project under one management makes for the most efficient production. And so it can be with the publications manager in charge of all aspects of the process. A responsible manager can unify the three primary components of a successful project: people, time, and money.

THE LEAD COMMUNICATOR

Critical to all of the publications manager's roles is clear and frequent contact with others: the client, the creative team, the print shop, the mail house. You're the lead communicator, explaining the project, the schedule, the budget.

You'll introduce the players who need to work together. For instance, if your designer has never worked with your printer before, make sure they talk before any work begins. That introduction will open communication between them, help make them comfortable with each other, and encourage them to freely ask questions about formats, capabilities, and so on. When time and circumstances allow, your client should meet the photographer who'll be shooting company personnel or the writer who'll be interviewing executives. Often top brass or other subjects will call on the client with questions, so he should be prepared.

As the publications manager, you'll be the scheduler, motivator, and supervisor—all reliant on strong communications skills. (The team members you manage might not report directly to you, which is sometimes a special challenge in itself within a company bureaucracy.) You'll make sure they stay within budget—or alert you in advance if things are sliding off track—and you'll negotiate the use and ownership rights of their work.

For everyone's utmost comfort level, an all-hands meeting can be the best way to kick off the project. Putting a face to a name makes communication easier and one's sense of accountability stronger. Keep in mind that as a publications manager, you're structuring a team of creative talent and vendors who not only require your guidance but might need to be motivated as well. Setting a clear path early on will help them understand your direction as questions or problems arise. Serving as a coordinating liaison among these various camps focuses everyone's attention on the shared goal of a publication that's on time, on budget, and on message.

THE MULTITASKER

Expand your goal beyond getting a publication produced; get it produced with the utmost quality, efficiency, and cost-effectiveness. Again drawing from Drucker, successful management means having a hand in as many of the project's activities as possible.

Here's a look at all your possible responsibilities, which will vary from project to project. I've categorized them, generally, by the several different roles that are often compressed into the position of publications manager.

Don't be overwhelmed by the length of these lists and the breadth of knowledge represented here. This is a foundation that will grow upward as you gain experience. You can rely on members of your creative team, your vendors, and networking colleagues in the industry for advice. "Speak to your peers and predecessors," recommends Jill Howry, principal of Howry Design Associates. "Research agencies such as AIGA and local listings for project management groups."

In many cases, these duties can be handled by others you'll be managing. For example, an experienced designer could be your printer liaison. So take heart: This comprehensive inventory is meant as a primer.

The Publications Manager as Account Executive

Account executives (AEs) traditionally are equal parts sales and service professionals. They seek out new markets and clients, sell them on a new project or service, and then act as the prime contact throughout the process, usually (and pragmatically) to keep sales expanding. Which is fine: It's a business, and without someone closing deals, those of us not involved would go hungry.

As businesses are streamlined, AEs more often act like pure sales reps, with publications managers assuming much of the ongoing client contact and service responsibilities during projects. If this isn't the case in your situation, you might want to suggest changing to a more flexible model that allows you direct client contact. This would get you quicker answers during the publications process and give the account executives more time for sales prospecting, benefiting the entire operation.

Client educator. Chapter 4 discusses gauging the need to educate your client about the publications process. His understanding of what will happen—and how, why, and when—is the basis of your strong relationship. It can make the difference between efficient publications development and disjointed steps that never quite mesh because of the client's interference or delinquency. With your client you'll be not only educator but also presenter, adviser, constant updater, and perhaps hand-holder.

Proposal writer. Part of the account executive aspect of your job includes development and presentation of the project proposal to the client. This is a sort of mapping out of how the publication plan will be executed. You'll walk your client through the proposal to answer any questions that arise. It's all about continuous communication for maximum clarity.

Creative team builder and manager. It's your responsibility to build and motivate the creative team. This is especially important when creative contributors are off site, working on their own, and especially challenging if you're coordinating staff members who don't report directly to you. Again, communication is key. The best publications manager is deemed a valued adviser by the professionals on the project, relaying information clearly from client to team members, representing the talent to ensure the creative product maintains its quality and integrity.

Conceptualizer. In your account executive role, you might be involved in development of concepts for the publication. Here's where your knowledge of the client, his organization, his communication need, and his audience will contribute directly to the graphic and editorial solution.

Concept presenter. Regardless of your involvement in creating the concepts, you'll present them for the client's review, discussion, and selection. You'll be the voice of the designer primarily, explaining his approaches to the communication and how they deliver the audience message.

Testing coordinator. Testing of concepts can be an important step in the publications process when you must guarantee a specific audience call to action. It might be your task to facilitate focus groups or another method of advance review by readers to help ensure the project's effectiveness.

Learned adviser. As the team leader and chief communicator among all the players involved, you'll be called on to answer myriad questions about the project, the creative work, the schedule, the budget, the printing, the delivery. You'll need that dual vision of the trees and the forest.

The Publications Manager as Project Manager

After all, what does a project manager do that you shouldn't? You'll be expected to know everything about everything. You are the go-to guy, the font of all information about the project: Where are we? What about? Why didn't? The buck stops at your desk, and that, my friends, is management. So wrap a phone around your head and get to work.

The key to mastery of all this is curiosity. By constantly asking questions and reconfirming answers, you'll have the best chance of knowing where the project actually stands at any given moment. You can't rely on vendors' updates if they are just their hopes or guesses. Plenty of great scheduling and budget management software is available to significantly support your project manager role. But you'll also need to keep your hand in and your voice heard.

Like the AE roles you might assume, you'll pick up all of the tasks advertised for project managers:

Resource expert. To be an accomplished publications manager, you must have an understanding of the needs of and interdependencies among the writer, the designer, the printer, and so on. What are their strengths and challenges? How much time do they require to meet project objectives? To maintain smooth flow, you'll represent their needs to others on whom they depend to get their own jobs done.

Traffic manager. Imagine literally carrying the project from department to department, your eye constantly on the clock, and then on out the door, and you'll have a good idea of how trafficking works. You'll be responsible for ensuring the draft is done on time so the designer can begin his layout, for getting the art to the printer by the deadline to keep your project's place in the queue, and for obtaining client signoff on the prepress proofs before he goes on vacation.

Meeting facilitator. Communicating with individuals to assess their needs is important. So is getting as many members of the team as practical in the same room to discuss firsthand how they affect each other. This builds a united feeling, as opposed to an us-and-them attitude within the team. Knowing each other strengthens accountability. It's your job to remind everyone that you're all in this together.

Scheduler. The project manager is probably most associated with managing time effectively. Keeping the publication on track will enable people to perform their tasks well and keep the project within budget. You'll need to focus on the daily schedules of individuals, checking in and prompting as needed, and if necessary making adjustments to meet the fixed deadline.

Budget manager. A project manager typically is fed the budget and is responsible for managing it. In this part of your role, you'll make sure that estimates meet budget requirements and the project stays on course so invoices match allowable estimate variances. Time really is money. You'll manage the amount of time team members spend on their part of the project. And you'll communicate the budget to members of your team as appropriate—for example, to the designer to ensure the job's specifications don't overrun the funds available.

Standards monitor. Throughout development phases of the publication, you'll check copy and design against the client company's editorial and graphic standards to ensure adherence.

Proofing coordinator. Circulation of prepress proofs among client and creative reviewers needs to adhere to the schedule that will maintain the allotted press time. This seemingly simple task can be a challenging step if the client doesn't know how important it is for him to provide a timely turnaround.

Distribution coordinator. After the ink is dry, you still need to get the job into the audience's hands. The project manager must coordinate shipment from the printer to the client or distribution to readers by a mail department or facility. You'll have to find out when the vendor needs your printed materials, envelopes, labels or mail list, and so on, to process and send the publication out the door on time.

Process evaluator. A good project manager knows what's working and what needs fixing. The best can foresee potential glitches and make adjustments before they become problems. He should evaluate the efficiency of the publications process on an ongoing basis, clearing roadblocks as they arise and reviewing the overall project to smooth the flow in the future.

The Publications Manager as Production Manager

Whereas human resources skills were needed in most of the previous roles, the production manager must have a current understanding of prepress, production, and printing. Good production managers always seem ready to jump onto a press and make the adjustments themselves. That level of expertise isn't necessary; however, you will need to stay abreast of the trends in the print and related industries that could impact quality, efficiency, and cost. Novice publications managers can turn to production vendors, professional associations, trade literature, and industry counterparts for advice on the latest in technology, its benefits and potential pitfalls.

Industry insider. In this role, you will need a general understanding of what's happening in the various production vendors' industries. You'll need to stay current with new technology and know where it's available. You should have a good grasp of standard business terms and practices regarding art ownership, proofs provided, corrections to proofs, delivery, and so on.

Vendor locator. The production manager will probably identify the appropriate printer for the job. He'll evaluate the vendor's capabilities, experience, quality consistency, and service before awarding the contract and continue to do so throughout the relationship. Ongoing open communication is a key component of the production manager's role. By maintaining an amiable partnership with the printer, the manager encourages the vendor to offer time- and cost-saving suggestions for producing print jobs.

Quality controller. You and/or the designer on the job will attend a press check to uphold your printing standards, such as color matching. This critical step ideally should be executed by someone with solid press proofing skills.

The Publications Manager as Business Manager

Within your team, you'll be responsible for the majority of the business details, most likely taking care of contracts, release forms, and invoices. You'll be responsible for figuring out the most cost-effective way to set up your relationships with freelancers and vendors. You may even have a role to play in accounts payable, no matter who signs the checks.

Contractor. In addition to identifying creative and production resources, as business manager you'll be responsible for negotiating property usage, rights, and payment terms. You'll need to review

---

The Eight Steps of the Publications Management Process

Concept: the idea for communicating a specific message to a defined audience

Proposal: the blueprint for producing the project

Planning: the identification of resources, and the creation of a schedule and a budget

Creative development: the writing, design, and photography/illustration

Testing: the advance critique of your concept with an audience sample

Production: the printing and finishing of the publication

Distribution: the mailing or shipping of the printed piece to the client or audience members

Follow-up testing: the postproduction evaluation of the publication's effectiveness and of the publications process

---

contracts—and run them by the legal department if applicable—to ensure they spell out every detail that is essential to your project.

Accounts payable manager (sort of). To ensure good work relationships going forward, take an interest in seeing that your valuable resources are paid according to the agreed-upon terms. By assuming responsibility and acting as an advocate within your organization, you'll keep your free-lancers and vendors happy if ever there's a problem.

FIFTEEN TENETS OF GOOD PUBLICATIONS MANAGEMENT

Rolling all these responsibilities into one position necessitates diligently managing yourself as well as other people, time, and money. Remember these tenets of publications management to keep yourself, as well as the job, on track.

Show up prepared. Come to the table with an understanding of the client's company or product and his audience. Be ready with all the questions you'll need to have answered in order to fully grasp his communication challenge.

Be curious: Ask questions. Turn to your creative talent and your vendors, and ask them to explain the choices they made and what you need to know and do to be an effective publications manager. Why are the photos cropped that way? What should I look for at the press check? Where can a reliable mail house be found?

Educate yourself. You're part of a community. Join associations in communications, marketing, design, or your specialization, and use their member benefits and networking opportunities to learn more about how to accomplish your goals. Contact other sole proprietors or counterparts at other companies for advice. And read: Keeping up on the latest in design, technology, printing, direct mail, and so on, will help you make time- and cost-saving choices and stay active instead of reactive.

Educate your client. Managing a project is much easier when the client understands his role in the process. Your client's committed and aware involvement will help the project stay on schedule and within budget.

Create agendas. Never enter a conference room without one. Agendas keep meetings efficient and ensure no topics are overlooked. You should review accountabilities and deadlines before you leave the scene.

Know the audience. Do your homework. Ask your client. Test the concepts. Make sure you can create a communication solution that answers the audience's need.

Make a smart schedule. Plan a schedule with everyone's buy-in upfront. Getting time commitments from all resources before the timeline is finalized and before work begins will—or should—mean that everyone can truly stick to the schedule. Don't figure you can make up lost time later on—you might just build a pressure cooker and go over budget.

Build a better budget. Just as with your smart schedule, the better budget is one that reflects realistic input from your writer, designer, photographer, printer, mail house, and anyone else involved. Make sure estimates are in writing, and ask questions to identify what's included and what's not. Otherwise you might encounter billing surprises. If your client is supplying you with the budget, make sure you're confident the project can be completed within his parameters before agreeing.

Sign a contract. Write comprehensive details about the project and the resource's deliverables in the contract or letter of agreement. You might think you and the vendor heard the same due date, the same word count, the same fee amount, only to learn differently when the invoice arrives and the arguing ensues. This is especially important if you're hiring a friend.

Think twice. It's surprising how often taking a minute to re-review pays off.

Get it in writing. Everything—absolutely everything. Estimates, schedules, budgets, contract terms and conditions, release forms, meeting notes, detailed invoices—you name it. If you think you own the art or hold the copyright, for example, think again. Negotiate up front for ownership and future use of creative materials. The client will proofread the blueline, right? Maybe not. Make sure responsibilities are spelled out in ink from the get-go.

Give advance notice. Step up. Don't wait until the last minute, hoping a situation will correct itself. Let the impacted party know as soon as you know. For example, if an illustrator blows a deadline, which might hold up a designer, it's important to notify the printer and find out what options are available.

Don't pass the buck. You're responsible for the smooth production of the job, so take responsibility for it. No client wants to hear you whine about the writer who's late with his copy.

Follow up. Don't leave someone hanging—your writer, your designer, your printer, your client. Respond promptly with the needed information—or at least check in to say you're on the case. Talk with your client after the job is delivered to gauge his satisfaction with the piece and the process. Send samples to your freelancers and vendors. Follow up with thank-you notes whenever possible. It's all about building your own good public relations.

Expect the unexpected. Even when you're sure the outcome will be A, B, or C, it could be Q. Sometimes it just is what it is, and you have to do the best job you can under the circumstances. You'll be ahead of the curve if you start with the number-one tenet: Show up prepared.

2

Conducting a Communications Audit

. . . in the end the communicator will be confronted with the old problem of what to say and how to say it.
—Edward R. Murrow

As my friend Lonnie always said, "Say *whaaat?*" It sounds so yesterday, but it sums it up. In publications management, it's question one: Say what? And to find the answer, let's start, at least for this chapter, with another question: What's already been said?

To best position your shiny new publication, you'll need to know all about your client's communication habits and the culture to which he's accustomed. You'll need to understand what the client has tried and what competitors have done to get similar messages to the same target audience. Gathering this information is an audit.

That's the basis of publications management: coordinating the process that facilitates saying what needs to be communicated and doing so in a style and format that drives the message home. It can be a problem, for sure, without the appropriate tools and knowledge to manage each step effectively. Or it can be an opportunity to create influential publications that address the communication needs you must carefully identify before you begin. Pinpointing those needs and whether they've truly been answered in the past requires a thorough study of the pieces in place. Your first step in determining what to say and how to say it is to conduct a communications audit.

WHAT IS A COMMUNICATIONS AUDIT?

An audit entails an inventory and analysis of publications—and frequently other modes of communication—against their objectives to ascertain their success. Its purpose is to identify the collection's strengths and weaknesses. This is accomplished by a thorough review and assessment of all of your client's communications to date, and for our purposes a look at what competitors are up to.

Your goal is to establish what's been done, what's in place, what's worked, and what hasn't. Your objectives will be to draw on past successes—and learn from mistakes—and to begin to build a consistent framework for future projects.

Ideally a publications audit should be part of an organization's comprehensive communications strategy, analyzing messages delivered by phone, print, electronic (e-mail as well as Web site), and in-person communications, such as meetings. For the purpose of laying a strong foundation for your print publications, we'll focus on the analysis of printed pieces.

By understanding the mission and auditing the existing communications used by your organization or your client company, you can assess the cohesiveness of word, image, and message. This will enable you to determine the effectiveness of past publications. It will also provide guidance on creating a new integrated family of publications going forward that clearly represent the mission and reinforce the brand in the mind of the audience.

An audit also can help you assess the success of publications management steps. Ask the client whether publications were produced on time and within cost parameters. If the answers are negative, discuss how schedules and budgets were established, who managed (or mismanaged) them, and where bottlenecks occurred. This information will help you discover not only the effectiveness of the publication but of the process as well.

WHEN SHOULD YOU AUDIT?

If your company or client has never conducted a communications audit, do so before moving ahead on the newly assigned publication. Depending on time available, this might need to be a fairly cursory review of what has been produced in the past, what is currently in use, and what has and has not been successful in meeting goals. At the very least, this exercise will familiarize you with graphic and editorial direction, audience needs as the client sees them, overall communication goals, and the client's mission—important information on which to base your new assignment.

An in-depth audit is called for especially in times of change: a new program or product launch, a merger, or other redirection. Review past introductory materials and interview management about whether the literature met the business objectives. This will tell you whether the foundation laid by past publications was sound or a new approach should be created.

Many communications, such as annual reports and internal employee publications, deliver information about change. This information could include an upturn or downturn in performance or a personnel restructuring. Such critical messages need to be delivered in a manner that will bring about the desired audience response, say, continued commitment to the organization.

Communications published prior to the change should be reviewed in detail to determine whether their approach needs to be altered to achieve the appropriate perception and action. An example is the practice of producing obviously expensive annual reports in times of corporate health, which usually is acceptable. During a time of negative change, however, high-end specifications might not sit well with shareholders concerned about company expenditures. The new annual report should be tailored to suit the condition of the organization and the expectations of the audience.

WHO SHOULD ADMINISTER THE AUDIT?

Consider recommending that your client or the organization you work for hire a communications or marketing consultant to administer the audit. An outside company would bring a broader scope of experi-

---

No Mission Statement?

Start by asking your client a few questions:

- Who are you?
- What do you stand for?
- What are your values?
- What is your purpose?
- Who are your customers?
- How would you summarize yourself in a brief statement to customers?
- What do you offer them that is unusual or unique?
- How do you stack up against your competition?

---

ence, objectivity, and possibly greater credibility to the task.

Budget, however, and the time you have to devote to an audit might require conducting the audit yourself for a client or with a team inside your company. You might need to move quickly on your own if a new or updated publication must be produced within a tight time frame and you need to view a snapshot of the foundation already laid for print communications. Keep in mind the additional time that will be required of you, as well as any staffers with other commitments who will be involved in the audit. Factor the audit and the time needed into your publication schedule.

HOW SHOULD YOU AUDIT?

A communications audit can be a time-consuming exercise, but it need not be complicated. Follow this basic formula to understand the communication environment in which you'll be operating and to establish a framework for future publications. The audit can be as simple as this five-step process.

A Roadmap for Your Audit
Examples of audit business objectives include:

- Ensure the consistency of graphic style and editorial tone among the publications.

- Compare the delivery of content with readers' information-gathering habits.

- Determine the appropriateness of design specifications to the message and the audience.

- Evaluate the appropriateness of the actual communication vehicles in place for delivery of the client's message or messages.

- Identify messages or information that is missing from the publication family that the audience needs to hear.

- Look for redundancies of information among different publications.

- Cite the existence of or identify the need for reader feedback forums.

- Review the time needed to deliver each communication and compare it with the original schedule; identify bottlenecks or cases of slippage.

- Review the cost to produce each communication and compare it with the original budget; identify circumstances that put you over the original allotment.

STEP ONE: DETERMINE AUDIT OBJECTIVES

Consider all of the information you want to gain from your audit and compose corresponding business objectives. These will be your roadmap through the audit and evaluation. Without objectives in mind, your process might meander, wasting time and resulting in scattered and vague recommendations.

STEP TWO: REVIEW THE MISSION STATEMENT

If your organization or your client already has a mission statement, get it and read it. It's a snapshot of a company and its values, an encapsulation of its purpose and what it has to offer its customers or the community. More than deepening your understanding of the client, the mission statement will help you devise the appropriate message, concept, style, and tone for all communications.

Some semblance of a mission statement or statement of purpose will be the measure of whether the messages of past publications were clear and delivered successfully.

STEP THREE: GATHER THE COMMUNICATIONS

Inventory all of the publications being used internally and with outside audiences. There might be a few, or there could be hundreds.

A small business with a narrowly defined audience, for example, might dictate a set of only a few print vehicles, perhaps a small family of product brochures, letterhead, and business cards. But a larger organization, with its multiple audiences, communicates with several layers of employees, customers, and other stakeholders. For these internal and external groups—many with additional subsets having differing needs—several different types of publications might exist.

In addition to the client's communications, review competitors' publications to gauge how your collection stacks up. For example, you might discover that another company's brand is consistently positioned more prominently than yours. From that observation you could conclude that your client's pieces need a stronger, more distinguishable brand presence to help readers immediately identify the company.

STEP FOUR: ANALYZE THE INVENTORY

If possible, line up all of the pieces across a table. If you're working with a team of reviewers, encourage them to speak their observations aloud as they occur. Take copious notes. I find it's helpful to write a brief description of each publication gathered. A just-the-facts kind of document, listing title, audience, purpose, and status (active or its place within history) to stay organized. These notes will be the basis for your recommendations at the end of the auditing process. Participants shouldn't edit their comments but speak freely about their initial impressions; these casual observations will closely represent readers' first-glance reactions.

Remember, the goal here for the curious publications manager is to understand what the client has been doing and how and why it has or hasn't worked. Even if the communications are perfectly consistent, the review can still provide direction. For example, let's say all of a client's various publications appeared utterly alike in tone, message, and execution, completely in sync. This probably points toward a very detailed style manual or a very organized client. By creating a publication that goes against the status quo, your message might get needed attention.

After noting your reviewers' first impressions, prompt them with a few questions: What's the general understanding, if any, of the company? Do all of the publications appear to support that opinion? Do they all seem to be from the same company? What's their relationship to competitors' efforts? Are there similarities or threads that link various grouped publications to other

---

Audiences and Publications to Audit

Employees
- Prospects—recruitment brochure, job application forms
- New hires—orientation binder, employee handbook, benefits brochure
- Existing workers—event fliers, weekly branch newsletter, monthly corporate magazine
- Managers—weekly management newsletter, training manuals, employee-evaluation instructions and forms, business cards, memos, correspondence, letterhead suite

Customers
- Prospects—direct mail, coupons, company capabilities brochure, catalog, advertisements
- Existing customers—monthly newsletter, product brochures, catalog, referral coupons, special-offer direct mail, billing communications
- Customers who have defected—welcome-back direct mail

Other stakeholders
- Investors—prospectus
- Management board and shareholders—annual report, quarterly performance reports, meeting and voting literature
- Media—press packets and releases

groups, or do the publications look like they could have been sent by a variety of communicators? Even the preschool game of "which of these doesn't belong" can generate some useful insight.

Then, regroup the publications, say by audience versus message, and ask similar questions. When your reviewers see the entire range of publications that a consumer might see and not simply all of the brochures used to gain prospective sales, their observations could change.

Take a look at the publications you've gathered from more than one perspective. Look at them in toto, and then group them by type (see the list above) and by target audience. For example, a hospital's neurosurgery publications might all be well coordinated. However, when you look at the range of communications a patient might see, including admissions, radiology, and so on, you could discern a mixed group. By regrouping in different ways and trying to see the range of messages a client publishes, you'll often notice inconsistencies that can dilute those messages.

Even if you're looking at what appears to be a cohesive family of publications, your work is not complete. They may hang together, use similar design elements, typefaces, or artwork. But to ensure thorough consistency, you'll want to take a close look, dissecting each communication's visual and verbal elements.

Do the collective publications communicate a consistent brand when viewed together? Do they communicate a coordinated and clear identity to readers? Disparity can cause confusion among audience members about your intended relationship with them. A hodgepodge of graphic treatments prevents individual publications from reinforcing each other and working together to further brand recognition with the audience.

This issue is of particular importance for a company with communications from a variety of suboffices or departments, as well as for an organization promoting several different products. The work of different locations needs to be coordinated so they follow the same graphic and editorial standards to present a common look and tone. Each product in a large line needs to be identified with its umbrella brand. In both cases, attention to coordinating the efforts of different factions will result in the cohesive identity that will keep clear and high-impact communication with customers.

Know Your Audience's Habits

Attracting audience attention to the brand is essential, and your audit will tell you whether you have a consistent brand presentation. Once you've determined whether your audience recognizes your client as the communicator, examine whether your publications address the readers' behavior. The essential question: How do they gather information?

If your audience turns to the Internet more frequently than it reads printed materials, you'll want to evaluate the length and detail of copy in your publications. Are your readers busy professionals who tend to glean for the most important facts? If so, you'll want to review your work for visual and verbal clues that guide the audience to those critical bits of information. For your audit recommendations, make a note of how your publications conform to the way the audience collects what it needs to know.

After establishing whether the communications mesh with reader habits, dig deeper to consider whether they're answering audience needs. What does the audience expect of your publications? There are three broad categories of information delivered to readers: good to know, useful to know for the future, and need to know and act on now. As part of your communications audit, ask which type of information your audience anticipates obtaining from a given publication. If immediate action is required of your readers, is the editorial clear about what steps to take and does the visual formatting convey a sense of urgency and showcase the details necessary for the audience to act?

During your audit, ask whether there are a graphics standards manual and an editorial style guide. These are important roadmaps for ensuring all publications look, sound, and feel essentially the same. Consistent formatting of graphics and editorial style not only projects a coordinated image of the client company but also helps guide readers through your publications to the information they want and need.

Review each publication in your collection to determine whether it adheres to the stated visual and editorial standards. If these guides do not exist, develop some for reference on future publications. Establish a few basic guidelines for graphics and copy to adhere to—such as developing consistent use of the company logo, identifying primary and secondary palettes to be used, and deciding which editorial style guide (AP, *Chicago Manual of Style, Words into Type,* etc.; see appendix B) to use going forward. Revising publications to meet uniform standards would ensure the clear communication of the company or product whenever a publication is printed. Depending on your timing needs, for now you might need to focus on consistency as you move forward.

In some cases, inconsistency could be appropriate and effective. During the audit, see whether some publications veer from the set standards. Ask whether there's a valid purpose for that deviation. For instance, the majority of a company's publications might adhere to editorial tone and guidelines, and to design standards. But the format of the customer newsletter might have a different design and tone to engage the reader, suiting multiple levels of information with differing degrees of importance. A different graphic approach may make sense for a publication that is unique within the family of communications.

It's important to go beyond checking conformity to your rules for graphics and language. Take a look at whether the visual presentation and editorial tone are appropriate for the audience within the context of each publication.

Some publications are targeted to a diverse audience with varying needs, whereas others must serve more than one audience category. Discuss the audiences of each publication as you conduct your audit and whether the piece effectively and appropriately speaks to each.

The magazine for a diverse workforce is an example of a communication that must address the needs of many who comprise a single audience category. A print ad for a children's toy must address two audiences: the child as well as the parent or other adult who might purchase the product. Graphics and copy should engage the fancy of the youngster and be understandable by that age group while explaining the benefits of the item to the mature buyer.

Whether a publication prompted a purchase or achieved another desired response from the audience is a critical question of the audit. What was the call to action, and was the communication effective in realizing that action?

The success of some communications could be obvious, especially when the call to action was objectively measurable. A product presentation kit might have increased sales by 10 percent, for example. Perhaps an invitation helped to sell out an event. Refer to the written list of purposes to start you on your examination of whether each piece fulfilled its mission.

In other, more subjectively defined cases, you could require additional research to determine the effectiveness of a publication. Internal interviews, constituent focus groups, and user questionnaires are examples of testing you could conduct to gauge whether print materials met goals such as consumer recognition of a brand or understanding of your client organization's services (e.g., see chapter 8).

To help you obtain ongoing data, consider whether including a reader-feedback mechanism would be appropriate for any of the audit's publications. A periodical could encourage comments and letters, for example, or feature an annual readership survey to capture the audience's opinions on editorial content and organization. This type of information will help you better define the purpose of future publications based on reader needs.

As you proceed with your audit, evaluate the appropriateness of each format or type of publication to the purpose and the message. News in a long monthly magazine, for example, could be delivered to its busy audience in a more succinct quarterly newsletter that saves your client time and money. Look, too, for any redundancies of information delivery that could signal that a communication is no longer needed.

Be on the lookout for publications that are needed but are not part of the mix. Some information might be lost in a large publication and need to be pulled out to stand on its own. Your audit might uncover missing messages that require the development of new vehicles. For example, the collection might cover communication with prospective and existing customers but ignore the audience of those who have defected. In this case, a letter or more comprehensive direct-mail campaign could be in order to encourage the return of these former customers.

Your audit should evaluate not only the effectiveness of publications but of the process as well. Reliable creative resources and vendors, adherence to schedule, and economic production are all areas to assess. For example, publications aren't effective if they deliver their messages to audiences late, and budget-breaking showpieces can tax resources needed for other, mundane but critical, communications. Walk through the publications process for each piece and identify any glitches that should be addressed before work begins on the next project.

STEP FIVE: WRITE YOUR RECOMMENDATIONS

Now it's time to consolidate what you've learned, formulate recommendations, and document the proposed next steps for your client. That might sound exhausting in theory, but you've already done a lot of the work. Rely on your audit objectives and research as your foundation. Explain to your client that the audit recommendations are a practical how-to guide that will benefit future publications.

Construct the document by listing the original objectives and writing a sentence or two summarizing your findings under each objective. Follow this with the step or steps you recommend on the basis of your findings. For example:

Objective. Ensure the consistency of graphic style and editorial tone among the publications.

Findings. Design elements were consistent within each company department but were inconsistent among the departments. For example, although the human resources department's orientation materials and the marketing department's product brochures clearly represented families of publications, the two sets of publications appeared to be from separate companies when laid side by side.

Recommendations. Call a meeting of department representatives to review the established brand, and graphic and editorial standards, and discuss the need for and value of a single, strong, cohesive identity. Channel the publications projects of all departments through a central communications officer to ensure coordination.

Keep your findings and recommendations brief. The shorter the steps, the more actionable they will appear to your client. It's about quality, not quantity.

Provide specific examples where possible. This will give a practical context and help decision-makers understand your recommendations. Include a few relevant physical samples in your presentation package.

Make reasonable recommendations. If a full-fledged graphics standards manual cannot be developed before the next publication is due, suggest the establishment of basic guidelines for the upcoming job that can be fleshed out as soon as doable.

Remember that these are recommendations only. Based on a number of factors, including time, people, and money available, your client or company might not be able to act on all of your proposals. And as is sometimes the case amid bureaucracy, they might simply not get around to it.

3

Creating Clear Concepts

There is nothing worse than a sharp image of a fuzzy concept.
—ANSEL ADAMS

The graphic design or production values of a publication may solicit "oohs" and "aahs." But does it communicate a distinct message to the target audience? A clear concept addresses the purpose of a publication or a brand identity; it carries the right message to the reader and can help achieve a specific audience response. An effective publication can't be just cutting edge; it has to deliver. A clear concept brings content into a purposeful focus.

In this chapter you'll read about the research needed to create, qualify, and present a concept. Conjuring up a concept can sound daunting; sometimes the very word is treated like magic. If you think of a concept in its most basic, *Webster's Collegiate* definition, "an abstract thought generalized from particular instances," it's much more approachable. It's just an idea.

Every publication, every thing created, begins with a concept, an idea for hire. It's a solution or approach employed to solve a problem or create an opportunity. When you are managing a print publication, your concept, like any good solution, will have to address all of the particular instances or relevant needs to be met. An early key task in directing a successful publication is uncovering those needs. Your task is to define all of the publication needs, even those your client might not know he had. This initial fact-gathering will provide the criteria to create a serviceable concept as well as help make the many smaller decisions that occur during any creative process.

Here the publications manager has to play the role of reporter, gathering the who, what, and why of the publication need, as well as the how many, when, and how much. Because the purposes of communications vary widely, it would be impractical to create a definitive checklist of all the needs to consider. By applying your reporter's questions within a categorical framework, you should be able to qualify and manage all the information you'll need to give your team direction. You'll have the facts; you'll be able to create a communication concept based on fact rather than fancy. A clear understanding of the core issues and criteria on which you base your concept will help you explain its validity and defend it against frivolous alterations.

The information you gather is the foundation on which to base decisions not only concerning overarching conceptual direction but also practical decisions about design dictated by distribution and budget. The accuracy of this foundation data is essential to developing a clear picture of what a publication or logo is meant to accomplish and what resources will be available. Gather data from reliable sources. When possible, check key assumptions with the project's decision-makers. In doing so, you'll also be developing a comfort level and common language with your colleagues that can go a long way in ensuring the publication's success.

All of this might sound rather complicated for a modest-sized brochure; it is and it isn't. Knowing your client's needs is essential no matter what the project. Understanding the core data will enable you to create a clear conceptual solution to those needs rather than just guess at what might look appealing.

Once established, much of the foundation data will apply to other, similar publications for the same client and need to be updated only when they change direction or target a new audience or market. The information may apply to families of publications or even all the publications of a company for a period of time. It's necessary to establish a base of knowledge so you'll know where to make adjustments in the future.

The role of publications managers encompasses a wide range of titles and skill sets, including account executives, graphic designers, art and creative directors, and production and project managers. That's to say some professionals with those titles end up managing publications from their initiation through delivery, while others with specific publications management responsibilities are asked to take on the task of creative direction. Because of this diversity, some of the following steps might not be your direct responsibility. Even if this is the case, read on; understanding the role of each team member will only help in your position as overseer.

PROFILE THE CLIENT

Chances are you know a lot about your client. You might even work for the same company and interact daily. If you haven't interacted with him recently or are new to the organization, a bit of research will provide a starting point to your understanding of his needs.

Conduct as much independent research as possible before meeting about a specific project. This familiarity can help you ask pertinent questions, enabling you to move the process forward smoothly and economically.

Be curious. Information on clients and their industries is available in a variety of places. It is useful to have an understanding of the specific client company or organization, its top competitors or organizations providing similar services, and the industry or market sector in which it operates.

A review of Web-based and print communications by the client and related enterprises will provide valuable background information and help you refine your questions when meeting to determine a project's needs.

You'll want to develop a profile of who your client company is and what it might expect or need. After you qualify your client-profile test with knowledgeable insiders, you'll be ready to participate actively

---

Who Are These Guys?

- How long has the company been in existence?
- What are the mission and goals of the company?
- What products/services are offered by the organization? How are they sold/distributed?
- What audiences/customers are served by the company? Are multiple audiences involved? Consider, for example, the company that sells products through distributors to customers.
- Does the client have a strong graphic identity? Is the client company consistent in its public presentation?
- How well known is the identity or brand? How does your client company distinguish its brand?
- How do competitors distinguish their brands? What is the competition saying to your audience?
- What is the current perception of the client company? Is a change in perception needed?
- How can you ensure that your communication represents the client company appropriately?

In Reverse: MINI MotoringGear Spring/Summer 2005 Catalog

50,000feet, INC., NEW YORK/CHICAGO

"With most of our work at 50,000feet, we try to create artifacts that have value beyond just their ability to sell product," says the firm's executive creative director, Jack Sichterman. "For MINI Cooper, that approach is mandatory, because MINI owners have come to expect more from their ownership experience. For the 'motorer,' MINI is much more than a car or a product. It's a way of life."

Sichterman says that the design for the MINI MotoringGear catalog is a direct manifestation of that philosophy. "It provides a useful sales tool, but it also provides content that delivers on the promise of the MINI brand. The piece is easy for both dealers and customers to use," he says, "and it's also fun and informative." For example, opposite the leather driving gloves is content about making decisions by playing "rock, paper, scissors," which is done with the hands—a natural connection.

"This 'utility-entertainment' split personality has been delivered literally, in a 128-page book that can be read from either direction," says Sichterman. "You shop for gear in one. You motor in the other. The result is a catalog that broke through the direct mail clutter and is finding its way into MINI owners' glove boxes."

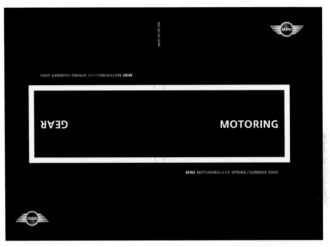

Art director: Tracy West
Writer: Reid Armbruster
Creative directors: Ken Fox, Jack Sichterman
Illustrators: Daniela Markova,
    Jonathan Sarmiento
Client: MINI Cooper
Copyright: © 2007 BMW of North America, LLC

with real questions when you meet the project's decision-makers. You'll be more efficient, demonstrate your interest in their well-being, and instill confidence in your ability to manage this valuable communication effectively.

DEFINE THE PROJECT

The primary purpose of your first client meeting is usually to define what the client has identified as his need, his desired solution, and the resources he's willing to expend to make it happen. It's like a job interview. Most clients appreciate a prepared, organized approach even if they are leading the discussion. Take notes that apply to your profile data and ask questions that either qualify or confirm the information being provided.

You'll gather information that will help you develop concepts for the publication project. Compose your questions in advance to keep the meeting focused, and use your time and that of your client efficiently.

Depending on the complexity of the project, consider having the writer and designer—and possibly other members of the creative team—attend the meeting. This will allow them to hear firsthand the project scope and client ideas. Often this is not necessary for a project with a fairly simple purpose and message that's being developed for a client you know well. For example, you probably could gather information from your client solo if you're developing that invitation or producing the second issue of an employee newsletter.

On the other hand, for a more challenging project, including members of your team in early meetings will give them the chance to ask questions directly, aiding clear communication. Bringing another professional into the process can help in gathering detailed information about processes that aren't your direct responsibility.

It's useful to remember that you are a professional manager; your expertise is in organization and in coordinating the entire team. You probably aren't, nor need you be, an expert in every technical area of each team member's craft. Bringing additional expertise to the table with you can be helpful, especially when being asked to meet monumental challenges. Allowing your colleagues to hear the urgency or the unusual circumstances of a project directly from a client can foster a shared ownership of an extraordinary need, and they'll be less likely to interpret your heightened concern as irrational panic.

The Fundamentals

Obviously you'll have a slightly altered menu of questions, depending on whether you're designing, say, an invitation package for a local fundraising event versus a major corporation's capabilities brochure. However, each will spring from the same basic reporter's questions. Ask as much as necessary to provide a clear understanding of what is expected.

Begin with the fundamentals: Why is the communication needed? Who is the audience that is receiving the publication? What is the message you want to deliver? And what do you want the audience to do?

Beyond this Joe Friday "just the facts" approach, in order to create a concept, your team will need as many other clues as can be teased from your client. Sometimes a seemingly innocuous phrase will spark that solution.

Preparing and asking these types of questions will help you grasp the scope, challenges, and opportunities of the project. The client's specific requirements will be reflected in the sound concepts you present, and your solutions will reflect your client's direction as well as the audience's needs.

Use Me: Art Explorers Portfolios
WIDGETS & STONE,
CHATTANOOGA, TN

"We wanted to create a piece that didn't feel sacred in the sense that you couldn't write in it or that you'd get it wrong and it would somehow be ruined," art director Matt Greenwell says, describing the Art Explorers kits that he and Paul Rustand designed for younger visitors at the Hunter Museum of American Art. The Widgets & Stone designers based the format of the project, now a showcase piece for the museum, on how the audience of families and children would use it and how they could get the most out of their museum experience with Art Explorers.

"The idea is that it's something that kids take with them through the museum and that belongs to them. The chipboard material that we used for the covers functions as a portfolio surface so that they can write on the individual pages," Greenwell explains. "Paul and I both have kids. We thought about the kinds of things that kids like to do and how they use drawing as a tool for learning and for recording thoughts and ideas. In our experience, that process is often nonlinear and unstructured, and Art Explorers is designed to encourage a less rigid interaction with the content. Images that we've included from the museum's collection are placed as if in a scrapbook. The effort was to create a sense of immediacy and accessibility."

To make the piece interactive with the museum experience, "all of the sections are keyed to specific galleries, and encourage kids and their families to look at particular works and answer questions through a combination of writing and drawing. The hope is that kids take Art Explorers home and the families keep the book as a kind of continually evolving record of their museum visits—to be the first step in a lifelong love for the arts."

Designers: Paul Rustand, Matt Greenwell
Illustrator: David Young
Client: Hunter Museum of American Art

"You have to figure out what the real message is that you need to impart and how to do that most effectively," says former *Wendy's Magazine* editor Beth Swanson, now an independent consultant for internal corporate communications and public relations. "There are so many different ways you can go in terms of developing how to say something. But if you don't know what your purpose is, you may end up with an article that's unusable.

"My number-one piece of advice is to make sure you get the content right," Swanson says. "Do research. Know the kind of content your audience is looking for and what's most helpful to them in terms of how to present it. Be specific about what action they need to take and why. You can't think that just sharing news is going to light a fire under anyone."

To flesh out the facts and to precisely gauge where the client believes he is headed with a particular project, you'll need to dig a little deeper. Explore preconceived notions about what the client wants to see and read in the piece (see sidebar at left).

This early information serves to bring the project into focus. Then you should be able to define the resources you'll employ.

DEVELOP CONCEPTUAL SOLUTIONS

So often, truly creative solutions to communication problems are dismissed as intuition. "She just came up with it!" Intuition might be a valid explanation of inspiration as long as it's qualified as the intuition of a talented, well-prepared mind that is applied to a specific situation. All of your fact-gathering will pay off when you can assimilate, organize, and synthesize the facts, needs, and desires of your client into the communication you're developing. Then *voila*: a concept.

Digital entrepreneurs dream of the "killer app," applying a new or existing technology in a revolutionary way that is appreciated by a large segment of the market. That isn't much different from what you're trying to achieve in your communication concept. Rarely are you

---

Quiz Your Client

These questions should provide most of the background information you and your team will need to develop a publication solution that answers the client's needs.

- What words would the client use to describe the company?

- What are the demographics of the company's target audience?

- How are audience members affiliated with the organization? Is there more than one audience group?

- What communications would the client say have worked in the past and why?

- What specific components of publications has the client liked?

- What has the editorial tone of past publications been? Are specific changes needed in the editorial direction?

- What has the graphic style of past communications been? Are specific changes needed in the graphic design direction?

- How has the company measured the success of past communications, and what have the results been?

- What is the purpose of the new publication? What audience response or action is desired?

- Have similar communications shared a theme or related themes?

- Is the audience familiar with the information? Will the piece be delivering news, or has the information been available through other means? Will the publication maintain or change the status quo?

- Is the company planning significant changes, say, in structure, in growth or downsizing, or in product, that might influence the direction of the project?

- What is the schedule? Turnaround time will be an important factor in developing a workable concept.

- What budget is available for the publication? Equally as important as schedule, knowing your financial resources will guide your publication ideas from the start.

- How will the publication be distributed?

Ready, Aim, . . . :
Target Bookmarked Logo
WINK, MINNEAPOLIS, MN

"It's conceptual, of course, by its nature," says Wink principal Richard Boynton, "but I think that something simple and intuitive just happens. Those always seem to be the ones that work the best."

The design firm was working with several names supplied by Target's copywriter for the new mark for the company's online book club. "Bookmarked" was one of them, and it was in the back of the creative team members' minds throughout the conceptual phase.

"We had done several logos that incorporated a book illustration. A couple of them had a book standing up that looked like it was on a shelf, a book lying down. That's when I noticed we had a stack of two books that made a B, but it didn't have a crossbar going through it," Boynton remembers. "Of course, the idea of including the bookmark just seemed a natural progression to creating the crossbar—and it also gave a place for the Target logo."

Because the book club identity would always appear in the context of a Target store or its Web site, Boynton says, including the company logo was not a requirement, but it would be extremely helpful. "It built in an inherent equity even though it was a new venture for them. Adding the Target bull's-eye made the program seem not just temporary but as though it would be around for a while."

Coordinating with Target's "very clean aesthetic" was, of course, a requirement. "We knew that whatever we did would have to fit within that. Then there's the Target red that was a prerequisite. The red creates the visual congruity.

"It just had to be fun, accessible, appropriate to what the content would be. Trademarks that are deliberate, that are simple like that, they always seem to be the ones that just come out of a weird intuitive sense. If you overthink designing logos, when you try to build too much into them, you end up with these very complex things that don't work."

Creative directors: Richard Boynton, Scott Thares, and Jason Langer (Target)
Designer: Richard Boynton
Illustrator: Richard Boynton
Client: Target

inventing a wholly new approach (I can't recall when this has happened, but want to respect those who thought that they had). You're much more likely to be sifting through all of the possible options to find one that fits the situation.

You've already begun by defining the publication needs. Now distill the objective criteria into a few sentences, a project overview. Include the fundamentals—why? who? what?—in your overview. When communicating the project to others on your team, including your clients, listen for any possible misconceptions. Adjust the project overview so that you are describing the criteria as clearly as possible. Remember the fundamental here: Put it in writing. Having a written project overview will allow all team members to qualify what they hear, and they'll be able to participate fully and be better able to understand how proposed concepts serve the client's need.

Several sound methods for conceiving ideas will form your ultimate concept, even when you're going it largely alone. But make sure that you don't allow yourself to work completely in a vacuum—even if your work structure might be set up for that secluded situation.

The methods for conceptualizing are easy to employ. Begin by looking around. Could it get any more basic? Look at what's current, what's cutting-edge in your project's industry. What's the competition doing? What has your client done in the past? What's effective and what has fallen on its face?

Collect samples of product brochures, annual reports, catalogs, direct mail postcards, customer newsletters, and anything else that catches your attention. Often you'll find workable solutions in seemingly unrelated projects. Over time your collection of exemplary publications will serve as a valuable reference stash that you can raid for inspiration, direction, or even quick solutions.

As you're looking around, record what is effective with consumers, even if it doesn't seem to immediately relate to your communication. Reach beyond the industry to the type of publication you'll be developing, look at what's *au courant* in bigger arenas. What's the latest, and how might it influence your publication approach? Fashion movements, fads, buzzwords, catch phrases, even colors and shapes rise or fall in popularity. And since you're building a print communication, trends affecting printed materials are especially relevant. For instance, what books are on the best-seller list? What magazine categories—celebrity, home projects, race car driving—are thriving? What's on TV? Is your audience "watching the detectives" or addicted to reality competitions? All of these stimuli can impact how your reader interprets your message, so work with it.

Ask your colleagues and your clients what relevant concepts—in any relatable medium—have caught their eye. Then probe: Ask them what has been the attracting element—color, white space, size, photography, clever language, clutter, sparseness? After you've done your research and collected opinions, you might decide to play it safe and follow the pack or turn the trend on its head.

Qualify the publications you've chosen: What distinguishes those you admire? Ask your ad hoc reviewers to choose favorites among similar publications and have them explain why. What visual and verbal components spark their interest? And what's the emotional appeal?

Now, how do you apply your observations to your concept? Refer back to the project's statement of purpose and return to your publication's goals. When conceptualizing a solution, the more definitive your ultimate objectives, the easier it will be to evaluate effectiveness. Your idea will need to directly address the challenge that mandates a communication in the first place.

The Art of Brainstorming

Everyone knows how to toss around their great ideas. That's called brainstorming, right? Well, sort of. Formal brainstorming sessions are designed to generate large numbers of ideas—good, bad, and otherwise. It isn't necessarily a process for determining which solution best solves a problem. The primary purpose is to generate a range of possibilities from every conceivable angle, then sort through them later to determine their value.

Brainstorming can be a highly structured, contemplative exercise or it can take the form of a lively conversation, a sort of group free-association session. Jill Howry, principal of Howry Design Associates, endorses the latter: "The more voices heard in the meeting, the better—nothing held back."

Whichever method you choose, here are a few guidelines that will help you get the most from a brainstorming exercise. The basic steps are: stating the problem, generating ideas, and a collective review of possible solutions. The collective review is important because you'll want to have participants see and hear about solutions that might involve directions radically different from their own. Such new directions could clear paths leading to solutions unimaginable without those stimuli.

FACILITATE AS AN EQUAL

A session facilitator is responsible for maintaining guidelines and encouraging participation. He can participate, as an equal, as long as he doesn't play a dominant role in the last review step. The facilitator will:

- Maintain a relaxed, respectful environment.
- Describe the brainstorming process. Review the short sections below and paraphrase them so team members feel comfortable with your faith in the value of the process.
- Distribute writing/drawing materials to each member.
- Give a description of the why, who, and what: the need, the audience, and the call to action.
- Be ready to answer any questions with factual data. Try to provide the client's criteria without interpretation.
- Monitor time: Keep sessions in which participants generate ideas on their own in brief, ten to fifteen minute rounds, before a short break.
- Start with two rounds and add more if you sense the team has more to offer.

BE ENCOURAGING

Brainstorming and other group-participation exercises can be a challenge for some. The goal here is to free all members' minds and encourage them to explore ideas that aren't obvious without the fear of looking silly or stupid. These anxieties can keep some people from joining in. Unless you have full participation, you risk having good ideas lost. Keep the atmosphere loose, safe, and fun.

SUSPEND JUDGMENT: THERE ARE NO BAD IDEAS

Don't edit yourself or others; you have to be able to set ego aside. Try to overcome performance anxieties and encourage an environment that allows everyone to feel secure offering any idea—and supporting it. Editing of selections comes later.

Evaluating which possible solution best answers the problem's criteria may be better made outside. Keeping value judgments separate from the creative sessions can avoid chilling team members' participation in future sessions.

MORE IS MORE

It's all about quantity. Let it fly. Keep the ideas raw. If you or other participants think of a variation or refinement, offer it as a separate idea.

MAKE AN ARTIFACT

If you're conducting a lively free-for-all exchange, assign a note-taker so that early ideas aren't lost to the last ones expressed. If you're asking participants to present ideas on paper, be sure to preserve them. Avoid the crumpled-paper dismissal.

If brainstormers are drafting their ideas for presentation, after each round have members read or explain their ideas, then post them around the room. Treating all ideas offered with uniform respect throughout the process will foster a sense of equality among participants and encourage them to offer their thoughts freely without fear of rejection.

REVIEW AND REPEAT AS NECESSARY

Together, team members should have a chance to review all of the ideas generated. This can be an exciting moment as participants see entirely different perspectives. A newfound one often leads to radically altered ideas in subsequent brainstorming rounds.

Next, list words that describe the successful communications and current trends you've identified. Try to associate them with your objectives and audience. You're in search of a hook—visual or verbal or both—that will make the message click with readers immediately. In effect, you're brainstorming with yourself. Write down all of your ideas—possible headlines, images, unusual publication formats—without editing or censoring them.

Many, if not most, of the ideas might miss the mark, and that's OK. Each one you put to paper—or screen—has the potential to launch or link to another, more suitable idea. You'll find that you pick up momentum when you let go of prejudging your thoughts. This is free-association time; you can weed out the duds later.

Now that you have several raw ideas, judge them against the communication criteria and client needs you researched, and the testing of sample publications you conducted. Compare their visual and verbal elements with those effective components you identified in your client's other publications and those you identified as exemplary. Ask which communicate the message with the greatest impact to the audience, and allow those that aren't so strong and clear to fall by the wayside, no matter how clever they may immediately seem. Caution: Cleverness can obscure clarity. Hold onto the few concepts that warrant being taken to the next step.

A Concept Overview Should Include

- The purpose of the piece. Example: to increase attendance at this year's gala by 20 percent to meet the fundraising goal of $120,000.

- An encapsulation of the communication's message. Example: The company has enjoyed a positive fiscal year due to reasons A, B, and C. It will continue its three-year plan to meet objectives X, Y, and Z.

- The intended audience or audiences.

- The working title or tagline, which might evolve as the project proceeds, either to work better with the design or to better position the message of the publication.

- An initial design description or general specifications. Example: 44-page plus cover, 5-color plus varnish, 15 to 20 bleed photos, 32 pages coated stock, 12 pages uncoated stock for financials.

- An overview of the schedule. You might only be able to include the delivery date at this stage. If possible, include key dates or time frames for copy, design, photography, final approval, press date, and delivery.

- Names and contact information for you, the publications manager; the client and final approver; the creative team members; and the printer, if known.

Before investing too much in an idea, test it. Share your solution with a few coworkers or colleagues. This need not be formal; you're just trying to bomb-proof your idea, to uncover any obvious faults before you stake your reputation on it. The reviewers don't have to be your peers; heck, grab the delivery guy if he represents your audience. Show the few headlines you've selected from your solo brainstorming. If you're not a designer and haven't drawn up sketches, try to briefly describe the look of the publication. Ask the same questions you posed about the sample publications. Bottom line: What works for them and why? And be as specific as possible.

Your next step might be back to the drawing board for refinements—or to try all over again. Don't get discouraged. Let the comments sift through your brain as your subconscious works on the problem. Start afresh and resume your brainstorming. Spark new ideas by exploring the opposite of some of your original ones—or at least try to give them a twist. It's OK to use the thesaurus to discover other words that might better connect with the audience. It's OK to use a common catchphrase or cliché and replace a word to create a new, appropriate message. These techniques can help warm up your brain. Rinse and repeat.

More Than a T-Shirt:
Hanes Beefy-T 2004 Logo

HENDERSONBROMSTEADART,
WINSTON-SALEM, NC

"Beefy-T has a fairly strong brand presence in the T-shirt trade," says HBA principal Hayes Henderson. "People tend to look for the new thing that comes out each year" for the company's giveaways.

What began as "knocking around T-shirt ideas for Hanes" birthed something far bigger—from "one little sketch at the bottom page of someone's sketchbook," says Henderson. "Once everyone saw it, we realized it was too good of a mark not to be used in a bigger way than just a T-shirt graphic.

"We were thinking about the broader theme for the trade event that [Hanes attends] each year and their marketing and trade campaign for the new season. What we initially started working on wasn't so much a logo idea as a theme for the season." The team came up with a butcher shop theme, which lent itself to a wealth of "peripheral

ideas that make for interesting little direct mails or clever double meanings on things as far as language goes.

"All of the butcher shop themes sort of spiraled around this little cut of meat, literally the Beefy-T logo," says Henderson. That logo, used fairly extensively for the 2004 season, met phenomenal success with business customers, who continued to ask about the T-bone steak mark long after it was retired.

Creative director: Hayes Henderson
Designer: Will Hackley
Client: Hanes

Don't bank on the success of a single concept. You can do your research, interview your client, and define your audience, but there's no magic wand for conjuring a perfect solution that is guaranteed to work with your readers—or to satisfy your client. Fully develop at least two, preferably three. At the same time, refrain from presenting too many concepts, which could overwhelm your client and muddle your task. Take a close look at your solutions against the criteria you set for the publication and ensure that your concepts truly answer the need.

SOLIDIFY THE CONCEPTS

Once you've identified a couple of workable conceptual solutions, it's time to reduce them to writing. And "reduce" is the key: Keep it short. Make it easy to grasp so that when you leave your client's office, he has a good chance of sending your message forth without too much distortion.

Don't assume that everyone has the same understanding of the concept. If you explained the idea to someone and your client explained the idea to someone, how consistent would the explanations be? The safe alternative to assumption: Solidify the communication approach in everyone's mind—yours, the client's, the writer's, and the designer's—with a succinct written concept overview. This document will keep everyone focused on solving the same problem.

What's the Real Problem?

Here are a few questions that will help define client criticisms:

- Are you happy with the size and positioning of the logo or brand?
- Do you think the text is easily read?
- What attracts your eye first?
- Does the piece look like it comes from your company? If yes, why (this may help the two of you discern what else is right with the design)? If not, why not (are the colors too bold, for example, or are there too many elements on the page, making it look like it's intended for a too-young audience)?
- Do you like the palette?
- Do you like the style of photography? If not, would you prefer more active shots instead of posed portraits? Does the close cropping around the head shots look too *avant garde*?
- Do you like the size of the publication? Do you think a traditional, standard size would be more in keeping with the tenor of the company?

PRESENT THE CONCEPTS

In an ideal situation, you'll be presenting to the decision-maker face to face (e.g., see chapter 4). This will allow an in-person exchange of questions and answers, and perhaps will further client direction and concept development.

Depending on a number of factors, such as the turn-around requirement, the complexity of the project, and perhaps your longstanding, comfortable relationship with the client, concepts could be e-mailed in PDF form directly from you or the designer to the reviewer.

Regardless of the method you choose to present your solutions to your client, it is essential that your initial design compositions (comps) stand alone as much as possible. It's likely that these materials will be retained by the client and shown by him to others, so the comps need to be clearly explained and understood.

If you are presenting your concepts to a client subordinate who will then carry your ideas to a higher-up, be sure to pitch your presentation in concise language that can be relayed easily. Present only the concepts that you and your team believe in and can support. Don't go into the client review meeting with a mangy dog hoping that the decision-maker doesn't choose it. If you show it, they may just choose it, so don't show it.

Sometimes it's a temptation to present additional yet lesser concepts for quantity's sake. But your goal is quality. What if a client is sold on superficial comps you know are not fully developed or truly

Inside Job: Hambly & Woolley Letterhead Kit and Moving Announcement

HAMBLY & WOOLLEY, INC., TORONTO, CANADA

When Hambly & Woolley prepared to move its offices a few years ago, the principals and husband and wife Bob Hambly and Barb Woolley saw it as the opportune time for revamping as well as reprinting their stationery. They wanted to keep their longtime signature pig (HAMbly) and sheep (WOOLley) but as they told their designers, "It's time that they manifested themselves in a new way, and we don't know what that is. You guys know us really well." Hambly and Woolley wanted the entire studio of twelve represented in the identity program, not just the pig and sheep duo. When they turned the redesign project over to five designers, Hambly says, "We actually treated it like a regular job with an outside client.

As a group, we had a healthy discussion about what we were looking at and what their thinking was behind it. I think they originally showed us about fifteen design ideas and we narrowed it down to maybe three or four and said, 'here are some things where we'd like to see some refinements.' We went to another round and brought everybody back. Though it was narrowed down to a smaller group of designers, we still incorporated everybody's feedback because it was going to represent all of us."

Next the whole project team "just did what designers love to do. We got down to a working session where we would run back and forth to the computer and try different things and bring it in and look at it. What was the color palette going to be? What fonts were we going to use? What paper stock? How did we envision this being printed? What process?"

Creative director: Bob Hambly
Art director: Barb Woolley
Designer: Emese Ungar-Walker

Thanks to: Dominic and Kristin
Client: Hambly & Woolley, Inc.
Copyright: © Hambly & Woolley, Inc.

"For a lot of the work that we do around visual identities, we mine the creative powers of as many designers here as possible," he says. "We're not the kind of studio that gives a job to one person. Especially not with visual identities. I think when you go back to a client you need to go back with a range of things."

Although the designers at first worked individually on their concepts, the teamwork and brainstorming soon began. "They had got together as a group and not only talked about their ideas but consolidated how visually it was going to be presented, and it was consistent," Hambly says. "They pooled their efforts. They went through the process that we normally do with a client.

Hambly admits that you can't afford to have everyone involved in all aspects of the process for most jobs, but "we have done some bigger identities where we went through the same process. As you know, designers tend to live somewhat in little vacuums, especially with the computer. We've done everything we can to try to encourage designers not only to talk to one another but for us to talk as a group. It's a great way to come to terms with your strengths and your weaknesses, to be able to defend your work, and that's the culture here." The team's consensus on the new letterhead suite? "It was nice that everybody, to some degree, touched it."

grounded in the mission of the communication? You'll be stuck with a concept that can grow less and less effective, even while you try to make it work as the publication process proceeds.

When presenting concept comps to your clients, discuss the verbal and visual solutions—and how they work together effectively. If at all possible, review your presentation with your creative team first. Your role is to explore with the client what he responds to positively or negatively and why. And your responsibility is to represent the thinking of the team and to understand the types of changes that might compromise the effectiveness of the concept.

Sometimes you'll work with a client who is inexperienced at reviewing design comps. Perhaps he simply doesn't know what to look for or how to articulate why he just doesn't like a design. Maybe there's not enough visual detail for the reviewer to envision how the final piece will look.

He may try to compensate for this lack of knowledge with an overly authoritative tone or by fixating on one element, say, a background color he doesn't care for. Many times I've been in review sessions that have begun with the client saying, "This is all wrong" or "I have a lot of changes on this." It has turned out, though, that the only problem was an easily adjusted element. Many clients tend to unconsciously exaggerate problems because they seize on the negative. It's your job to guide the client–designer relationship and to steer communications in a positive direction that will result in the most effective design.

When working with a client who has difficulty approaching the review of a design or explaining what doesn't work for him, you'll need to ask questions to unearth what the problem really is.

In your review conversation, use nontechnical terms the client will understand. By engaging the client and asking questions he can answer, you'll create a safe environment for discussion that will make him more comfortable and help you both arrive at what the design concerns actually are.

It is not your duty to agree with everything your client says or to make wholesale changes based on his comments. The result might be a muddled concept that no longer communicates the message clearly or speaks to the audience. Furthermore, you don't want to return to your team with a new tagline that doesn't work or a new design that has taken pieces from three different approaches that don't mesh. This will make for frustrated freelancers as well as a disjointed, ineffective concept. You'll employ testing as needed to allow your readers to help select the strongest concept (e.g., see chapter 8).

Clients can be eager to discuss the concept presented and develop it further. These discussions often can refine your idea and strengthen your solution. However, be prepared for their wish to integrate components from several solutions, a sort of "one from column A, two from column B" approach. It's commonplace for clients to want to take standout elements from one concept and apply them to another. This is why it can be important to bring your creative team to the presentation or to be fully confident that you can represent the reasoning behind the concepts and not allow the design integrity to be compromised.

Including the Creative Team

Depending on the import and complexity of the project—and on your comfort level—have the designer and the writer attend the concept review meeting to represent their thoughts behind a visual or editorial approach. This must be done diplomatically. Make clear that the meeting is not a forum for ego-driven argument or stolid defense of a concept, but for elaboration on a communication solution as needed.

Special Delivery:
Deborah Kelb CPA Letterhead

COMMERCIAL ARTISAN,
INDIANAPOLIS, IN

"Take something that you would just assume would not be special, and try and make it special. We always look for that opportunity." Principal James Sholly put that philosophy to work when he and partner and brother Jon Sholly conceptualized a humorous letterhead for their CPA, Deborah Kelb.

"Deborah had an identity that she had been using that was really about as dry as you could get," James Sholly says. "I think she had it typeset at Kinko's or Office Depot or some place like that, where you just sort of get the bold Helvetica type and it's black and shiny."

In a way, the idea for a suite reminiscent of IRS forms came from Deborah herself. "One thing she had done that I thought was really clever was to get her phone number, which is 466-1040. To have that number was a fun clue—with everything else being so banal. The concept just sprang out of that.

"We thought, 'Let's just go for it and see what she thinks,' and it ended up working out." Asked whether the letterhead has been heart-stopping for any of Deborah's clients, James Sholly says that as soon as they realize what it is about, "they're delighted."

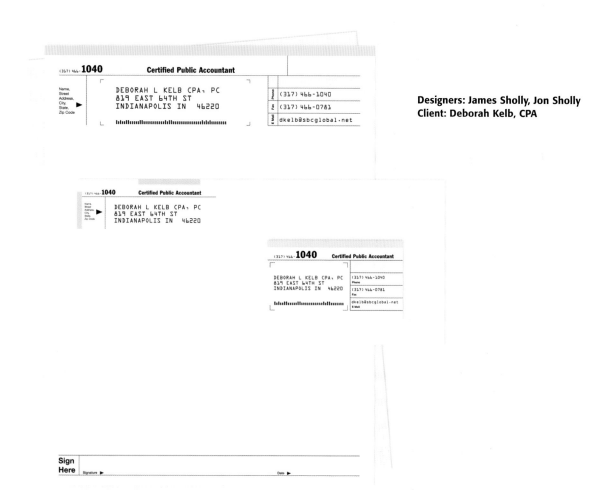

Designers: James Sholly, Jon Sholly
Client: Deborah Kelb, CPA

Make It Happen:
"What Moves You?" Postcards
nFUSION GROUP, AUSTIN, TX

Art director Megan Berryman, of nFusion Group, set out to involve the audience emotionally in this series of fundraising event postcards for the local Hill Country Ride for AIDS. "As the designer, I worked with the copywriter to come up with the line, 'What Moves You?' The concept was based around your finding out what moves yourself in order to make this ride happen and in order to help cure AIDS."

The purpose of the postcard series of six, Berryman says, was not only to "get people geared up to attend the kick-off party and save the ride date." Its deeper audience call to action was a psychological one, a challenge to become involved. "We wanted something that was small, that wasn't as big as a brochure," to draw attention. "Each person on the front had a key statement about what moved them," prompting readers to think about the idea for themselves. An accompanying poster, part of the multicomponent campaign collateral package for the event, featured fifty-plus people pictured in small squares, each with a reflective word that reinforced the concept.

The ride is a challenge. So is living with AIDS. I work every day with people living with HIV and AIDS. I see their ups and downs, good days and bad, joys and many tears. THE RIDE makes such a difference in their daily lives. So I've volunteered for five years, making sure riders cross the finish line safely and have all the support they need. Just like the people I work with every day.

— Anitha Thomisee

I rode for the first time last year. I did it in the spirit of my FRIENDS Ricky and Richard — who are no longer with us. If they were still alive they would be riding right next to me, or at least yelling for me on the side of the road. We have to keep fighting so that one day there isn't a reason to ride.

— John Pitzer

Art director and designer: Megan Berryman
Photographer: Scott Van Osdol
Paper donation: Unisource & Fox River
Printers: Horizon Graphics, The Lithoprint Company
Ride director: David Smith
Austin Advertising Federation
Client: Hill Country Ride for AIDS

RIDE WEEKEND APRIL 30-MAY 1, 2005   WWW.HILLCOUNTRYRIDE.ORG   (512) 965.RIDE   WHAT MOVES YOU?

HILL COUNTRY RIDE FOR AIDS

Review your agenda with your team members well in advance of the meeting. This will give them a chance to weigh in. Define how each participant should and shouldn't contribute. The designer should explain, for example, how purple complements the company brand colors, not simply that purple is the only color that will work. Of course, the client may simply hate purple. There you are.

Explain that the concept might be developed further during the meeting. This isn't a contest. Often the most creative ideas begin as disjointed thoughts from different and clashing perspectives.

Effective concept development can be accomplished best as a team working together in a solution-oriented manner. Keep in mind that the client probably has the best understanding of what the brand is trying to represent and what the reality of the brand perception is.

4

Educating and Managing Clients

If you have a good relationship with your customer, the business process flows that much more smoothly.
—RICHARD PRATT

Your most unhappy customers are your greatest source of learning.
—BILL GATES

Sometimes you're buying, sometimes you're selling. As a publications manager, in some cases you're the client and other times you're serving a client.

In this chapter we'll focus on how to educate your client about the publications process, how to assess his communications needs, and when to hold your client's hand. We'll also explore what your expectations should be when you're the client of creative and production vendors.

Your relationships with clients or customers can be internal. If you are creating a publication for your supervisor or for another department in your company, these are examples of internal clients. For the same project, you might be managing the work of a company writer or designer.

Try viewing your work for inside higher-ups and your collaboration with colleagues as client relationships. This will help you develop a professional demeanor to which others will respond positively, whether you're wearing your publications manager hat or filling the client role.

If you're a sole proprietor or a member of a design or communications firm, most or all of your clients will be external. Again, the creative professionals you call on might be part of your company, or you might contract external resources and vendors to complete the project for your external client.

Above all, says consultant to creative professionals Emily Ruth Cohen, "Being honest with the client is important because it will encourage him to be honest with you. Apologize rather than make an excuse. Or if you feel the client is taking advantage of you, you need to tell him that—if he's subtly enlarging the project, doing 'scope creep,' you need to tell him that."

HOW MUCH DOES YOUR CLIENT KNOW?

Gauge your internal or external client's experience with the publications process. This will help you determine how extensively you need to educate him, and perhaps additional project contributors and approvers. You should discuss your responsibilities, the client's role, the publications process, and past client projects and experiences.

Client management "is a big part of the job," says the Story Board's Barry Nelson. "Any good publications manager needs to do a fair amount of educational work, to make sure the sources and approvers know that the first thing we have to do is get the story read, or else what's the point?

Is the Grass Greener?

"We produce about 250 projects out of here a year—which is a lot of work," says Jim Ales, design director for the Monterey Bay Aquarium. But for each of those projects "we are not reinventing the wheel, we are working within our established brand."

Ales notes that he has been on both sides of the client fence, running his own design business for ten years and heading up design at the aquarium for more than a decade. "The art of managing an internal design department," he says, "begins with patience and understanding. Here, you can't walk away from your problems. Like family, you have to work things out. There's a lot of forgiving on both sides."

A significant part of Ales's job is training his internal clients (the aquarium has 450 full-time employees)—from marketing to membership, from life sciences to education—in the brand. "A strong brand requires twenty-four-hour maintenance," he says. "It takes a lot of fortitude to maintain our position as a nationally recognized and respected brand."

Ales developed a PowerPoint brand presentation, which illustrates the purpose and importance of quality and consistency in messaging and design. He meets with each department (fifteen in all) periodically as part of his internal "brand education" program. "The level of sophistication varies greatly within the organization," he says. "My approach is to teach and partner, rather than isolate my clients."

In addition to education, working within an established system aids the three design team members with their client relationships. "We have a work order [e.g., see appendix A], which clients fill out as the starting point in the process. Most projects require a face-to-face meeting. We talk about the purpose of the project, who's the intended audience, what are the results you're looking for."

"I hate to see a communications program get so compromised trying to please approvers that it loses its focus on readers and comes out sounding so corporate, with its stories all playing out from a management point of view."

If you're dealing with an internal client you've worked with before, you probably have an idea of his publications process experience. If you're just beginning a relationship with an internal client, say, a department head, or with an external client, perhaps a college development officer, talk with your new customer about his past publication experiences. Employ diplomacy to avoid insulting or embarrassing him. A client might be sensitive over his lack of knowledge about communications management. Cohen notes that it's so important to "realize that the client is not the enemy. A lot of complaints that design firms and in-house departments have involve the client, but most are actually about the processes, about staffing, or about structure. You have to educate the client." Try to set the client at ease by positioning your relationship as a partnership: You'll guide the process and involve the client as much as he desires.

Cohen says that if publications managers can "embrace their role in streamlining and improve their business and management skills, it'll go a long way in making projects more economical and more successful."

Your client needs to be familiar with the basic process steps so he'll know what to expect and when. Knowing the approximate time frame and cost associated with each phase of developing a publication will raise his comfort level and limit your hand-holding duties. And when you clearly define schedule and budget factors that could impact the project, you'll motivate your client to respect deadlines and avoid last-minute changes. Also, define his responsibilities for the project, such as content contribution and timely reviews, versus your tasks, including, for example, contracting a writer and schedule management. This will enable you to work together as partners more efficiently and amicably.

EXPLAIN YOUR RESPONSIBILITIES

First, explain your role and services. As a publications manager, your responsibilities and tasks—whether you perform them yourself or call on other internal or external resources to do so—likely will include the following. Don't let this lengthy list overwhelm you; not all of these items will apply to every project, and in later chapters you'll learn how to manage each step one at a time. These steps appear approximately in chronological order. Give your client an overview of what you'll be providing and coordinating for the given job.

Interview the client. You'll need to learn about the department's or company's mission statement, goals, and communication needs. This information will form the framework for the publication you're managing.

Define the publication basics. When you begin planning the specific printed piece, first determine the purpose, audience, and message (e.g., see chapter 3).

Determine the delivery date. If the client will be handling distribution to readers, discuss when he needs the publication delivered to his site or mail house. If you will be responsible for getting the piece to readers, determine the delivery date. Ask whether there are multiple addresses for shipment so you can make accommodations in your production schedule (e.g., see chapter 10).

Develop a working schedule. Several factors will influence the schedule you create, including the scope and complexity of the project, the availability and needs of internal creative professionals or free-lancers, and the delivery date.

Client tasks will be included in the schedule. Be sure to allow the client (and all project team members) to review a draft schedule so he can give input and make recommendations for adjustments before the calendar is completed. Copy everyone involved on the final schedule.

Develop a working budget. First obtain from your client any information about the budget that has been allotted for the publication. Try to determine at least a ballpark figure or range that he has in mind. You should not have to guess what resources the client has available for the project.

Depending on your budget experience, don't immediately commit to producing the publication within the client's budget. You'll need to gather estimates from any external creative resources, and production and distribution vendors first. Explain that you'll provide an estimate to the client and that upon his approval of the cost, you'll be managing the project so it does not exceed the budget.

Prepare a proposal. Creation of a proposal and its contents will depend on whether the project is for an internal or external client. One might not be necessary for a publication you're managing for your company. Still, consider an abbreviated document for internal review to make sure you and the client are on the same page.

The proposal will spell out your understanding of the project, a general description of your recommended solution, approximate schedule and budget, everything that is included in the cost, information about individuals on the project team, if known at this stage, as well as other information as needed (e.g., see chapter 5). Your client must review and sign off on the proposal before any development work begins.

Compose a client contract. If you're working with an external client, make sure a contract is signed before any development takes place. The contract should specify not only details concerning your primary role of, say, designer (including scope of project, payment amount and terms, and deadline), but also your publications management responsibilities and fees (including management of vendors, for example, and proof-review coordination).

Client Collaboration: Digital Learning Group Branding Package

EVINS DESIGN, BALTIMORE, MD

"I think it's a two-way street," is how Julia Evins, principal of Evins Design, describes client education. "You educate each other. Designing for a client and a business that is not your own is an education every time. I live vicariously through their projects."

Evins enjoyed "a real collaboration" with client Christie Timms, founder of Digital Learning Group, when the new company was ready to create a compelling brand. "What I appreciated so much was that Christie spent the time to do this right," says Evins. "She knew what she wanted. She gave great feedback. She didn't rush the process. When you have a great client, the ideas seem to come so much easier."

Christie E. Timms
EXECUTIVE DIRECTOR

Digital Learning Group

Post Office Box 15
Ellicott City, Maryland 21041
PHONE 410.795.8850
FAX 410.750.9720 (CALL)
ctimms@digitallearninggroup.org

Asking comprehensive questions, often on more than one occasion, is Evins's formula for kicking off the project right: "Ultimately, you need to know where they want to go with this company, what kind of product will they have, who's the audience for these products. For example, one might assume that Digital Learning Group was potentially geared toward children's learning. But the client made it clear that DLG would work with all age groups in any kind of media. We needed to create a logo brand that could represent a varied and growing product."

Evins says that normally she shows "no more than three logo concepts. But in this case, I believe I presented five. The original logo concept had a few options—three hands, four hands, different colors. After a few rounds of revisions, mostly showing the hands in different configurations, we settled on the DLG logo with three hands.

"I wanted the logo to feel 'aspirational' and suggest modern modes of learning. The three hands reach up, perhaps answering a question; I wanted this logo to have an upward flow. The hand colors connect and interact with each other and give the logo an approachable feel. [It conveys] that DLG is about a wide range of people using technology to learn and grow."

Her best work, says Evins, comes "when the client and the designer work together . . . [though] not every client wants a collaborative process. I may come up with the initial ideas or I may take their copy and rework the order—try to create some consistencies in text/headline.

"Or I may see a great idea buried in the middle of the copy. I try to show the client we have this great concept that we should bring to the surface. And the client is often receptive. You have to be open to the feedback you receive. Even feedback that may not work can open you up to something that does work.

"I often have to remind myself that until you show the work, they're taking an educated guess that you're going to deliver for them," Evins continues. "I do try to explain what to expect from the process. I tell them what the next steps will be—initial concepts, feedback from the client, revision time, approving the logo design, and then building out the package of collaterals. I give a timeline. The more information about the process you can give the client, the more comfortable they will be."

Digital Learning Group

1643 Liberty Road, Suite 106 • Eldersburg, Maryland 21784 • PHONE 410.795.8850 • FAX 410.795.8851

···Extensive Interactive Digital Experiences

Beyond our award-winning credentials in instructional design, video production and interactive digital media, Digital Learning Group possesses extensive experience reaching diverse student populations ranging from preschool age children to adults. We have created unique, hands-on professional development programs for teachers, multimedia instruction for job placement candidates, services for child care providers and families, and interactive experiential websites and educational resources for K-12 and adult classrooms.

Online Field Trips and Interactives

Computer screen journeys transport middle school students to new and distant worlds through virtual museum spaces. Highly interactive technologies invite visitors to explore history, earth science, art and commerce with streaming video, flash animation, decision-making modules, adaptive building programs, and multi-layered content. Lesson plans, primary source documents, links for further research, and fun family and class activities are included.

USA Today:
"Early one of the best literary sites we've seen in years."

Education World:
A+
"Dramatic, highly interactive site. A real winner."

Bay Trippers

Visitors join an archeological dig, experience a virtual sailing excursion, discover flora and fauna, and examine dangers impacting the health of the Chesapeake Bay.

Knowing Poe

Edgar Allan Poe's writings evoke images beyond the printed word. This site allows students to experience Poe's mysterious life and haunting works.

Picasso

Pablo Picasso single-handedly changed the face of 20th-century art. Students explore his early influences to further appreciate his vision and contribution.

Store Alert

Use interactive tools to learn what tobacco companies are doing to market products in convenience stores and what local communities can do about it.

Sense and Dollars

Planning tools illustrate spending and saving cause and effect. Families learn about credit cards, investment programs and personal economics.

Words for Work

A state-of-the-art multimedia program that develops vocational English language skills. This quick-start program prepares Latinos for jobs in occupations such as healthcare and construction.

Accolades
Our projects have won awards from major media festivals, including a National Emmy for an award-winning community service campaign, CINE Golden Eagles for video documentaries, and distinctions from many major education website for quality interactive learning resources.

Designer: Julia Evins
Printers: Cavanaugh Press (brochure), Woodberry
** Graphics (letterhead and business papers)**
Client: Digital Learning Group

Contact and contract creative resources. If the publication is for an internal client, you might be working with an inside writer and designer. If external resources are needed, you'll probably be responsible for contacting one or more freelancers to discuss different development phases of the project. (Alternatively, your client might ask you to work with freelancers he's hired in the past.)

In addition, you'll gather estimates from those creative professionals. You might make the decisions on who to hire, taking estimates into consideration as well as other factors (e.g., see chapter 7). You will decide with your client which of you will handle freelancer billing and payment. If this is to be your responsibility, depending on your own payment terms, you could be compensating resources directly and then receiving client reimbursement. In this case include an additional fee for this upfront out-of-pocket expense and your management of the logistics. Disclose this fee to your client so he can make an educated decision about whether to handle payment of freelancers and other vendors directly.

Coordinate client–talent meetings. If your client will be more involved with selection and payment of a freelancer you recommend, you'll arrange a meeting between them on the client's request. Remember that you will be coordinating the creative product. Make sure you have the opportunity to offer your input on the appropriate person for the job.

Conduct interviews. Collecting content for copywriting could be one of your responsibilities. You or an internal or external writer might need to conduct research or interview the client, other company personnel, or external parties.

Develop copy. Initial copy concepts, perhaps a publication theme, tagline, or major headlines, should be developed in conjunction with the design concepts when possible. You'll present first, second (as needed), and final drafts of the copy for client corrections and conduct or coordinate fact-checking (depending on who is responsible for this task).

Develop design. You'll manage creation of the graphic concepts for client review (e.g., see chapter 3). After approval, you'll oversee development of design drafts, complete layouts, and final designs for changes and signoff.

Arrange photo shoots. Depending on art to be included in the piece, you might coordinate a photo shoot or contract illustration. This could involve photographer or artist interviews and selection, photo subject scheduling, and location logistics, as well as presenting proofs and making selection recommendations to your client (e.g., see chapter 7).

Negotiate rights. You should determine the usage rights required for the publication at hand and future projects as well. You'll be responsible for educating your client about all creative copyrights, licensing, and ownership (e.g., see chapter 7).

Coordinate testing. To ensure the success of your communication, you and your client might decide to conduct testing with a readership sample. Surveys, focus groups, or other testing methods will help you hone your message and graphics to effectively call your audience to action. As the publications manager, you'll recommend the method and either coordinate the testing logistics or contract a market research vendor (e.g., see chapter 8).

Contract production. Your company or client might have an established relationship with a printer, box manufacturer, mail house, or other production or distribution vendor. Or you could be in charge of selecting and managing these vendors (e.g., see chapters 9 and 10).

Manage production. As the coordinator of an internal print shop or outside printing company, you'll manage estimating, scheduling, proofs, and press checks.

Circulate proofs. Your client's review of prepress proofs must be completed on schedule to maintain your place in the print queue. Find out in advance when proofs will be delivered to your site, and arrange for your client and other approvers to be available for efficient turnaround. Make sure reviewers understand the costs involved with last-stage changes.

Coordinate distribution. You'll work with an internal mail house, or external printer or distributor to send out the finished publication. You'll need to accommodate shipping time and cost in your schedule and budget, and possibly coordinate delivery to several sites (e.g., see chapter 10).

Conduct follow-up testing. To evaluate the effectiveness of the publication, consider postdelivery audience testing. This would be especially valuable for printed materials with measurable objectives, such as some direct mail. You also should test ongoing publications, such as newsletters, periodically to gauge reader satisfaction and gather input for improvement.

COMMUNICATE YOUR CAPABILITIES IN WRITING

Your own capabilities brochure can spell out your services in writing for your client. This valuable educational tool will reinforce what you've discussed with the client. He can use the brochure as a reference throughout the development of the publication. This document differs from the traditional capabilities brochure that showcases a design firm's work, today typically presented online instead of in printed form. It focuses on the publications process and who needs to do what, and it can include examples of relevant projects.

It needn't be elaborate; it could be a simple Word document depending on your time and your design experience. Regardless of its format, you should try to include these basics: a brief introduction highlighting the brochure contents, a statement of your commitment to a smooth process or your work philosophy, an overview of a publications manager's responsibilities, a client's responsibilities, and the major process steps and the approximate time frame required for each.

Also consider including your background as it relates to publications management. If you have a team of creative and production professionals with whom you work, either in your department or in your external network, think about including their background information, too: names, credentials, experience, and some clients or company projects. If you're creating a more elaborate package, it's a good idea to design it in a way that's easy to update—for example, by containing different information sections on separately printed sheets.

Your Twenty Management Tasks

1. Interview the client.
2. Define the publication basics.
3. Determine the delivery date.
4. Develop a working schedule.
5. Develop a working budget.
6. Prepare a proposal.
7. Compose a client contract.
8. Contact and contract creative resources.
9. Coordinate client–talent meetings.
10. Conduct interviews.
11. Develop copy.
12. Develop design.
13. Arrange photo shoots.
14. Negotiate rights.
15. Coordinate testing.
16. Contract production.
17. Manage production.
18. Circulate proofs.
19. Coordinate distribution.
20. Conduct follow-up testing.

Go Ahead, Laugh:
Ph.D Self-promotion Book
Ph.D, SANTA MONICA, CA

"Humor is essential just for getting through life," says Ph.D creative director Mick Hodgson. "It breaks down any barriers." This was the philosophy behind the firm's *Terms and Conditions* self-promotion book, an LOL take on the traditional capabilities brochure.

The diminutive—read "handy"—reference presents dictionary-style definitions of thirty-nine words such as "brand," "integrity," "presentation," "solution," and "type." "Personality," for example, is described as "(1) We create personalities, not brands. Personalities are more accessible, less scientific than brands, and people relate to personalities better. (2) You might not need a logo, but you definitely need a personality. (3) In the old days, people would say, 'I don't need much, just a business card.' They didn't realize the amount of thought that goes into capturing the personality in such a small space."

Scattered among the clearly client-education (but still very funny) pages are quips including "Elevenses: When the tea arrives" and "Lofty: When the work gets awkward, designers turn to layers of meaning to obscure it."

The book, says Hodgson, is used both for client education and good client relations: "When you're asked what you specialize in, we talk about 'visual personality,' which is our take on branding. That's how we prefer to refer to our work.

"We get to the point where we understand who a client is, whether it's an individual or a big corporation, then we translate that into a visual personality, which other people would call developing a brand." Clients are excited by the idea of what their visual personality is, "so the book helps in that sense." The reaction to *Terms and Conditions*? Very positive—and a laugh.

Art directors: Clive Piercy, Michael Hodgson
Designers: Clive Piercy, Carol Kono
Client: Ph.D
Copyright: © 2005 Ph.D

eighteen

A brief introduction to **cockney** rhyming slang

How's yer father?

china	mate
frog	road
Tilbury	socks
butcher's	look
whistle	suit
Brahms	drunk
trouble	wife
apples	stairs
Lilian	fish
Henry	door
jam	car
titfer	hat
ice cream	man

1: slang

china plate (mate) frog and toad (road) Tilbury Docks (socks) butcher's hook (look) whistle and flute (suit)

Brahms and Liszt (pissed) trouble and strife (wife) apples and pears (stairs)

Lilian Gish (fish) Henry Moore (door) jamjar (car) tit for tat (hat) ice-cream freezer (geezer)

Idea
19.

1: a transcendent entity that is a real pattern of which existing things are imperfect representations : a plan for action : 2: a visible representation of a conception 3: an entity (as a thought, concept, sensation, or image) actually or potentially present to consciousness 4: a formulated thought or opinion 5: whatever is known or supposed about something 6: the central meaning or chief end of a particular action or situation

(**1**) Our business: Coming up with solutions that clients can take ownership of.
(**2**) Preconceived idea: Contradiction in terms
(**3**) The trick is to take ownership of ideas without getting possessive about them.
(**4**) Sometimes the best idea is the one that's flawed.

Less is more.
True, though in ways and for reasons that are hard to explain. Has something to do with encapsulation. Not necessarily minimalist at all. Can lead to things that are colorful and bright and loud and noisy. We prefer Milton Glaser's variation…
just enough is more

22.

ENOUGH *1: occurring in such quantity, quality, or scope as to fully meet demands, needs, or expectations*

1: devoted in character and spirit : noble : elevated in status : superior 2: having a haughty overbearing manner : supercilious 3: rising to a great height : impressively high, remote, esoteric

TWENTY-THREE

Lofty

When the work gets awkward, designers turn to layers of meaning to obscure it.

The Client's Role

Discuss the role your client will play during the process, and reiterate highlights of this information in your capabilities brochure. It's important for any client to be aware of his involvement in development of the publication before work begins. This will allow him to clear his calendar for such scheduled tasks as copy, design, and proof reviews. It also will give him the chance to communicate with others in his organization about their necessary contributions, from providing content resources to posing for photos to eyeballing comps and finals, if they're among the decision-makers.

Depending on the project and your agreement, your client's responsibilities and tasks will include most or all of the following:

Be available. Nothing's more frustrating than trying to track down a client who doesn't respond promptly to phone calls or e-mails. Equally important is his reasonable availability for meetings to discuss the project at the start and mid-progress, and for review of bluelines and color proofs. Without the client's commitment to be available to you and project team members as needed, the job will be in danger of veering off course.

Answer questions. You'll need a wealth of information at the outset and throughout publication development. Your client's duty is to supply that information, from audience demographics to delivery date. If he doesn't have the answer, your client is responsible for obtaining it from the appropriate, reliable source in a timely fashion. You won't be able to proceed effi-

---

Work Out the Details

Be aware of the minutiae that can bedevil an otherwise sound plan of action. Discuss these issues with your client before beginning the project. Note that fee-associated issues relate primarily to external clients; however, they also might impact your internal client's budget, depending on your company cost center system, so bring them up as needed.

All work phases must be signed by the client as evidence of review and release before work can proceed.

- The client's required usage/ownership of all creative elements and production materials published or created for the project must be determined before negotiations with artists and vendors.

- Internal information and documents provided to you, the publications manager, or to creative freelancers or production vendors will be honored as confidential. Is a confidentiality or nondisclosure agreement (e.g., see appendix A) required? Include that document as an addendum to the contract.

- Responsibility for fact-checking and final proofreading needs to be assigned to you, your designate, or, preferably, the client. Note this in your contract.

- If your client fails to adhere to the approved schedule, delivery might be delayed and budget impacted. Include this in your written agreement.

- Explain that rush charges might be incurred if changes or delays tighten the schedule. Define your own rush-charge policy, if applicable, and those of your resources, if known. This, also, should be part of your contract.

- Notify the client that there will be additional fees for changes beyond the project's scope or at late stages—for example, the request for a fourth copy draft or accommodation of a new photo at the prepress-proof stage. Add this to the contract.

- Define the out-of-pocket expenses for which you'll charge separately, such as mileage, travel, long-distance phone, and overnight mailings.

- Determine payment responsibility for third-party vendors, and add this to the written agreement.

- If you're handling invoices from freelancers and vendors, add a 10 to 20 percent administrative fee. More detail for the contract.

- Work out your fee schedule. Spell out your terms in the contract. Also explain any finance charge you'll apply for late payment.

- Tell the client that you will invoice and expect payment for work completed if the project ends before completion. Make sure this is written in the contract.

- In addition, be sure to gather contact information in advance for the client, any freelancers and vendors contracted by the client, and an accounts payable representative.

---

ciently without knowing what graphic standards exist, who's to be interviewed, the required quantity, and multiple other details.

Meet with the team. Decide with your client whether it would be valuable for him and perhaps others to sit down with project team members. This will depend on the complexity of the project, the client's involvement in hiring freelancers, the interaction between company personnel and creative resources for interviews and photo shoots, and other factors.

Provide information. You'll need at least basic information from your client to write copy—for example, an event's date, time, and location. It might be your client's responsibility to provide more comprehensive research or reference materials for content generation or to write the copy.

Act as a liaison. Your client should introduce you or your creative team members to any company people who will be interviewed or photographed. This liaison role should reach beyond providing you a name and a number. Your client should give the contact an advance heads-up by phone or e-mail about who will be getting in touch and why; for example, freelance writer Jane Connor will be calling you to arrange a time for a phone interview about the information technology (IT) department.

An in-person introduction might be more fitting for the comfort of everyone involved, such as the meeting of an executive and a photographer. Depending on the import of the project, say, an annual report or creation of a new company brand, it may be appropriate for your client to present the major team players to management members who will be contributing to or signing off on the job.

Adhere to schedules. Your production schedule should include all dates for your client's deliverables, including provision of reference material; meetings; and copy, design, and proofs turnarounds. Impress upon your client that upholding his responsibility to meet these deadlines will help ensure the publication stays on course. Depending on his other commitments, ability to focus on the project, and so on, consider reminding your client about when he'll receive a draft and when his comments are due throughout the development process.

"Additionally, if a client makes a late change," says Kinimod principal Dominik D'Angelo, "I am very honest about the impact that change will have on the budget and timeline. I clearly state the consequences and let the client decide whether the change is worth delaying the delivery of the project or increasing its cost."

Involve decision-makers. Ideally you'll work directly with the person who has the final say-so, but this isn't always the case. Your client contact might not be the ultimate decision-maker. Or he could be one of several.

"I will only work directly with a decision-maker," says D'Angelo. "Sometimes this is not the person who solicited your work or decided to hire you. Many times, the real decision-maker is very busy and shielded by other people. You have to fight for this person's time and attention—it is absolutely crucial to the success of any project."

Jill Howry, principal of Howry Design Associates, agrees. She involves critical parties from the start. "We are clear up front that the decision-makers need to attend the kick-off meeting—preferably the CEO," she says. "We write a creative brief and get signoff early on before design work begins. We want everyone's input at one meeting because it makes the process much more efficient."

It's your client's responsibility to secure initial buy-in and final signoff from everyone who has a say in the project. If other reviewers are not present during meetings, your client will need to present the appropriate project elements to them and obtain input within the agreed-upon schedule.

Prepare the Reader: *MFAH Today* Magazine Redesign

PENTAGRAM DESIGN, AUSTIN, TX

MFAH Today "got a lot of attention for us," says Pentagram Design creative director DJ Stout. "People really loved it, and the client [Museum of Fine Arts, Houston] loved it. The idea was to use this vast collection, this great resource to build the magazine."

The previous version was "the normal museum members' publication," Stout says, more like "a catalog than a magazine, and not a very interesting format." The museum director "had the sense that people weren't reading the publication and he wanted it to be more vital, something that people actually read. He gave us the challenge to rework" what was essentially a newsletter with a calendar into a magazine. The new publication should add "value to your experience as a member of the museum as opposed to just regurgitated press releases."

Pentagram hired a writer and editor to develop in-depth, entertaining editorial for the new, thematic publication designed by the firm. "We made it larger, we made it very visual," Stout says. The premiere issue focused on African art, reflecting two exhibitions on traditional art as well as contemporary art. "It was all about their devotion to African art," says Stout. "There was a story about their big African gold collection, another about contemporary artists. A lot of the photos were from the collection, but they weren't necessarily representative of the shows."

The museum, however, elected not to continue the new *Today* magazine. "I think that a lot of the membership got it and didn't know what it was. Maybe they thought it was a special brochure about up-and-coming African exhibits. This was so different. I think that the audience was probably used to the magazine performing one particular function. Now all of a sudden it was a real magazine."

Introducing and explaining the retooled publication would have gone a long way toward ensuring its future, Stout believes. "They should have sent a letter with it from the director of the museum on his official letterhead saying, 'Here's your new magazine. We've reworked it to try to make it better for you'—then they probably would have gotten a better response."

Art director: DJ Stout
Designer: Erin Mayes
Client: Museum of Fine Arts, Houston

African Art Now

FORM HAS FUNCTION

Communicate project scope changes. It's critical that your client alert you to any changes in direction as soon as they occur. Upper management might broaden the scope—for example, adding articles to a newsletter. Alternatively, the client could decide to decrease the pages of the publication, cutting out photos of a facility pegged to shut down. Let him know in advance that significant changes to the project could impact schedule and budget, and that additional money might not buy delivery on the original due date. The contract will need to include an addendum or be rewritten to detail the project's new direction and the resulting changes in timing and fees.

Fact-check and proof copy. You or your copywriter should check the accuracy of information, style, and format. Be sure that the client or someone he designates is the ultimate authority for fact-checking company information and for proofreading for typos, grammatical errors, and so on. Specify this responsibility in the contract.

Review proofs. Your client will be responsible for reviewing bluelines and other press proofs thoroughly and according to schedule. Agree in advance to a process for communicating desired changes before marking up the proof; discuss the cost ramifications of late-stage, unnecessary changes before they're in the blueline, for example, and avoid conflicting written comments from multiple reviewers. Your client should sign the printer's release-to-press form or initial the proofs as the final approver.

Coordinate the review process. If client colleagues or managers will be reviewing proofs as well, have your client coordinate their schedules and collection of comments.

Attend press checks. Depending on your client's publications process experience and desired involvement in the project, accompanying you or your designer on a press check could be among his responsibilities.

Pay contracted workers. You'll decide with your client in advance whether you or he will handle freelancer and vendor billing, and payment according to their terms.

Define the Major Phases

Your capabilities brochure should identify and explain the major phases of publications development. This information should include an approximate time range for each process step. The time allotted should reflect what is feasible for your internal communications department or other company resources, or for the external freelancers or firms and production vendors you hire. Ask your creative resources and vendors for input on what ranges are reasonable.

Your usual workload and other client commitments also influence the schedules you communicate. State that these are broad time frames for general reference only and that project requirements could necessitate shorter or longer turnarounds. Also note that some steps can be executed concurrently.

Tailor the time periods below to reflect the type of work in which you or your group specialize. There will be significant variance in time needed for, say, quick production of company fliers, report formatting, and production versus annual reports and company identity packages. It might be appropriate to reduce the listed time frames of weeks to days. The steps that are not included in your process should be omitted from your capabilities brochure.

Here are basic process steps, what's involved in each, and flexible time frames to consider and then adapt to your capabilities document:

Research. Gathering information from materials provided by the client, from company or outside interviews, or from your own print or online resources may be needed to support your initial concepts or as copy fodder. In addition, you might be responsible for researching or analyzing audience demographics: One to two weeks.

Concepts. Considering your projects could range from letterhead suites using established branding to new-product brochures, your concepts time frame should be broad: One to four weeks. As appropriate to your services, note that farther-reaching assignments, such as company logos/identity systems, can take several months.

Testing. Holding focus groups or conducting surveys or other testing can occur at various development phases—for example, after concepts, copy, or designs are created: One to three weeks.

Writing. After your research and interviews are completed, allot time for draft development. You'll establish in advance how many drafts will be included in the project's fee, typically two or three. In your capabilities brochure, it's helpful to specify a time frame for each draft: First draft, one to three weeks; second draft, one to two weeks; third draft (final corrections), one week.

Design. This phase can be performed in conjunction with copy development or after a final or near-final draft is supplied to the graphic artist. Again, specify ranges for the agreed-upon number of rounds: Initial layout, one to three weeks; second design, one to two weeks; final changes to design, one week.

> ### Define Your Client's Practical Experience
>
> The following questions are designed to help you assess your client's comfort level with various process steps:
>
> - What publications have you led inside your company (your internal client) or managed for your company or product (your external client)?
> - Tell me about the process you've followed managing publications on your own, with internal or contracted publications managers, or with creative professionals who have also served as publications managers.
> - Do you determine communications needs primarily on your own or with other company personnel?
> - What involvement have you had and would you like to have in the development of concepts?
> - To whom and how do you make presentations? Have creative resources been involved in those presentations?
> - How many presentations do you expect to include in a project's contract?
> - What input do you wish to contribute to the project?
> - Have you contracted creative, production, or distribution vendors in the past?
> - Do you have a pool of external resources with whom you work on publications?
> - Do you have writing, editing, design, production, or distribution experience?
> - How comfortable are you reviewing or overseeing those publication phases?
> - How do you conduct reviews and signoffs in your company?
> - Have you developed project schedules and budgets, and how do you try to manage them?
> - Have you negotiated ownership/usage rights for creative work?
> - What rights do you typically negotiate and why?
> - What negatives have occurred with past projects that you wish to correct for future publications?

Photography. Include coordination and scouting as well as execution in your photography time frame. A shoot could range from a single portrait to a half-day of on-site action shots to several days in the studio or at a variety of locations: Arrangements and scouting, two days to two weeks; photo shoot, one hour to two weeks.

Illustration. This process step will include concepts, roughs, and finals: One to three weeks.

Printing. Allow for prepress proofs review and special finishing, such as folding or binding, and additional handling, including collating or inserting pamphlets into folder pockets: One to three weeks.

Shipping to client. Figure in time needed to get your finished publications from the printer to your or your client's facility or a contracted mail house—for example, if you're located on the East Coast and using a company print shop in California: Same day to one week.

Delivery to readers. Determine this time frame depending on whether you work with an in-house or outside mail house; whether you'll deliver to one location, such as a meeting site, or thousands of homes; the type of shipping you'll use, such as overnight mail versus bulk mail; and other factors: Two days to two weeks.

DEFINE THE PROJECT SCOPE

You might need to guide your client through the discussion about his specific communication needs. These questions range from the basics about message and audience to such particulars as fact-checking and future editions. Use them as a guide to laying the groundwork for your project.

"Ideally, we gather key stakeholders together for what we call a Customer Experience workshop," says Yang Kim, principal of BBK Studio. "This workshop is an opportunity to define goals, audiences, customer path, and priorities.

"We run through exercises that help identify brand attributes and points of differentiation. We ask participants questions like, 'If your company had a leading role in a movie, who would play the part?' or 'If your company were a dog, what breed would it be?'"

References

First identify what's already in place that will dictate the publication's creative content. To aid your understanding of the client's company (or department, product, or event, etc.), ask for reference materials, including existing publications. What are the company's branding and usage guidelines? Do editorial style and design standards manuals exist for my use and distribution? What educational company literature and past projects may I use for reference?

Foundation Facts

Howry asks these two key questions at the beginning of the project kick-off meeting: "One, who is the audience for the publication? Two, what is the main message (in one sentence) to that audience? Another good question to ask is whether there are any misconceptions out there that need to be clearly addressed."

Remember the why-who-what concept formula discussed in chapter 3. This information will form the foundation of your initial concepts.

Precedent

Ask your client about what already printed material might influence the design or editorial tone. You'll need to understand the new publication's context. That's something the novice client might not think to explain unprompted. Fitting the new piece into a family can be a challenge if the original concept is lacking or a time-saver if the solution in place is functional. Will this publication be part of a family of communications? Is this a new publication, an updated version, or part of an existing collection of publications? Does a design template exist?

Client Vision

Your client or his managers might have a vision for the publication, however limited or ungrounded that might be. Be sure to explore that before your team begins concept brainstorming. A client might not share his ideas proactively but wait to respond to concepts and present his ideas at that later stage. That can be a significant setback. Ask upfront whether the client already has a concept, specifications, or a format in mind for his publication.

Specific Needs and Logistics

Even questions that seem obvious to you might not have been considered by your client. How many copies does he really need? If he seems to be guessing or gives you a broad range, you'll need to help him determine his precise needs based on primary audience count and any additional ancillary or future uses for the publication.

You'll also want to be sure the due date is realistic, both in terms of time required to produce the piece and when it's genuinely needed. Talk with your client about what can be accomplished on his timeline and whether alternative delivery options might meet his needs.

The distribution method might impact the delivery date. Ask about what system has been used in the past and whether there are in-house mail services or an established relationship with an external distributor. You'll need this information before you can develop your schedule.

Ten Project Questions for Your Client

Define the following project criteria with your client upfront. Answering these questions will prevent interruptions and redundancies in the work flow.

1. What is the total—or ballpark—budget?

2. When is the final job to be delivered? Does delivery need to coincide with an event? Can a portion of the publications be delivered on a selected date, with the balance to be delivered subsequently?

3. Who are all the internal and external resources required for creative development and production? What are their schedule needs in relation to those of the client? Should the client meet some or all of these resources?

4. Who is the audience for the project? What are the audience demographics, including age, gender, education, profession, income, common interest, common membership, and so on?

5. What is the message of the publication? What specific response does the client want from the audience—for example, brand or product awareness, contribution, purchase, or other call to action?

6. Based on the audience profile and the publication's purpose, what mood or tone is appropriate? What should the design and production convey, and how will the editorial content support that feel and look? How will word and image work together? Is there any market research to support these decisions or does research need to be conducted? Does the client have any preconceived notions about the copy or the design that should be discussed and evaluated in advance? Do any other factors need to be considered—such as the economy or the current status of the client's company—before a suitable concept can be developed?

7. Will this be a single, stand-alone piece or does it need to work with existing or forthcoming publications? Should it conform to an existing identity or editorial style and graphic standards? If the client believes this will be an isolated publication, explore whether this is in fact possible or whether the client might be expecting too many objectives or too long a shelf-life for the project. Explore in advance whether the publication or some elements of it could be used for additional purposes.

8. What envelopes or packaging are required and how will this impact the budget? Ensure the packaging will adhere to postal regulations, as appropriate, and will facilitate cost-effective and timely delivery.

9. Does the client have a distribution system in place, or will you administer fulfillment and distribution? Will the job require unusual shipment methods, say, to ensure same-day delivery to audience members nationwide?

10. How can you and the client test the effectiveness of the publication? Outline specific objectives for the publication, and determine whether comp-stage testing and/or postdistribution surveying will be necessary.

Allowable cost is a given, too, right? Don't be surprised if a client doesn't bring a budget to the table. You will need at least a ballpark range before you can begin developing concepts. Make sure he understands that meeting both the delivery deadline and the budget depends on adhering to the schedule, one of his most important responsibilities.

Discussing schedule, quantity, and budget with your client also will reveal his education needs. For example, is he planning on printing a low run that will make the unit cost soar? Is he expecting a twelve-page, four-color newsletter to be written, designed, and printed in two weeks? Does he understand that the number of colors, photography, page count, stock, and so on, all will add to the bill? Your in-depth conversation will enable you to get the answers you need and help inform your client about what can be accomplished when and for how much. Be sure the client understands that deviation from the schedule might impact the delivery date and budget, including rush charges incurred by you or other contracted resources.

Project Team

You might have a team of resources in mind; however, your client could have strong ties with writers, designers, or printers with whom you'll need to work. Your internal client might have a firm on retainer that will provide data or creative input to the project. If you'll be selecting and contracting freelancers and vendors, on the other hand, find out from your client whether he'll want to meet the project players. This could be especially valuable for a larger project, say, an annual report, versus a modest product brochure.

Content Creation

You might be relying on your client for copy information, or you or your writer could be responsible for editing a provided draft. Make sure you understand what details must not be disclosed outside; communicate this with your project team.

Research and interviews could be among your team's tasks. In that case, make sure your client will serve as a liaison between you and the inside contacts. After writing is complete, who will have final say on checking the facts and proofing the copy?

Ownership

Your client might be familiar with usage rights and ownership, or he might not. Now's the time to find out and to make sure he understands that his company does not own

---

Who's Responsible?

CONTENT

- Who are my resources for publication content?
- Will any proprietary information, verbal or visual, be required for the publication?
- Will you or someone in your company be providing a draft or serving as an editor?
- Will I or my contracted writer need to conduct research or interviews to obtain content?
- Will you accept fact-checking and final proofing responsibilities?

RIGHTS

- What rights do you wish to hold for creative elements, such as dies or art files delivered to the printer?
- Do you need me to negotiate those rights?
- Are payments for those rights included in your budget?

FUTURE EDITIONS

- Have you thought of future revisions needed for the publication?
- Are there other uses for the publication that might increase quantity and budget, but ultimately save money?
- Are there elements of the publication that might be used for other pieces from your company to the same or different audiences for cost effectiveness and time efficiency?

the photo, the film, the die, and so on, unless negotiated in advance. Discuss with him the possible advantages to licensing multiple-use rights of images. They could be used for other publications and the company Web site, for example. Explain that the budget will need to include any costs associated with purchasing additional rights or with buyouts.

Future Editions and Additional Uses

Discuss a realistic shelf-life for the piece—one year? three years?—and what revision needs there will be when it's time for changes and reprinting. This can help your team make decisions about copy placement and design now, making it easier to update later. In addition, explore all of the possible uses for the publication beyond its primary purpose. If an annual report could be included in an employee-recruitment package, for example, decide now to print 11,000 instead of 10,000. This will alleviate the need to reprint a short and costly run later or to create separate material about the company already included in the annual report.

Last, ask your client whether certain sections or elements might be appropriate for other projects. For example, explore additional uses for photography and negotiate multiple-use rights. Or overprint a signature that details company products to bind separately as a customer publication. This type of forward thinking can save money and time.

HOW ARE *YOU* DOING?

Internal client perceptions of you and your work are critical to your firm footing or advancement in the company. In a corporation, for example, as a communications professional, you're not likely contributing directly to the bottom line; therefore, you might find yourself in the position of justifying your existence. Be proactive.

Understanding and improving client perceptions can be extra challenging if you find yourself in the role of publications manager by default. If you're a writer or designer, for example, and there is not a project coordinator or traffic person in your communications department, you might be called on to serve as publications manager as well.

Begin by taking a hard look at the current perception of your work or your department's work. Do clients deem you as competent, or better, as an expert in your field? Have you succeeded in producing jobs on time and within budget?

Regardless of your past performance, clients might misunderstand your skills or be overlooking the value of your services. Investigate whether any previous or potential clients are seeking external communications professionals to perform work you can execute. Are you aware of a department newsletter that's developed and produced outside the company, for example?

This is a clear indication of either a poor perception of your abilities or a lack of awareness of your or your department's function—or even your presence. Now's the time to create and circulate that capabilities brochure. This document need not be for external clients only. It will serve as a sort of calling card and as a reminder of the creative- and production-management role you can fulfill, and the writing and design services that team members can provide. If appropriate, share your brochure with senior management. They should be interested in the cost- and time-savings that an efficient internal process affords the company.

The Artist as Client: Joe Comick Photography Promo Book

HENDERSONBROMSTEADART,
WINSTON-SALEM, NC

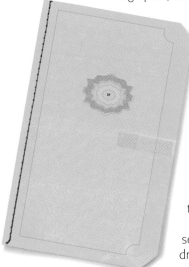

Joe Comick, "pretty much a generalist" photographer, according to HBA principal Hayes Henderson, was ready to step up his own photography marketing. He turned to HENDERSONBROMSTEADART, with which he'd worked extensively. How did the firm collaborate with a client whose own creative work was the feature of the publication?

Comick shot "this series of photography of dresses for Givenchy and wanted to, in some way, use them in his promotion. Instead of mixing these in with other photos, we talked him into really concentrating" on the fashion photography, Henderson says. "We pushed him hard to make this the focus because it was beautiful photography."

The creative team conceptualized "a format that highlighted the photography aesthetically. There was a certain delicate frail quality but a minorly disturbing sense to it as well. In the photography there were a darkness and a lightness playing out at the same time. We tried to do the same thing with the book."

Henderson points to the promo's "delicate and hand-drawn flourishes and fleur-de-lis" and handwriting, all in keeping with the fine quality of the art. And "the side stitching is a cloth stitch; it seemed like it made it a little more hand-tooled, it pertained to [the fashion theme].

"We incorporated writing to cobble together the photography with some sort of string of a storyline . . . but not smother the photography in concept."

Creative director: Hayes Henderson
Designer: Michelle White
Photographer: Joe Comick
Copywriter: Michelle White
Client: Joe Comick

Meet with clients you've worked with as well as prospects to explain your role, to learn about their communication needs, and to try to secure projects. Explain the cost benefits of work performed by internal resources like you and other creative professionals. It's a time-saver, too: You'll manage the hiring, schedule and budget, development and production, and delivery instead of your client.

To help explain to clients the advantages of working with you internally, obtain the cost of a publication that's been produced or cost out a theoretical job. As appropriate, include estimates for research, writing, and editing; design; photography; printing and special handling; distribution; and management of creative resources and vendors. Compare these numbers with what's spent when the project is created in-house. Keep your manager apprised of your efforts to raise your profile—and to get the green light if necessary.

Maintain high marks from internal and external clients by proactively and frequently soliciting their suggestions. Postproject surveys are good public relations. They show that you care about your clients' satisfaction and want to ensure that you meet their needs by delivering superior work according to their objectives. The results will demonstrate where ongoing perception of your services stands and what areas require improvement.

Unsatisfactory results might indicate a need for altering your process or contracting more reliable vendors. You could conclude that you need to be more involved in the publications process—for example, attending a press check or micromanaging the designer who falls behind schedule. The survey also might show the need to review your client's performance. For example, did late approvals impact the delivery date? Or did untimely changes impact the schedule and budget?

If results are less than glowing, follow up to discuss the survey findings with your client. This attentiveness will demonstrate your commitment to improving service quality. It also will give you the chance to correct, diplomatically, any misconceptions about the project. Does the client understand, for example, that his proofing errors resulted in an unsatisfactory product? More important, listen to your client, reexplain parts of the process and responsibilities if necessary, and act on his suggestions for making the publications process seamless and convenient for him.

Cohen says, "I'm also a big believer in underpromising and overdelivering. You can promise something and give clients much more, and they're going to love you. When you deliver the additional work, however, you have to tell them that you're giving them much more. Otherwise, you are giving them free work without getting the client's recognition."

WHEN YOU'RE THE CLIENT

When calling on internal resources and contracting external vendors, you'll be playing a dual role as both manager and client.

As the publications manager, you'll budget time and fees; coordinate conceptualization, writing, photography/illustration, and design; negotiate rights and ownership; and work with print and mail house reps to ensure timeliness and quality.

As the client, you'll be updated on progress; have presentations made to you; receive creative work at progressive phases of development for your review and comment, changes, and signoff; and have your product delivered to you or distributed to readers.

Wearing two different hats in a single relationship can take some getting used to. In subsequent chapters, we'll continue to discuss in detail your role as publications manager. The best way to approach your role as client is to define your expectations of those reporting to you.

What You Should Expect

Realistic schedule input. Don't assume that the schedule you create on your own will accommodate the needs of creative pros and vendors. Get their input first and consider their other obligations when you prepare the project's calendar. What you should expect from team members is accurate estimation of the time needed to complete their tasks. They should not underestimate their timing needs to secure a job they actually can't complete.

Adherence to schedule. If they commit to turnarounds and approve your schedule, your writer, designer, photographer/illustrator, printer, and mail house should have no reason to miss their deadlines.

A capped fee. Negotiate a project fee estimate or limited range with an agreed-to maximum. Do not accept open-ended per-hour billing, which can lead to surprises beyond your budget. If the project's scope changes, you'll probably need to renegotiate the fee; again, cap it.

Proactive updates. A good creative or production resource will keep you posted on where his part of the project stands. He'll confirm, for example, that you'll receive a PDF of his second design layout by noon tomorrow, as scheduled. Or your writer will report in to let you know that an interview went well.

Reasonable availability. If a freelancer or vendor accepted a job, he needs to be available to meet with you to kick off the project. Client meetings also might be required. Your resources should make every effort to accommodate the scheduling needs of you and your clients.

Responsiveness. You don't have time to place repeated phone calls or send multiple e-mails to seek answers from your hires. It's their responsibility to respond to your queries without delay. In addition, they should inform you if they will be unavailable at any time due to another commitment.

Advance notice of problems. Learning about problems at the last minute can throw a project severely off track because you'll have no time to devise a plan B. You should expect notification of any difficulties as soon as they occur—or better yet, as soon as they're anticipated. Then together you can try to resolve the situation before it impacts schedule or budget—or at least to limit that impact.

Adherence to guidelines. If you've delivered an editorial style guide or graphics standards manual, your freelancer should ensure his work follows the rules. In addition, work should be delivered in the format and by the means you request.

Professionalism. In many cases, a project team member could be representing you. A writer could interview client company managers, a designer could present comps to executives, and a photographer might shoot employees at the workplace. Professionalism with all of your clients and colleagues is mandatory. Prepare your freelancers for the people, situations, and environments they'll be dealing with.

Professionalism among team members will also keep the process smooth. For example, a writer might work with a designer to cut some copy to accommodate space available. A photographer could discuss the appropriate artistic mood with your art director. And a designer probably would deal directly with the printing rep to ensure the art meets the printer's equipment capabilities.

No excuses. Or surprises. Or whining. Just as your client doesn't want to hear your complaints or excuses for missed deadlines or other problems, neither should you tolerate that unprofessionalism from the people you contract. And no client wants to hear that his project is being bumped—even for a single day—by another client's rush job. Do the work. Take responsibility.

A backup plan. The best professionals will have a backup colleague in place if an emergency occurs and they cannot complete the job.

A detailed invoice. Discuss with your freelancers and production vendors that you expect bills with details that reflect your contract: project name, description of work performed, dates the work was performed, subtotals per task (if appropriate), and the total fee.

5

Creating a Practical Proposal

Reduce your plan to writing. The moment you complete this,
you will have definitely given concrete form to the intangible desire.
—NAPOLEON HILL

Wowing clients with your beautiful design comps isn't enough. You also should explain how the publication will be executed in a proposal. Writing and presenting a clear, comprehensive publication strategy will illustrate your preparedness for the job. The act of developing this detailed document also will bring focus to your planning.

The proposal is proof that you've thoroughly considered all of the development phases, from concept to creative development, from production to delivery. It will ensure that you and your client share the same vision for the project. In addition, this critical document can serve as a reference throughout the process to make certain the communication needs are met successfully. An easily understood proposal can help keep your concept clear when it's explained second- and third-hand. (For comparison with a design creative brief, see sidebar on page 62.)

The degree of background information about you, your resources, your portfolio, your understanding of the client's company, and so on, will depend on your history with the client. These factors, plus the project's complexity, will also help you determine whether the proposal needs to be presented in person. In creating a simpler publication for an established client, for example, you might e-mail a basic proposal explaining the concept, creative team, schedule, and estimate.

If you're in charge of producing an internal publication, you'll be guided by the expected method of presenting a proposal for a project. But even if plans are typically communicated orally in your organization, consider backing up the presentation in written form. A written proposal can help gain buy-in from all direct and indirect internal clients.

Communicating in this way with everyone who will be involved in the development process or reviews can only help your cause. Distributing a proposal will allow time upfront for questions. It can also serve as a project-long reference that you and your clients share.

The project proposal is your presentation of the communication solution and your strategy for delivering it. It can be brief for a simple project or experienced client, or it can contain detailed information explaining the assignment or helping educate a novice client or one with whom you're about to begin a relationship.

PROPOSAL COMPONENTS

Especially valuable for the new client, a full proposal answers the reporter's questions about the project, such as what is the concept, who is the audience, how will the publication be created, and when will it be delivered. It explains the responsibilities of the client—for example, providing facts for copywriting and reviewing proofs. And it can introduce the creative and production team members.

The proposal is an essential tool when you're in competition for a project; it will serve as the enduring "first-round" impression on the client and enable him to remember and compare you with other contenders. Some sections of the proposal are suggested for inclusion in the capabilities brochure (e.g., see chapter 4); this is in order that each document can stand alone.

Below are several sections you might include in your proposal. To determine what to include, consider the complexity of the project, your client's familiarity with the publications process, and with you and the team you're proposing, and who else might be reviewing the proposal.

The Creative Brief

Emily Ruth Cohen, consultant to creative professionals, considers the creative brief the most important document in the process. She says, "It expresses your value, illustrating that you think strategically and asked the right questions to get that information from the client, that you listened. It shows that you have the ability to write and are able to present ideas in a professional manner, and understand the client's needs.

"The creative brief can be very simple. In most cases, it doesn't have to be more than three or four pages. It provides a clear set of expectations and defines measurable objectives. It summarizes as comprehensively and concisely as possible both the business objectives and creative strategies, and the requirements of the project and the relationship."

Cohen explains that clients can't always define the creative strategy: "They know their business objectives. What you need to define clearly is how their business objectives—for instance, raising awareness or generating sales leads—link to the creative strategies you propose.

"The brief also guides the approval and decision process. You want to define the attributes and the goals so that if, in the middle of a presentation, a client says he doesn't like blue, you can say, 'Let's look at the creative brief and see if this blue meets your objectives.' In doing so, you're able to turn a subjective opinion into an objective decision. Designers complain that clients make very subjective decisions. The creative brief mediates these types of disagreements."

Letter to the client. Thank the prospective client for the opportunity to present the proposal. Include a brief overview of the topics covered in the proposal.

Background and business objectives. You should draw on your research about the client to demonstrate that you understand the purpose and vision of his organization, its unique challenges, and its goals going forward. Illustrating your knowledge in the proposal will help substantiate both your concept and your competence to execute a project that will meet the communication need.

Communication need. Define the need that the communication is meant to address.

Audience. Identify the readership. Explain the relationship between the target audience and the client organization. Explore whether that relationship needs to be strengthened or altered by the communication to be developed.

Call to action. Describe the desired audience action, such as purchasing a product, or the impact the communication should have on readers, such as increasing their awareness of the client's brand.

Concept or concepts. The crux of your proposal, of course, is describing the concept, your idea for delivering the appropriate message to the targeted audience. You probably will be supplying more than a single solution.

Explain what the message is and through what graphic and editorial means it will be delivered. Explore the publication's verbal theme, possibly including sample headlines or taglines. Describe the graphic approach, perhaps including preliminary specs, suggested photography or other art, and if an integral part of the piece, plans for packaging.

Include printouts of any visual materials you have already presented; these will illustrate your concept as the proposal is passed along.

Distribution method or methods. Explain how you or a vendor will get the publication into the hands of the readers or several reader groups.

Audience testing. You might recommend that testing concepts with audience samples be conducted. Explain who would be overseeing the testing, say, your team or an outside market research company. Discuss the recommended test method—for example, a focus group.

Follow-up testing. Suggest methods for gauging whether the objectives of the publication were met. Recommending this step will demonstrate your commitment to creating a successful communication solution.

Responsibilities. Define the basic roles of both you and your client. This will help the novice client in particular, by outlining tasks such as providing information for content, reviewing drafts, and meeting approval deadlines. Also explain the services you'll be providing, from management of the creative team through coordination of mailing the printed piece.

Steps and time frames. Delineate the steps of the publications process. Depending on the project, the steps might include research, creative development (writing, design, and photography), testing, printing, and delivery. If the scope of the project is not yet precisely defined, you can estimate the time frame associated with each step—for example, one to two weeks to complete the first draft. If the job is well defined and its delivery date is known, try to include a more specific working schedule. Review what each process step entails and why the given time frame is needed.

Where Do We Stand?

Include the following types of information in project updates:

- Project title, such as Charles University Prospectus
- Confirmed headline
- Confirmed specifications
- Steps completed and the dates completed
- Any change in scope of the project
- Any outstanding issues that need resolution, such as reference materials to be identified or a late review by the client
- Next steps, such as fact-checking by the client or the final prepress design with all photography and other elements in place, with dates
- Confirmation that the budget and schedule are on track or documentation of why these need to be adjusted or why they were adjusted

Approval process. Tell the client what he will be reviewing—for example, two drafts, two rounds of design, and prepress proofs. Emphasize the importance of timely turnaround, and explain the stages when changes will negatively impact the schedule and budget.

Estimated costs. Your knowledge of project details—and of your client's budget—will influence whether you include broad-range estimates or more definitive costs for each step. Items you'll estimate include research, writing, and editing; design; photography/illustration; printing; and mailing. Qualify your estimates as projections that will be confirmed or adjusted and submitted for final approval before work begins.

Clarify what is included in the estimate. For example, design might include refinement of the concept, three rounds of layout and revisions, design proofs for client review, and preparation of art for the printer. Publications management tasks included might be listed as client communication and meetings, schedule creation and maintenance, contracting and managing the writer and designer, printer coordination, prepress proof review, and a press check.

Also specify what is not included in the estimate. You might not have bids for photography at this stage, for example; explain that the price will come later. Clarify that client changes beyond the agreed number of design rounds will be charged per additional hour.

Change-of-scope statement. State that your concept plan and all estimates are based on the project as it's defined at the time of the proposal. Note that any significant change in scope will require a new budget for the client's signoff before work begins or continues.

Your credentials. Note your education, experience, clients, awards, and so on. Refer the client to your online portfolio. Include references, contacts, and possibly testimonials from other clients.

The team. If the creative professionals you'll be contracting are known, include their names, experience, and relevant projects.

Proposal conditions. Specify the period of time the proposal and estimates will be valid. Cite your invoice payment terms, hourly rate for extra client changes beyond initial project scope, and whether elements of the finished product will be licensed to the client for limited or unlimited use unless negotiated otherwise.

TRACK YOUR PROJECT'S PROGRESS

Consider creating written progress reports or updates (see sidebar on page 63) at critical points of the project, especially if it's complex or will be created over the long term, or if your client relationship warrants it. These concise documents communicate status and reiterate next steps. They serve as reminders of the responsibilities of clients, of your resources, and of yourself that still need to be carried out.

You likely know the level of information and involvement your internal clients require or to which they are accustomed. Even if those are minimal, ask yourself whether this type of documentation will further understanding, ensure all parties are in ongoing agreement, and aid you in the event of project change or end-stage changes or questions.

Circulate progress reports to your client or clients and to relevant creative and production team members. Keep each written update on file with other project plans and documents, such as budget, schedule, estimates, contracts, and so on.

A progress report can take any form, but it should be convenient, inclusive, yet succinct. Your report could be a simple memo or in milestone chart form. Time your reports at a few critical junctures in the publications process, such as after draft and layout are complete and at the prepress stage, as well as when bottlenecks appear in the process. This will document what or who is causing the delay, which might impact budget and delivery, and hopefully will spur responsible parties to action to resolve the problem.

When issues need to be resolved or when problems have arisen that impact budget or schedule, it's especially important to have the client initial a copy of the progress report to document his awareness of the project's status.

6

Planning: People, Time, and Money

Planning is bringing the future into the present so that you can do something about it now.
—ALAN LAKEIN

Let our advance worrying become advance thinking and planning.
—WINSTON CHURCHILL

As head of the project, you'll plan and manage people, time, and money. Who's on the team? What's the schedule? How much will the job cost? Careful planning is an essential requirement if any publications process is to proceed smoothly.

Organizing the job, identifying internal and external resources required, scheduling each publication phase, and developing a budget are critical preliminary steps. They should involve client decision-makers and the creative and production team members to ensure everyone understands and signs off on your overall plan.

In this chapter you'll learn how to plan all the specifics within these three basic categories—people, time, and money—for your publication. And you'll look beyond your publication in progress to plan for a future edition or update. You'll save time and money when the new version is required. You also might discover additional uses for the original piece, requiring relatively minor revisions.

When you've accomplished your planning phase, you can make the most of your opportunity to move the audience to action. One last item to keep in mind while you read on: Plans change.

ORGANIZE THE PROJECT

First things first: Get organized. Set up a central electronic or physical file—or both—that contains all the information, notes, and documents pertaining to the project.

You can create a file for each job with sections, as appropriate, for contact information, client company information, project overview, proposal, concept brief, new job request form, schedule, budget, estimates, and contracts. This can take a physical form or be several documents in a computer folder. Having both formats can facilitate your communication with others.

Create a Job Request Form

To start your project off in an organized fashion, complete a job request form or new job order (e.g., see appendix A). This sheet or two of information is a snapshot of the project, with brief information that's easy to glean for your fast reference: client, project purpose and audience, preliminary specs, team members, delivery, and so on. The document will serve as a quick reference as creative work begins on the publication. You'll have gathered a lot of this information during your initial client interviews; some information may not be known at this early stage. These fundamentals will be fleshed out as you obtain additional data and the project evolves.

Your client can fill out the form, depending on his familiarity with basic publication needs and your process. You could decide instead to complete the request with your client—a good educational exercise—or to fill it out on your own. With an established client, this may be reviewed at your initial project meeting.

The job request form can include such elements as:

Descriptive title. Include a working title or descriptive slug so everyone involved knows what job you're talking about: for example, "Capshaw Letterhead Suite" or "Johnson Annual Report."

Client. Place the name and contact information where you can see it.

Department to be billed. If the job is internal, note the name or code of the department responsible for payment.

New job versus reprint/revision. If the project is a revision of an existing publication, attach a sample of the piece being reprinted with no changes or to be revised.

Primary audience. Include a brief audience statement or description, such as "new customers" or "children ages 8–12." This information would have been obtained during your first client interview.

Primary purpose. Again, a succinct statement of message or audience call to action is sufficient here—for example, "to explain the claims process" or "invitation to spring dance." And again, info gathered previously.

Secondary audience. Make sure the possibility of additional audiences is considered from the get-go, when you first discuss the project with your client. Perhaps the secondary audience is "parents and grandparents" who will be purchasing products for "children ages 8–12."

Secondary purpose. With a secondary audience typically comes a secondary purpose. From the example above, this purpose is to influence adults to buy.

Expected shelf-life. How long is the publication expected to be valid? For example, will the product brochure be updated in a year, when prices increase? Is the catalog seasonal, to be replaced in the fall with a new edition?

Other applications. Consider upfront other possible uses for the piece. This may impact your quantity and might influence your design as well. For example, an annual report might be overprinted to be used in an executive-recruitment package.

Event-specific. Note whether the publication is tied to, say, a conference or a grand opening, as communicated by your client during your first project review. This will impact the distribution method and the delivery date, below.

Distribution method. Knowing ahead of time how the communication will get into the hands of readers will guide the design and decisions about packaging and scheduling.

Graphic precedence. Find out whether the new project needs to adhere to a graphic standards manual and/or whether the piece will be part of a family or series with an established template to follow. Write "manual" on the job form as a reminder or "see sample" and attach the publication that preceded the new job.

Editorial precedence. Just as with graphics, check to see whether there's an established headline or boilerplate copy. Make a note and attach a sample. Reference an editorial style guide as needed.

Photography/illustration. If you have planned art with your client, note on the form whether photography or illustration will be required. This notation will be a reminder that you'll need to get going on planning in short order.

Information sources. Where will you turn for background or for content fodder? List contact people or references to be supplied by the client.

Quantity. Include the run or a range discussed with your client. Consider the quantity for other uses of the publication determined by you and your client.

Initial delivery date/balance due. Write down the delivery date; if unknown, try to establish as tight a time frame as possible. The project might allow delivery of an initial quantity, say, 500 copies for an annual conference, and delivery of the balance at a later date. Asking about this type of flexibility when planning begins can impact your schedule favorably by adding production time.

Deliver to. Note the contact name, address, and phone, or write "mail list" or whatever is appropriate for alternative distribution.

Finished size, flat size. If known, include the size or approximate size. The finished size is that of the folded piece; the flat size is the size of the publication unfolded. For example, a flat size of 8½" × 11" folded down in half would have a finished size of 8½" × 5½".

Pages/panels. Note or estimate the number of pages or in the case of a folded piece, the total number of panels.

Folds/binding. Note the number and type of fold or binding.

Cover stock. Note the name and/or the weight of the stock you'll use for the cover if decided. If it's to follow a previously printed piece, write down "see sample" and attach the earlier publication.

Text stock. Make the same notes as you did for the cover stock.

Printing. Try to include basic, preliminary specifications, such as the number of ink colors and varnishes or other coatings, for the publication. These specs can be grouped for each stock (cover, text, inserts, etc.) or section of the piece (cover, narrative, financial tables, color photography section, etc.). If you're revising an existing publication and want to maintain the established production values—stocks, colors, binding, finishing, and so on—you can contact the printer who produced the last version for exact specs.

Separations. For an uncomplicated project or a publication that just requires updating, you might know the number of photographs and their sizes even at this early stage. Note this information on the form.

Finishing. Here you'll note additional production requirements such as die-cuts, pockets, special trims, or slits to hold business cards, and so on.

Packaging. Note whether envelopes or other packaging will be required, plus any stock or size information you might have at this point.

Before you can begin to gather the specific creative and production people you'll manage, identify the types of resources you need on board to execute the tasks ahead. With the groundwork for your project defined, you'll have a better idea of who will be required to create your publication and you can move on to organizing your team.

IDENTIFY AND LOCATE NEEDED RESOURCES

Begin by listing and evaluating your available resources. Number one on the team: you. You'll be serving as the publications manager, creating a team of internal and/or external resources you'll shepherd through the process. Evaluate your own experience. What is your publications management background? Where can you turn for advice?

Educate yourself on the publications process: Use this book as a reference. Talk with managers and colleagues in your department or company and with counterparts at other organizations. Network with professionals in design, marketing, communications, and other trade associations. Join the organizations that support members of your profession (e.g., see appendix B). Membership benefits in these associations vary, but most provide access to resources online, free or discounted educational guides and courses, and events that offer the chance to network with professionals dealing with the same needs, problems, and concerns as you are.

Now on to your team members. Whether you'll be working with external or internal resources, you'll need to evaluate their appropriateness for the tasks ahead. As you interview prospective external team members, you will discern who should be part of the project based on several factors (e.g., see chapter 7). For an internal team, ask yourself who your resources are.

Say your marketing area has access to creative professionals working in another department. Do they have the experience needed to complete the project? For example, is there a young designer who is adept at publications from fliers to newsletters, but the upcoming task is the

---

Estimating Creative Time

"Scheduling creative correctly is tough at first," says Dominik D'Angelo, principal of Kinimod, Inc. "So much of the timing comes from experience with previously completed projects." Here's her typical process for estimating turnaround times for copy, design, and photography:

"The first thing I do for any larger project, and whenever possible, is to set the project due date two weeks before the client expects the publication to be delivered. This buffer allows enough time to address most unexpected problems. I use that date as the deadline by which I expect the publication to be delivered from the printer. I back up from that date to schedule in everything else.

"I usually receive copy from my clients and give them the date by which I need to receive it in order to deliver the project on time. The design process starts only after I receive the copy.

"For complex, multiple-page projects, I estimate two hours of design time per page. This estimate includes design layout time only, so for a 100-page art exhibition catalog, I estimate 200 hours of design time. For less complex projects, I estimate one hour per page.

"Design usually takes up the bulk of the time spent on a project other than printing, and these estimates immediately show whether it will be possible to deliver the project on time. If impossible, I know that the deadline needs to be readjusted, the scope of the project needs to be reduced, or additional designers need to be hired.

"Depending on the complexity of photography needed, I schedule in one hour of photographer time for extremely simple photos, half a day (four hours) for more elaborate photography, and a full day for very complex photo shoots. Consult a photographer before scheduling. Any retouching time should be scheduled in separately."

---

company's annual report? Evaluating your internal resources' experience will enable you to determine the support they'll require or whether you'll need to enlist other, external creative professionals to meet the job's demands.

Next list the external resources you'll require to develop and produce the publication, for example, a writer, a designer, a photographer, an illustrator, a printer, and a mail house.

If you're just beginning to build relationships with creative freelancers and print vendors, you'll need to locate a pool of available resources. Chapter 7 provides Web sites, organizations, and references for locating creative talents to meet the needs of your project. It also gives advice on evaluating which resource is best for you and how to manage your working relationships. Chapters 9 and 10 will help you through the same processes with printers and distribution vendors.

Part of the planning process is initiating relationships among team members who'll be working together. Consider at this early stage who will need to meet whom. And consider bringing the entire team together, with the client, at a kick-off session—especially for a particularly challenging project. Having your creative resources meet in advance of the project will help establish effective partnerships.

For example, have your designer meet your printing rep, even if you intend to be the point person with each of them. A comfortable relationship between them will encourage direct exchanges about required art formats, press sheet size, folding machine capabilities, and so on. Such exchanges among team members, especially about technical details, will ensure accountability and save you valuable time.

MAXIMIZE RESOURCE RELATIONSHIPS

Writing, design, photography, and printing for a family or ongoing series will have maximum continuity and production quality if you use the same resources for each piece, issue, or updated version. For example, assign a family of brochures this quarter as well as the updates next year to the same designer. Design will be consistent, and you could save on hours and therefore fees because the designer will already have laid the groundwork for next year's brochure set. Using the same printer for originals and updated publications will maintain quality, help ensure color matching from year to year, and save on film.

Contracting the same photographer, as well, will carry the tone and quality from one publication to its successor. You can try to anticipate photographs for the updated brochures or for future issues of, say, a newsletter—or for different publications entirely. Foresight will save on costs because you'll be paying for a single shoot, including one-time scouting, travel, and other expenses. In addition, perhaps all the photography can be shot in a day instead of paying for a five-hour "full day" on one shoot and a three-hour "half-day" shoot on another (e.g., see chapter 7).

Now, with the basics of the communication defined and your people resources identified, you can put dates to the development, production, and delivery steps in the publications process.

PLAN THE SCHEDULE

You've probably heard that a schedule for any project is most efficiently and reliably created by working backward from the completion or delivery date. Nice theory, but what exactly does this mean and how is it done?

Start by listing all the steps required to develop, produce, and deliver the publication. Depending on the project, you'll include some or all of the following: research, writing, design, photography/illustration, printing, and shipping to the client or delivery to readers.

Your next task is to estimate the time needed for each step. As you gain experience, you'll become more familiar with your creative and production resources, and better understand their processes and their schedule needs for a particular type of project. You'll get a feel for how much time is needed to complete each phase and be better positioned to estimate time requirements yourself. In the meantime, have each vendor provide an estimated time frame required for each step. Time available to complete a publications process step will depend on the length and complexity of the project, the availability of each creative or production resource, and the deadline. And there are multiple variables to consider before allotting time to each step (see sections that follow).

The client approval turnarounds for each step can be significant and often are the least controllable. Realistic allowances must be built into the schedule, giving decision-makers sufficient time to review the writing, design, photography, illustration, and prepress proofs. These approvals can run into bureaucratic delays that stall progress and strain delivery schedules.

Such delays aren't always dependent on the complexity of a given project; they tend to be more affected by discipline, or lack thereof, within the client organization. Try to uncover the possibility of these delays early; your client contact should be willing to share them with you. After all, you're trying to avoid a pressured situation that can result in costly rush charges or blown deadlines.

At the bottom of your schedule document, write in the delivery date—the day the project must be in the hands of the client or readers. Move up the chain of steps, plugging in the number of days and corresponding dates needed until you arrive at the required start date. Be mindful of holidays, as well as time zone differences. Remember that some steps can be performed concurrently.

You can complete your first draft of a schedule fairly quickly once you know needed time frames. You might discover, though, that to deliver the job on time, the process should have been kicked off weeks ago. Now it's time to review the schedule and tighten wherever possible.

Can you shave a day off the first draft? Did you remember that some tasks, such as design and photography, can overlap, possibly opening up time in your schedule? Can your client commit to faster review turnarounds? Or is he willing to pay rush charges to meet his desired delivery? Ask, too, whether that's a drop-dead date or whether there is any flexibility in his schedule.

Once you've coordinated each vendor's needs into a working version of a complete schedule (e.g., see appendix A), make sure that you review it with all team members in advance of sharing it with the client for his approval. If your initial schedule exercise reveals breathing room, consider adding days to the process steps or assigning an earlier date for delivery. This extra time can save you when the unexpected strikes. Allow yourself a little leeway for adjustment—for example, in case the printer requires additional time for creating a die or the client needs an extra day to complete reviews.

Take the following points into account when you're establishing the time needed for the creative, production, and delivery tasks.

Research

Copy might require reference-book or online research. Depending on the complexity of the topic and the length of the publication, research could require a few days or weeks for the writer to be knowledgeable enough to begin his draft. Books and Web sites might be provided by the client, or the responsibility for tracking down informational resources could be up to you or the writer, adding time to this phase. Consider whether the material will be all new to the writer, in which case more time should be allotted to allow for his learning curve, or whether he is familiar with the subject.

Research also might include interviews. Again, whether the client provides the subjects, or you or the writer needs to track them down will impact the research time frame. Before you compose the draft schedule, find out from your client the interviewees' availability. You can't assume, for example, that you can allot three days for interviews and simply assign dates to this task. Subjects might be busy executives whose meetings and travel interfere with that plan. You'll need to schedule around the people who will provide the writer with information for the copy. Enlist your client to serve as liaison between the writer and interviewees, explaining the importance of the sessions and taking responsibility for scheduling them as efficiently as possible.

The variable of availability will increase if the writer will be responsible for locating experts and others who will provide information for the draft. A vast network of resources could be required to answer all of the questions inherent in the assignment. You'll need to work with your writer to determine an appropriate future date that affords sufficient time for research at this in-depth level.

The location of interviewees, whether provided by the client or identified by the writer, also could require additional schedule time. Perhaps phone interviews will be sufficient. Or interviewing a subject in his environment with a photographer, or to gather comprehensive information or tour a facility might be required for the piece, again potentially adding days to the schedule.

Writing

Make sure your client understands the skill, talent, and time involved in creating even seemingly simple assignments. A solid draft can't be turned around in a day—well, it's not ideal anyway.

Regardless of the simplicity of the writing assignment, the schedule should allow time for at least two drafts. This will enable you and the client to ensure the piece is on track from the start, delivering the agreed-upon message to readers in a style to which they can relate. Remember to include draft review time for the client—and possibly his colleagues or superiors—as well as for any interviewees whose information should be fact-checked.

Base the total number of drafts required on (1) the client's expectations, (2) the project complexity, (3) the writer's familiarity with the topic, and (4) the writer's level of experience.

Try to gauge how involved in the editing of the drafts your client expects to be.

Sometimes a reviewer will make multiple changes that are really inconsequential, solely to "leave his mark" on the manuscript or to prove that he's done his job. If you believe that the client will be apt to make significant changes, add review days to the schedule. Also consider whether others on the client team will be reviewing the draft. Again, use your client as a liaison with other reviewers to ensure their availability when the draft is ready, as well as their understanding that timely review is required to stick to the schedule.

Project complexity might require you to plan for three or more drafts to ensure clarity and accuracy. If you have multiple drafts scheduled, treat each as a further level of refinement. The majority of changes concerning tone, direction, and content should be made and questions asked in the first review round. Second-draft comments should focus on newly generated material created in response to first-draft questions. The third round should center on ensuring factual accuracy and the technical edit for perfect grammar, punctuation, and spelling plus adherence to the client's editorial manual, if one exists.

A writer's in-depth knowledge of a publication's topic can save time on the schedule, especially the first draft. Expertise should be a prime hiring consideration. Time to conduct research on an unfamiliar subject can push the first-draft date out. For more on contracting the appropriate writer for the job, see chapter 7.

Experience typically means time saved. It's always a scheduling plus to contract a seasoned writer whose first draft is close to a final draft. Of course, you can't bank on that. You might not be able to locate a writer knowledgeable in a specialized field, or your budget might require you to hire a less experienced professional. Consider the amount of direction you'll need to give the writer during and after the first draft, and add time to the schedule accordingly.

Experienced writers are sought after and busy. Especially for long-term assignments, inquire about the writer's other jobs, obligations, and vacations and how they might impact the schedule for research and writing. If you're working with a writer burdened with several projects or if a freelancer is working on more than one concurrent assignment for you, compose your schedules to accommodate the added timing needs of your resource.

Consider your timing needs, too. "For an intricate project, schedule an assignment meeting with the writer. You also might meet to discuss draft reviews and changes needed. E-mail, instant messaging, and electronic conferencing have made communication with creative professionals easy even when they're based in faraway locations. But as stated earlier, keep in mind the impact of different time zones. If you're working on the East Coast and your writer is out West, specify the time zone on your schedule. Simply documenting the date could mean a lost day for you—or a late night—if your resource interprets noon in Pacific Time and e-mails the copy at 3 P.M. your time.

Design

A software program cannot just turn anyone into a designer. It's your job to educate your client to the fact that a design is not created or corrected by a few clicks of the mouse. And you must not let anyone make that unreasonable request of your designer.

When scheduling design, first consider the context of the project and what preparation the designer might need to do. If the client's publications follow a graphic standards manual, your designer will need to familiarize himself with its guidelines, such as color palette, logo use, grids, and so on. He also might need to review publication samples that have set the precedent for the new project. These tasks represent a relatively small investment of time, and working with an existing template will translate to less time on the design schedule. Far more hours will be required to create an original layout if there is no precedent-setting model.

Before work begins, the designer needs time to read the copy, if available. Designers should read and understand what they are communicating. This is a seemingly small, often overlooked, but critical step that could impact the design time you allot. Take it into account.

Next consider the design assignment itself. An invitation would take less time than a newsletter, right? Maybe. Take a close look at the elements within the assignment that must be created. Will there be photography or other components that need art direction? How many pages will there be? Work with your designer to estimate the number of hours needed per page. Be sure that the time you're scheduling for design allows completion of all the elements necessary.

Be aware of situations in which a single design element can impact the schedule greatly. This can happen, for example, when an elaborate photography concept is translated into the logistics of actually getting the pictures. The creation of a new logo will sometimes be introduced as part of a project. Designing a new mark for a company can easily rank among the most time-consuming of graphic design assignments in and of itself. Many clients—and publications managers—underestimate the research, trials, reviews, and refinements that typically go into creating a brand identity. A new logo that will identify an entire corporation probably will be applied to numerous communications of multiple media. Its import and longevity deserve and require extensive time and testing.

You've explored the elements that will be a part of the publication. Both the details involved and whether the piece will be original will help you decide on the number of design rounds to schedule. For a less complex project, figure on time for a first layout or rough plus its review, then a second, more refined design incorporating changes plus its review. Consider scheduling at least a third review for complex multilayered designs incorporating a large number of components that need to be evaluated in context with each other for consistency. Finally, schedule a prepress design stage for a last check before art goes to the printer. This review will be done by you or by both you and your client. Ideally this should take less time than previous reviews; significant design issues should have been resolved by this point, and you will probably find nothing more than minor graphic and editorial errors you missed earlier.

Again, remember: Plans change. As you schedule the design process, think about the expected involvement of the client and whether he is known for untimely changes. Major corrections and alterations during later rounds can require additional layouts for review. Try to plan your schedule accordingly, adding another go-round if you fear client holdups.

The designer's responsibilities might extend beyond design itself. If the planned publication includes photography or illustration, he may have to scout locations, manage photographers/illustrators, or review and edit images. Discuss the time needed for these tasks with the designer and make sure the schedule accommodates them. Depending on the project and the photographer, the designer also might need to attend the shoot, which could impact his available design time. Scanning, Photoshop work, and related tasks will also add hours to his schedule.

Budget, time, or logistics might dictate using stock photography or illustrations. Consider the hours needed by the designer to find appropriate art online and possibly contract for usage. Try to determine at the scheduling stage whether the designer will need unusual fonts or other design elements that will require research, adding more time to the schedule.

Budget will also help determine the level of experience you can afford in a designer. A professional with more years in the field typically will be able to deliver more finished designs at earlier stages, benefiting your schedule. To save on cost, however, you might need to add time to the process to accommodate a less experienced artist. Keep in mind specialization as you try to select the most appropriate person for the project (e.g., see chapter 7).

Developing a Schedule

"As with most people, we start with the ideal," says Yang Kim, principal of BBK Studio. Here's Kim's typical process for developing a publication schedule:

"We're usually working with an end delivery date, an event or a product launch. We back up the milestone dates from there.

"We plan time segments according to the activities: concept development, meetings, proofing, illustration/photography, production, etcetera. We will then build in review times for the clients, as well as internal meetings and reviews.

"All of this leads to the kick-off date, the date that we should start the project. Then we tighten dates where we can.

"Generally speaking, if the client is asking for an aggressive schedule, then we need them to be available for reviews and to make timely decisions."

Production Value:
Evergreen Sticker Brochure

zig, TORONTO, ONTARIO, CANADA

"You need to take into consideration what your client stands for and make sure that it is addressed," says Aimee Churchill, project manager for zig's Evergreen book, *Imagine your city with nature*. "For example, Evergreen tries to bring awareness and attention to including nature in urban spaces. They are very environmentally focused within a city, so [we needed to maintain] an urban perspective—their target market lives in cities—while promoting nature and green spaces." zig's response to the client's mission? "We were environmentally conscious of using recycled paper and materials."

The firm also needed to focus on the added financial challenge of working with a nonprofit. "Budget is always a concern dealing with nonprofit clients," Churchill says. "You almost always have a lot less money to work with.

"We looked at vendors we did a lot of business with. We sold them on the idea that we were looking to produce" an interactive and highly involving brochure with a center spread of nature stickers—trees, butterflies, and so on—that could be placed by readers in photos of urban settings throughout the book. "When it's an interesting project and it's for a good cause, vendors are willing to help out and lower their prices to meet your budget. In this case, we mentioned all the vendors involved with a thank-you in the back of the brochure for donating their time and services."

The complexity of design made for another challenge as well. Churchill says, "The specs did play a huge part in the production schedule. A work-back schedule was created at the beginning of the project; this included the photography, color corrections, and the printing of the book.

"Knowing the stickers would take longer than the rest of the booklet, they were sent into production a little bit ahead of time. By the time they were being kiss-cut, the rest of the book was finished printing. Sticking to the original schedule was important to meet our delivery date."

Imagine your city with nature.
Evergreen's commitment to Canada's cities 2005-2008

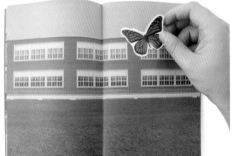

Creative directors: Elspeth Lynn, Lorraine Tao
Art directors: Paul Hogarth, Deborah Prenger
Copywriter: Jonathan Careless
Planner: Jennifer Breton
Project manager: Aimee Churchill
Photographers: Sandy Pereira, Michael Kohn
Client: Evergreen
Images: Courtesy of zig, Inc.

Remember that the popular pro might be tied up with other clients; check on his other projects lined up, as well as nonwork commitments, that coincide with the schedule. Don't make assumptions about mid-process availability.

In some cases, especially when you're collaborating with a designer in the same company, he might be working on more than one project for you. As the publications manager, it's up to you to ensure that the designer's time is prioritized according to your various publication needs. Compare the needs of the assignments in context with each other and compose the separate schedules to prevent deadline overlap. Keep in mind the time you'll need to effectively manage the design process, including meetings and review time. Include time for ongoing discussions with the designer.

When working with an external designer, address any time-zone considerations. Make sure it's understood whose clock the schedule follows so you can communicate efficiently.

Photography

Start by defining the nature of the assignment. How many photos are planned for the publication? Does the project call for a variety of candid shots or carefully staged and lighted portraits? Will people, products, or environments be the photo subjects? Is it studio work or location? Is location scouting required? How much travel is involved? If shots are to be taken outdoors, could bad weather cause delays? Each of these variables carries with it a time consideration.

At this stage try to account for any factors that may require time and resources so that you can create a realistic schedule and budget. Studio work, for example, can involve coordinating and scheduling portrait subjects, auditioning models, and locating products. Someone must be assigned to manage shooting day logistics, ensuring the client, the subjects, and the photographer feel comfortable with all aspects of the shoot.

If products will be shot in the studio, consider whether the designer or art director will be providing photo layouts or whether the photographer will be creating arrangements on his own, adding time to each shot. You or your designate will need to gather, deliver, and in some cases review each item with the photographer; add these hours to the schedule.

Coordination can be a significant part of a location shoot, too. As you prepare the schedule, consider travel time, location scouting, and the number of locations. Outdoor photography could be delayed by weather, obviously a factor you can't control. When possible, allow extra days in the photo time frame if shooting will be performed in a weather-variable location or seasons in which weather changes quickly.

If the appropriate, quality photographer has been contracted and the assignment has been reviewed with him in detail, there shouldn't be a need for a reshoot. But it does happen, so try to schedule time for this possibility.

Discuss the assignment, its requirements, and variables in detail with your photographer before guessing at a time frame. In addition, incorporate time into the schedule for photo shoot reviews by you, the client, and the designer.

Illustration

Artwork for your publication might involve one or several artists, depending on the concept for the piece. Certainly, managing the creative process with a single professional will require less time on your part and will reduce the chance of negative impact on the schedule.

It may be difficult for a client to visualize a finished work of art from an initial thumbnail sketch; therefore, several incremental illustration rounds can be helpful. Reviews at numerous points can help ensure that everyone is comfortable with the visual's direction throughout development. Schedule the review rounds according to the purpose and presence of an illustration in your publication. For example, an oil painting for an annual report cover would require reviews at multiple stages, whereas a simple spot illustration for an invitation might need a rough and a final only.

As with all creative resources, consider the artist's experience and other obligations during the course of the project.

Printing

Each publications step impacts the next. Because of its late-in-the-process position, printing vendors are most often asked to absorb the preceding delays and still meet their finish deadline. This isn't easy, because you've made a commitment not only with people but with machines. You're part of a queue, and if you drop out of line because art was delivered late to the printer, you can't always just pop back in. You might need to wait for the next opening days later to get your piece on press. Make sure you manage the schedule to avoid missing your press date.

Several parts of the printing process will impact your scheduling, including time for the vendor to run prepress proofs; for you, your designer, and the client to review the proofs; for a press check; for the print run; and for any finishing, such as trimming, die-cutting, or folding.

> ### Red-letter Production Dates
>
> - Delivery of final art to the printer
> - Prepress (blueline and possibly color) proofs to you/the client
> - Return of corrected or approved prepress proofs to the printer
> - Press check
> - Completed publications released for delivery or distribution

Keep in mind these pointers about prepress proofs: First, make sure your client knows that, ideally, only typos or inaccuracies should be corrected at the blueline proof stage. New art from your designer or prepared by the printer's design department will take time and add dollars. That's why careful review is so critical before art is released. Depending on your printing process, major changes at the proof stage can break the budget and can cause delays.

Second, make sure your client knows when he'll receive the proof and when it must be returned. It's a heart-stopping experience to see a lonely blueline lying on a desk in a dark office while the printer is waiting to make any corrections and run the job. Missing the return date can bump your job from the queue. That can mean rush charges or late delivery.

If you know from the start that you'll be on a tight schedule, avoid production bells and whistles that will add days to your publication calendar. New dies, intricate folds, embossing or foil stamping, and any handwork are examples of time-consuming extras. Make sure, too, that the design specs meet the capabilities of the printer. For example, a folded piece should be designed to be finished by machine instead of by hand, if possible. Find out whether the printer intends to send the project out to another vendor for any specialty work, adding time to the schedule and probably markup to the budget. Explore whether a different design or a different printer would be more appropriate and efficient.

In addition to the primary publication, schedule production of any packaging. Something as obvious as envelopes can be forgotten until the finished job is delivered and it's time to put the communication in the mail.

Shipping to the Client

Take into account the time needed to transport the finished products from the printer to your client's office or other final destination. Depending on the printer's location and what type of shipment the budget will allow, delivery could be from the same day the publications are finished drying to several weeks if they were printed overseas for cost savings.

Delivery to Readers

If your communications are to be distributed by a mail house, be sure the vendor has address information in advance of the deliverables. The distributor may need to complete time-consuming processing that can be done in advance. Make sure you include the time required for the vendor to collate, label, sort, and post the materials as well as time for mailing days.

Delivery time is especially important for time-sensitive or event-specific materials. Calculating the postpress time needed to get the publications into readers' hands is often left until late in the process or even overlooked. This situation can require the additional cost of expedited delivery.

MANAGE THE SCHEDULE

It bears repeating, once again: Plans change. An interview subject cancels. Rain washes out a photo shoot. The client finds factual errors in the blueline. The result? Your perfectly planned schedule takes a detour. Maybe you can make up the time lost fairly easily, but maybe your delivery date is in danger. You'll have to punt—or better, accept that things out of your control can happen and try to be prepared.

Preparation begins with client education (e.g., see chapter 4). A client who understands the time generally required for each development and production phase will be more likely to respect the final schedule and pass that on to other decision-makers. The time frames will reflect your ideal schedule. They'll need to be adjusted for tighter or rush schedules depending on project needs. Assign a time range to each process step and include these in your proposal (e.g., see appendix A).

When you review a schedule with your client, take the time to explain what's involved in each step. Be cautious about revealing the contingency days you've added to the timeline. Otherwise the leeway you've included to absorb mid-course correction can evaporate before you start. Simply saying "we have a bit of leeway on the design" could push a snowball downhill. It's your responsibility to create a schedule that works despite a wide range of variables, some of which are mentioned above. Adding time to guard against the unexpected is a viable strategy that needn't always be advertised.

When composing the schedule, along with input from the creative team and production vendors, you asked your client for realistic time frames and delivery date. Now, with a workable schedule in hand, you'll need to obtain his commitment.

Reinforce the importance of keeping due dates sacred. Suggest that the client post the schedule and write his deadlines on the calendar. Depending on your comfort with a new or inexperienced client, a bit of micromanaging might be useful. For instance, call ahead to remind him when a draft will arrive and on what day his corrections will be due.

Even though you've emphasized to your client that his time obligations are set in stone, remember that plans change. Recognizing potential problems early and planning a few fallback strategies can quell panic when a project begins to falter. Solidify relationships with more than one writer, designer, photographer, illustrator, and printer. You might need to call on one as a backup if a problem arises.

People get sick, lives go off track, and your deadline might lose priority. Sometimes vendors just flake out—it happens. No client, including you, likes to hear excuses. You can avoid making excuses to your client if you have a viable plan B—a backup resource—ready. To help focus freelancers' and vendors' attention on your deadline needs, it's a good idea to specify in the contract that late delivery of work—or a no-show—will have financial ramifications.

You might find that too often your clients are demanding that you and your team jump through hoops of fire. If you're working on your own or are part of a design or communications firm, you may find a client's needs unmanageable and can turn down the project. If you're working for an internal client, you probably don't have that option. In those cases, without a padded schedule, your project might squeak as you try to squeeze it through the tight time frame.

Your best option is to talk with the client. Explain that you're investigating rush fees that could be incurred to meet the unreasonable deadline, but that in order to feel confident in your ability to produce a quality piece that will reflect well on him, you'll need more time. Also tell him that you'll find out the availability of creative and production resources who can meet the fast-track turnarounds.

If your team is available and willing, and your client green-lights the extra cost, your job as publications manager just got a little more challenging. You'll need to crunch the schedule steps, then check in daily—or several times a day, if necessary—to make sure the draft and design are on target for meeting the art-to-printer delivery date. Keep the team pumped and you'll help push the rush project through. Also make sure you get your client's written signoff on the schedule, the budget, and all proofs in case the compressed schedule results in errors or other disappointments.

When the rush project is completed and you've caught your breath, take action. Don't wait for the next crazy project to be dropped on your desk at the last minute. Talk with your client about what you can do to help make his job more manageable. For example, offer to meet with him to discuss his publications needs for the rest of the year. Return with reasonable start dates. Explain that he'll be far less harried if he can arrange his own schedule to begin his communications in a more timely fashion.

Client education—and your offer to help—can go miles in making the situation better for him, for you, and for your resources. It's important not to become known among your creative and production resources as always having a rush job, or you might find your network weakening.

Encourage Ongoing Communication

Remember that the publications process steps are interconnected. Receipt of copy by the designer depends on the writer's adherence to the schedule. The job might lose its place in the press queue if the designer misses the deadline for art delivery to the printer. So depending on the size, complexity, and importance of the job, round up your writer, designer, photographer, and printing rep. This gathering is guaranteed to increase the degree of accountability each individual will feel to the other team members they now know personally. It also gives them the chance to ask each other questions about preferences, processes, and how they like to work.

As a follow-up to this introduction, consider holding update meetings among relevant team members to ensure the project stays on course. Certainly for a particularly long project, you'll want to hold progress sessions of some or all of your team members by phone conference, IM, or in person. You'll have the chance to reiterate the importance of adhering to the schedule. Remind people of their next steps and deliverables. Use names and specific situations to reinforce personal accountability: "George can start on the design when he receives your final draft on Tuesday, Malcolm." Give everyone the

Time and Money:
David Reed Exhibition Catalog
KINIMOD, INC., PHOENIX, AZ

"In essence, I had two different clients," says Kinimod principal Dominik D'Angelo. The Ulrich Museum was paying for production of the catalog, titled *Leave Yourself Behind*, "and David Reed and I made decisions as far as the concepts and the look of the publication went. The museum had approval, but we were the main decision-makers, which simplified the process."

Complicating the process were a tight schedule and a low budget. "The original goal was to have it completed in three months, which sounds like a lot of time," D'Angelo says. But it really was not because we had to collect all the images—and different people had different images. We had to get high-quality scans done. And we were dealing with three different people writing the essays." In addition, "because it was important for David to be a part of the design process, it took longer than it normally would. But even though David's involvement made the process more complex, it really was crucial in how successful the publication was."

D'Angelo plans each project schedule with an additional two weeks to accommodate surprises and mishaps (e.g., see sidebar on page 70). "The exhibition was opening in the very beginning of April, so I scheduled the print delivery to be on March 15," she says. To manage the schedule effectively, "I just tried to push everybody to meet their deadlines. That did not happen on the dot, so I got the things done that I could with the amount of information I had.

"The basis is a lot of communication between all the parties, and there were many parties. I was communicating with everybody consistently and continually to get things out on time."

The other planning hurdle was the scant $20,000 available for printing the piece, approximately 112 pages and about 10" wide and 13" high. "The size of the publication and the complexity of the printing process were going to be very expensive. There were many, many color reproductions of David's artwork, so color-matching was extremely important from the quality perspective. The catalog also had a dust cover that wrapped around; because of its size, it was difficult to execute. The paper I used was also a little bit difficult to work with."

Because of the budget limitations, D'Angelo could not work with a big printer that would have had more experience in these production areas. "I asked for a quote from a large national printer. The estimate was $60,000," she says. So she took another tack. "I had developed a very good relationship with a local printer, and I knew their quality of printing was great. But they are small, so the size and the scope of the publication were going to be challenging." The second estimate met the budget, and the designer did not need to adjust the specs in any way to accommodate the lower price. "The gap between a huge national printer and the local printer was amazingly large," she says.

Art director, designer: Dominik D'Angelo
Copywriters: Kevin Mullins, Richard Shiff, John Yau
Photographers: Christopher Burke Studio, Dennis Cowley,
    Dominik D'Angelo, Bevan Davies, James Dee,
    Frédéric Lanternier, Spike Mafford Photography,
    David Reed, reedstudio, Stephan Rohner,
    Christopher Stover-Brown
Clients: Ulrich Museum, David Reed
Copyright: © Ulrich Museum of Art

59

#456, 2001-02
opposite page: The Bar, detail

opportunity to discuss any potential problems they foresee and brainstorm ways to resolve them before they occur. A brief written progress report can also update your team members and your client on the project's status (e.g., see chapter 5).

Creative Management

Will such update meetings keep even your designer on task? Many people believe that creative individuals, especially graphic designers, cannot be reined in and kept to a schedule. The myth is that their heads are in the clouds, that they require unbridled space and open-ended time to create their art.

While there may be cases when extremely creative and unique solutions need to be invented, requiring an unpredictable amount of time, this is rare. As in any commercial enterprise, defining deliverables and meeting expectations are key to success. It's necessary to assign a time frame for coming up with an annual report concept, designing a book, or laying out a brochure. And once a schedule is established, the success of the process is largely dependent on each team member's meeting his obligations and moving the project forward.

If you inherit a designer in your department, or as part of an established team, who doesn't have the discipline you need to complete projects on time, address the problem directly. If appropriate, take the time to differentiate between the designer's talent and his inability to meet deadlines, and discuss specific methods for time-management. "You shouldn't expect a designer who's a procrastinator to manage a project," says Emily Ruth Cohen, consultant to creative professionals.

Helpful methods can include daily review meetings with you until he gets the hang of managing his own time better. You might suggest that he

---

"Pricing is an Art Form . . ."

. . . says Emily Ruth Cohen, renowned consultant to creative professionals. "It's something that should be done very thoughtfully." And although there are few absolute rules, Cohen offers these eight pointers and guidelines to consider when pricing a project for a client.

1. Establish a minimum fee for taking a new job. Consider all of the logistics involved and whether it's worth your while.
2. You can ask the client for his budget. There's absolutely nothing wrong with asking. Of course, he might not answer you. . . .
3. You shouldn't give out numbers without thinking about them and confirming them beforehand. Clients tend to fix on that first number and expect you to stick to it.
4. Before starting a relationship, you might offer this well-thought-out number as a way of qualifying a client's budget. You could discover that he's thinking a $1,000 logo while you're thinking $10,000.
5. A fee shouldn't be based solely on time. A client often wants that magical number, but there is no magic formula. I think too many design firms want to template everything. A brochure isn't always $1,000 a page.

   While it's easy to just say 'my logo fee is $5,000,' it isn't really true. A logo for an event or a gala is going to be different than the logo for a major corporation. And even if it took the same amount of time to develop those two examples, they aren't going to have equal value for the client.

   A designer could come up with an idea in two hours, or it could take four weeks because he's stuck. If each fee is based on a fixed hourly rate formula, clients will think of you as a vendor instead of a valued consultant.
6. Deciding the fee is also based on usage. Cohen cites an annual report design that was used for years beyond the initial project. The client got five years of value out of that, when the designer only based the price on the one year. So even with an annual report, you have to define use.
7. Consider the aggravation factor. Is the schedule tight? Is it really boring work? Is the client somebody who'll keep you on the phone incessantly? Is he somebody who can't make decisions? If you choose to take the project on despite red flags, add a percentage to the fee to cover that aggravation factor.
8. Finally: Don't lowball, don't underbid.

---

allot a certain amount of time to each task, set an alarm on his computer, and try to get comfortable with shorter-term deadlines that will keep him on track for the big due dates. You'll be going through the same education process with your designer that you conducted with your wayward client. With his practice and your perseverance—and as much patience as possible—eventually he'll adopt good—or at least better—self-scheduling habits.

Manage Yourself

You can use time- and project-management methods to help yourself, too, including software programs and visual aids. Think about what type of device will best accommodate the way you work and think. Perhaps your tool will be seen or used by others on the team; consider their information needs and work styles, as well.

Depending on your style, you can create schedules and track your publication's progress on a calendar, on a wall chart, or in Excel, Microsoft Project, or another project-management program. You might find it helpful to hang up a visual that charts all of the elements of a project in an open setting where editorial, art, and production personnel interact frequently. Include all the tasks, the due dates, and the responsible producers, and log the completion of each step. This is a great way to spot—or thwart—a bottleneck. It enables everyone to visit a central, visible tracking device to check the status of any part of the project at a glance. And public display encourages accountability.

"I think the best way to manage a project is with FTP sites," says Cohen. "Clients want electronic documentation so they can review past presentations, schedules, updates. You can document every single communication that's sent back and forth—the whole process.

"If you can afford it," Cohen advises, "use some kind of password-protected client-only accessible site. It goes a long way in managing client expectations."

Your people are in place, your schedule is set. Now on to creating and managing the budget that will fund the development, production, and delivery steps of the publications process.

PLAN AND MANAGE THE BUDGET

Perhaps the most important two words you'll hear—and ask—as a publications manager: "How much?"

Before you can start realistic publications planning, you need to know your client's financial resources. Put plainly: How much is he able and willing to spend? Ideally the client will say that he's willing to pay what it will cost, that he only cares about the quality and integrity of the work. Then you can set off to gather estimates for the perfect project. More likely you'll hear a round number or range with which to work. This is the norm, the sky is seldom the limit, and it's the publications manager's job to create a solution within the client's parameters of time and budget.

If you are dealing with a new client, be aware that his initial description of the lavish project envisioned compared with the budget offered can tell you a lot about his experience. And you'll get a feel for how accommodating the client might be in future negotiations, when you try to bring his expectations and budget into alignment.

You'll need to determine the budget available as definitively as possible. Although this seems an obvious point, budget is not always easy to pin down, due to variables ranging from internal politics to a client's budgeting process or cycle. But without at least a ballpark figure, you'll be guessing at what's available, planning for all sorts of possibilities, and may have to repeat the estimating

One Small Spark: AishSeattle Fundraising Brochure

HORNALL ANDERSON DESIGN WORKS, SEATTLE, WA

"There were definitely budget constraints" for the nonprofit AishSeattle fundraising project, says Hornall Anderson designer Yuri Shvets. "Basically, the overall project budget was broken down into creative direction/design and printing. However, since the client is nonprofit, a portion of the cost was deemed pro bono.

"Additionally, the budget was kept down because the print quantity for the

brochure was only 150 total. We enlisted the assistance of a printer we've used many times in the past, so we trusted them and the quality of their work. Full-bleed, black-and-white photography is used with large type and white space to emphasize the message

behind the piece without becoming cluttered," Shvets explains.

The brochure's "integral element"—an envelope-encased matchstick adhered to the back cover—"was very significant to the overall piece. Being a more tactile brochure gave it a connecting, engaging, and interactive look and feel in how the recipient related to it."

In order to incorporate the unique component and still "ensure the budget was as low as possible, part of the agreement was that the client would be responsible for assembling their brochures on an as-needed basis," Shvets says. "This consisted of slipping a matchstick into the glassine envelope, sealing it closed with double-sided tape, and then using the same tape to attach it to the back of the brochure.

HELP *spread* THE LIGHT.

THIS CAN *change* THE WORLD.

"It purposefully touches on both an emotional and an informational vein depending on from which direction you read the brochure. Incorporating a matchstick on the back cover nods to the notion that one spark can spread the light—their message of faith."

AishSeattle Fundraising Brochure

Art director: Jack Anderson
Designers: Yuri Shvets, Katha Dalton
Photographer: Sara Simon
Copywriter: AishSeattle
Client: AishSeattle

process until you uncover the budget. As frustrating as guessing too high and then whittling down your plans can be, guessing too low can preclude even considering great options and, if you are working for an external client, will cost you in lost profit.

When discussing the available budget for a project with your client, have your own broad range in mind if possible. This range is for *your* information—and will come from your printing rep and ultimately from your own increasing experience. If during an initial project discussion you are unsure whether a client's publication plan and budget will work together, don't commit to do the job at that price. Explain that you'll have to check out all the costs involved to make an accurate estimate. You might need to hold an eye-opening session with your client about basic creative and production costs.

If your client—internal or external—wants a blowout project but has a shoestring budget, determine what the end product must convey and begin adjusting to meet the budget. For example, will the message be as compelling with stock photography as with original art? Can you have the piece designed and written in such a way as to shave off four pages? Call in your designer and printer to help brainstorm some alternatives. Often the most creative and effective publications are those that demand resourceful, ingenious solutions and cost-cutting measures.

Once you have at least a dollar range for the project, list all the items that could have costs attached to them. Depending on the project, these might include:

Research. Budget for payment to writer, editor, or editorial assistant to gather information for the copy. Purchase of reference materials could be included.

Writing. Budget for the writer to complete the agreed number of drafts, incorporating your and the client's changes, and rewriting at each round as required. Time for working with the designer or for proofing could be included.

Photography. Budget for the estimated number of days of photography plus any time for scouting or travel anticipated. Inquire about additional dollars for assistants and cost for film and processing.

Photo-shoot coordination and review. Budget for your designer's or art director's time to create photo layouts, coordinate and possibly attend the photo shoot, and review the shoot and select photography (some of these tasks might be your responsibilities).

Photo research and purchase. As an alternative to new photography, you might need to budget for stock photos. Plan for designer research time and the estimated cost of art.

Illustration. Budget for the artist to complete the established number of illustration rounds.

Design. Budget for the designer to develop the chosen concept and the agreed number of design rounds.

Design tools purchase. If you know at the planning stage about special fonts, software programs, or other design tools that will be required to complete the project, build them into the budget now.

Design comp materials. Clarify whether your designer's fee includes materials for review comps and proofs, and budget accordingly.

Testing. Determine with your client whether concept, editorial, or design testing with an audience sample will be required. Your budget for testing will depend on the method and whether you or an external market research firm conducts the sessions (e.g., see chapter 8).

Stock. Find out the cost of the paper stock from your print rep, then price it with a stock house. If the printer markup is significant, consider purchasing and providing the stock yourself.

Envelopes or other packaging. Don't forget to budget for the envelopes. This is easily overlooked when no special design or printing is planned.

Long-term Concept:
Vivus Annual Report Series

HOWRY DESIGN ASSOCIATES, SAN FRANCISCO, CA

Vivus, Inc., is a pharmaceutical company that develops therapeutic products addressing obesity and sexual health. Howry Design's three-year series of reports for the company relies on a light and creative concept "to counteract a relatively serious subject," says Howry Design principal Jill Howry. "Our challenge was to do it in a way that was entertaining without being trite—or flippant.

"Vivus deals with these scientific issues every day. We created an approach [to their annual reports] that was less technical and more human and unexpected—you don't expect to see people vacuuming in pharmaceutical annual reports."

The idea behind the vintage photos was not only budget driven. "We wanted to use the low-tech style of vintage images because it juxtaposed the technological nature of the company's products. And we wanted these images to be mundane, to get the reader thinking of more exciting things that people could be doing instead. This graphic approach was entertaining and approachable.

"We try to do this every year, be a little more innovative, more conceptually compelling so it reels you in," Howry says.

Art director: Jill Howry
Designers: Craig Williamson (2002),
  Ty Whittington (2003, 2004)
Client: Vivus, Inc.

Arousal

VIVUS 2004 Annual Report

VIVUS, Inc., 1172 Castro Street, Mountain View, CA 94040

the little blue pill doesn't work for him.

vivus 02

SEX
HAS BEEN PROVEN TO BE GOOD
FOR YOUR HEALTH.

VIVUS 03

Dies. Obtain the cost for any dies needed for a non-standard-size pocket folder, for example, or a unique publication trim. Make sure the fee includes your ownership so you can send the dies to other vendors in the future if needed (e.g., see chapter 9).

Foil stamping, embossing, or other additional design elements. Make sure these items are noted in your print estimate request and included in the bid.

Printing. Be sure that the printing estimate matches the specifications of the project exactly and that the same specifications are shared with the client and designer.

Prepress proofs. Inquire whether the bluelines and color proofs you're requesting are included in the print estimate, and budget accordingly.

Press supervision. Include the fee for hours spent by your designer or art director at a press check.

Binding. Consider the postprinting production steps that will add to your budget.

Collating or other assembly. Plan ahead for handwork by your printer or other vendor.

Labeling and sorting. These and other tasks may be performed by a mail house or other distribution vendor.

Mailing or shipping. Include costs for postage if mailing the publications directly to readers or for shipping the lot to your client's facility or other location.

Storage. If delivery will be made in more than one shipment, budget for storage of the balance at your printer or mail house.

In addition, if you are the publications manager of various contributors to a publication, include your fees for project direction. Some consultants also charge an administrative fee for handling the logistics—and surprise out-of-pocket expenses—of coordinating several resources.

Obtain Several Estimates

Don't leap at the lowest estimate; a basement bargain could be a sign of an inexperienced vendor or of one who cuts corners that may cost you quality.

Consider not only price in making your choice but also reputation and professionalism, your previous work relationship, and how well the resource's specialization is suited to the project (e.g., see chapter 7).

When reviewing estimates, make sure you clarify vendor charges for often-overlooked or hidden costs in advance to avoid surprises at billing time. These can include:

Author's alterations. Make sure you understand that changes beyond the agreed-upon project scope will be corrected for an additional fee, typically charged by the hour by your designer or printer.

Overtime and rush charges. Find out each resource's overtime policy and hourly charge, as well as a range for rush charges.

Printing overs/unders. This is usually a 5 to 10 percent fail-safe quantity overrun or underrun instituted by the printer to cover production problems and other variables. You need to be aware that you might be paying for more publications than ordered or paying the full cost but receiving less product than you planned—and negotiate accordingly (e.g., see chapter 9).

Mark-up on hard costs. Some talent and vendors mark up materials, travel, and other fixed costs. Try to negotiate that the resource's profit should be reflected in his core estimate—his design, day rate, or printing bill—and not made by increasing out-of-pocket expenses whose real prices can be checked by the client.

Out-of-pocket expenses. These include phone bills, delivery charges, materials, travel, and so on. Make sure you clarify what the resource will bill for separately, and have your client approve those charges in advance.

To prevent invoice surprises, whenever possible negotiate fixed-fee or "closed" contracts with vendors. In other words, don't accept an hourly fee with an open-ended time frame. Distractions, the speed at which a vendor works, any number of variables can affect the amount of hours a task entails for different people. Instead, note that the estimate must be for a maximum charge. This will put the onus on the vendor to alert you, rather than bill you, if he feels he must work beyond the agreement.

Most estimates are valid only for a certain number of months or for a year. If you price out a job that's held for a long period, be sure to confirm all the estimates when the project is resurrected. In addition, recognize that material costs, such as for paper stock, can rise even if the estimate doesn't. Try to lock in these costs with your vendors.

Make clear to your creative talent and production vendors what percentage variance to the estimate, if applied, you will accept and that the estimate must cover the job from start to finish, including all expenses. Note in writing that the budget cannot be increased beyond the variance unless you are notified before further work is performed. It can be helpful to communicate your client's budget for design to the designer and for printing to the printer. In this way, each resource will be mindful of the job's financial limits. Ask your vendors to suggest ways to maintain and manage the budget.

Payment Terms

Arrange in advance the billing and payment terms with both clients and vendors, and get it in writing. The best circumstance from a publications management perspective would be to pay vendors upon delivery of satisfactory services/products; however, different vendors will have their own needs and systems. And as much as is practical, you should try to accommodate them. As mentioned before, many of the creative talents you employ are small businesses for which cash flow is vital. It is helpful to remember that as a contractor, you have the ability to set reasonable terms for payment to contracted vendors. As long as your terms are reasonable, for instance net 15 or 30, are stated clearly before work begins, and most important, strictly adhered to, you'll establish your good reputation in the community.

Change in Scope

At the outset, establish procedures to accommodate changes. Caution your client that any changes to a publication may affect its cost and deadline, that even seemingly minor changes to the printing specifications, the number of pages, quantities, design direction, earlier delivery date, and so on, can have a major impact. Any client changes should be communicated in writing to all relevant internal and external parties with the effect on budget noted. For example, if a client wishes a mid-project change that may alter delivery and/or cost, explain that you will need to investigate the time and budget ramifications. Report any impact the change will have in writing, and have the client sign off before proceeding.

It's a good idea to retain all memos, notes on all phone conversations and meetings with clients and vendors, and any follow-up documents on file until the project is completed.

Maintain and update a project specification and budget sheet so the current status of a job can be seen by glancing at a single page. Be sure to update the information and distribute the updates to all the team members and vendors so everyone even marginally involved is up to date. When vendors are made aware of changes, they can raise concerns promptly and help keep the project on track.

For instance, even a slight change in size could affect the design and printing costs, as well as the size of the envelopes needed, or it may push the mailing or distribution costs to a higher bracket. Such concerns will immediately be apparent to your vendor. By keeping the entire team in the loop, you'll benefit from everyone's experience.

PLAN FUTURE EDITIONS AND UPDATES

It's smart to plan for the next version of a current communication from the outset of the project. Your schedule and budget will benefit when you begin the updated publication. Here are several practical examples of how to accommodate the needs of future publications—or possible ones—while planning the project at hand.

Plan Years Ahead

For a three-year series of annual reports for a medical research institute, a marketing communications firm designed all of the covers at the start of the first project. The unified identity, with only slight variation, helped build recognition and tied the reports together from year to year. In addition, purchasing stock upfront for all of the covers avoided materials cost increases down the road. Printing 60,000 covers three up on the press sheet instead of 20,000 each year saved on the printer's make-ready (or setup—the bulk of the printing cost), so the cover unit cost was significantly lower.

Plan for Multiple Purposes

It's not every day that you can specifically identify future publication needs that could be satisfied by advance printing. You can realize efficiencies and savings by designing multipurpose pieces that can be used in combination with other publications. For instance, a simple folder that a health care corporation created to contain a family of coverage brochures was designed in a generic enough way that it could also be used for meeting presentations and employee orientation materials.

The publications manager considered how to make the piece easily customizable, postprinting. He interviewed the client about all of the possible uses for the piece over the next few years.

If you're a publications manager who's working in-house, contact all your internal clients to propose their use of a multipurpose publication. Obtain their commitments on quantities and budget to pool for a larger run of the piece. This type of advance planning will save you and your clients the time and money involved in creating different designs that could be addressed by a single solution.

Forecast Future Needs

Also think about how your initial design for a piece could impact future versions. If you don't plan ahead, you could either miss the opportunity for painless updating down the road or be stuck with a design that just won't work for new editions.

Of course, simply identifying future needs isn't the end; it is all about planning. You'll need to create a publication plan that elegantly incorporates both your current and future needs.

If a design is to be used to incorporate future changes, you'll need to anticipate what those changes might be and determine how flexible the design can be. For example, if a list of staff members is likely to change in updated versions, try to establish whether the list will remain similar in the number of entries or grow. And if growth is likely, how much growth? While you might not be able to gauge exactly what the future needs will be, you can come up with some probabilities and incorporate that flexibility into your design criteria now.

Investing in extra copies for future use could be wasteful if the design can't accommodate change. Such was the case with a multicomponent publication intended for long-term use. The design consisted of a two-pocket folder with several inserts, each a different height so that together the pieces were stepped. It was a nice display and easy visual organization.

The plan was that reprinting only one or a few inserts as needed would save significantly over reprinting an entire package or consolidated brochure. A problem arose when the amount of updated copy for one of the inserts increased by more than 30 percent—and therefore several inches—from the first year to the next and outgrew the original insert's size. Another problem arose when the information on one insert became obsolete, eliminating the need for that piece altogether. Each of these changes disrupted the step system, and the package had to be completely redesigned and reprinted.

A better plan would have been to forecast the ways in which content might change and create a design that would accommodate more or less verbal or visual information.

Several copy-organization and design alternatives can save you time and money when you're ready to update, say, brochures. In an overview or capabilities brochure that you can use for two or more years, you might try to identify and isolate all of the information unlikely to change yearly (this content could include copy about the company, the quality and durability of products, and the commitment to customer satisfaction). This will allow you to print additional years' quantities upfront and save on press setup and stock.

Or if the boilerplate copy is to appear in a series of brochures, design the pieces so the repeated information appears on the inside covers. This approach will allow you to overprint covers and store them for next year, updating only the text inside that changes. Make sure your printer maintains files, negatives, and plates for any materials that have a chance of being reused down the road.

Whenever you print parts of a publication family, or even pages of a single piece, separately or over time, it's critical to match inks and stocks to maintain the integrity of the collection. This will reflect on the company, the brand, and you as a publications manager. Use the same printer for updated editions or, when that's not possible, supply the new printer with last year's samples and make sure you or the designer attends the press check.

MAXIMIZE THE PRESS SHEET

Work with your designer and printing rep to maximize the use of your project's press sheet. This will help you save on stock costs and trim waste. Ask how different pieces with the same print specs can be laid out on the sheet to run the greatest number of pieces together.

Think ahead to other uses for the sheet, not only the current publications you need printed now. Look at the layout of the press sheet to see what space is available, paper that would normally be cut away and tossed. Consider how you could use that extra press room.

For example, card-stock folders could be arranged to run in a configuration that accommodates printing business cards and note cards at the same time. Even if there is not an immediately identifiable need for an additional piece, try not to waste that paper or printing make-ready cost. It wouldn't be unreasonable to design and print holiday cards in advance if time allows.

If you foresee the need to update only some "family" publications but not others, don't run them all together. Instead, group only those that likely will require revisions or restocking. In this way, you won't print additional unneeded copies of other pieces, and you'll lower the unit costs of the publications that need reprinting by running more.

7

Assembling the Creative Team

None of us is as smart as all of us.
—JAPANESE PROVERB

The best executive is the one who has sense enough to pick good men to do what he wants done,
and self-restraint enough to keep from meddling with them while they do it.
—THEODORE ROOSEVELT

Good news: You don't have to do it all. Sure, you hold responsibility for the success of your project and must perform multiple tasks. But remember that you'll call on creative resources and production vendors to design and deliver the job. Schedules and budgets can be significant management challenges. Just as important is building the competent team that shares your vision and enables you to meet the client's needs.

In this chapter you'll learn where to find resources for your team, how to select the best people for the job, and how to manage relationships with creative professionals: writers, designers, photographers, and illustrators.

Following this book as if you were bringing a project forward, you now understand the assignment, have devised a conceptual solution, and are on to identifying the creative talents available to make your vision real. I'll approach this chapter assuming you need to find creative talent. Some of you are employed by client companies or design firms that rely on in-house talent to provide creative services. Even if that's the case, I urge you to read on. At some point you may have to assemble a larger or more specialized team. Or it could end up being a regular part of—no jinx here—your next job.

As a matter of course, when you come across business communications or other publications that you consider effective, consider why each works and why it appeals to you. Short of an actual audit (e.g., see chapter 2), review your collected samples, organize a file, and note the names of the creative professionals involved to feed your database. This exercise will not only build a resource file for talent, techniques, and approaches but will hone your own communication skills in describing what you want to achieve with any given project.

Beginning with "the hunt," I'll suggest a few ways to survey the field and find out what creative resources are available. Then I'll review several guidelines for developing strong working relationships with writers, designers, and photographers/illustrators.

Talent for Hire

Brand strategy and design are handled within the Monterey Bay Aquarium design department. Illustration is the only creative that director Jim Ales contracts outside. Ann Caudle, who specializes in life science illustration and has worked with Ales for many years, illustrated the aquarium's Fish Fact Cards.

Ales places "quality of work" at the top of the criteria list when selecting freelancers.

Illustrator: Ann Caudle
Copyright: © Monterey Bay Aquarium

"Just as important," he says, "is their personal and professional attitude. It's very important that people you work with (1) know how to work with art directors and (2) bring project experience with them."

He also looks after the interests of his freelancers: "I'm most concerned with getting the best out of my vendors. We pay very well, and over the years have built an excellent reputation and mutual respect with our vendors."

THE HUNT: DIRECTORIES AND PROFESSION ANNUALS

Connecting with industry groups is a great way to find a large, organized talent pool. Every type of creative discipline is covered by at least one association that maintains a Web site featuring professionals' work. And many sponsor juried award annuals recognizing the best work in a wide range of categories. These are great sources for both talent and inspiration. I've included a listing of many professional resources in appendix B. Here are a few on which I've relied.

If you're looking for writing and editorial talent, turn to the American Society of Journalists and Authors (*www.asja.org*) and the Editorial Freelancers Association (*www.the-efa.org*). Both allow nonmembers to post project needs for application by members; the service is free to hiring parties. The International Association of Business Communicators (*www.iabc.com*) offers the same job-posting capability with the added feature of reviewing members' resumes.

You can search design portfolios online at the American Institute of Graphic Arts (*www.aiga.org*) and Communication Arts (*www.commarts.com*) sites. *Communication Arts* magazine also publishes design, photography, and illustration annuals that have become industry standards for excellence. These terrific annuals are available in print and interactive versions, which are both available for purchase at the Web site.

Photographers' portfolios are viewable at the American Society of Media Photographers (*www.asmp.org*), and illustrators' work can be seen on the Graphic Artists Guild site (*www.gag.org*). At *www.folioplanet.com*, the ArtistFinder™ feature lets you search for illustrators by name, review their work, and obtain contact information.

THE HUNT: WORD OF MOUTH

Unless you and any colleagues you might have all just stepped into your publications manager roles, you probably have at least some experience with creative pros. Swapping the names of those talented vendors falls within the highly trusted category of word of mouth. Again look around, ask questions. Naturally, most of your queries will be about successful, appealing work, and those involved will be glad to credit the team. After all, artists are glad for referrals, and their success reflects well on everyone involved.

Personal testimonies often provide added comfort because they usually include information about reliability and business practices that you won't see in work samples. Something along the lines of "yeah, it looks great, but what a pain" will raise an alarm that a portfolio review won't. For the most part, established professional creative talents are just that: professional. They operate as independent contactors or part of small service groups. And, like any small business, they wouldn't succeed by repeating mistakes. But a friendly caution from someone who has been through difficulties with a freelancer can save you from paying for new mistakes.

Printers are a great resource for creative talent recommendations. Printing reps make it their business to know all of the players in the community. They'll be able to tell you who are the superior designers and who's best suited for a range of work. The reps' self-interest operates to your advantage: They'll also guide you to designers and firms that deliver art to printers on time and in the right formats. Ask your trusted rep, who in the design community are smart and effective print managers? Managing details from the design table to press is paramount to your project's production quality. And ask about professionalism, too. If a printing rep finds a designer difficult to work with, you might encounter the same experience.

THE HUNT: OUTSOURCING THE SEARCH

To good success, many managers turn their design needs over to creative-talent placement firms. These agencies, acting as business and marketing representatives for freelancers, are able to take a lot of the business responsibility off the shoulders of the designers and art directors, writers and editors, photographers and illustrators, allowing them to concentrate on their craft.

Agency reps will discuss your job requirements, review the talent pool, and make recommendations about who's best suited to your job and who meets your fee requirements. Most reps will offer you an opportunity to meet candidates, review their portfolios, and personally gauge whether you feel comfortable working with them.

Whether you're looking for a creative professional for the first time or deciding on who among your past associates would be best for your assignment, you have myriad considerations and guidelines to keep in mind during the selection process, contracting, and relationship management. You want a reliable, professional resource to work with you on future projects.

It's important to remember, too, that you want to be a client with whom the creative talent will want to work again. The same word-of-mouth network operates in the freelance community about clients and employers. Clients who make unreasonable demands or are otherwise hard to work with are avoided, which limits their options when they need a specific resource on their creative team.

Each of the creative professions you're likely to draw from—writers, designers, and photographers/illustrators—differs from each other enough that I'll discuss them separately. Here again, even if you haven't yet or don't plan to hire a professional from one of these categories, it's still worth reviewing this material. Much of what is covered describes good practices that will benefit you elsewhere.

One other note: These creative vendors are professionals who bring with them knowledge and experience that can benefit you beyond a particular assignment. They're valuable resources, worth cultivating. In addition to alternate creative solutions, freelancers might suggest slight variations to your standard business arrangements, due to their status as independent small businesses. When possible, try to accommodate them, and if you aren't able to, let them know immediately. A bit of early, frank discussion about payment terms can avoid a predictable drain on their enthusiasm for your project.

EFFECTIVE RELATIONSHIPS WITH WRITERS

"It sings." That's how you want to feel when you read your writer's draft, that the words leap off the page. Would that it were always so. You will find some writers whose first drafts are nearly finished, requiring minimal changes to complete the copy phase of the publication. There will be others who need your more dedicated guidance to understand the audience, the angle, the message, and the mode. Regardless of the state of the first draft, however, remember that you can work together to develop it into inspiring music.

Selection Criteria

The writer you hire should have experience that's appropriate to your publication. Does that go without saying? No. Of course, it's the ideal situation. But you might not be able to base your selection solely on a writer with several years of relevant experience. That freelancer's experience might equate to a fee that will blow your budget. Less or broader experience might fit your funds more appropriately. If you're operating on a shoestring, consider novice or less experienced writers with limited yet strong samples.

Search freelance-writing Web sites for typical as well as individual writers' fees, which vary by region. The Editorial Freelancers Association (*www.the-efa.org*) lists rate ranges for tasks from writing to substantive copyediting, from transcribing to indexing. Colleagues and counterparts in other organizations, of course, are also a valuable resource for you when establishing your writing budget.

Review the candidate's portfolio with an eye to a tone appropriate for the type of writing you need. Whether that's a conversational tone for a human-interest story slated for a company newsletter or catchy copy for a direct-mail solicitation, the writing should be engaging and should appeal to your targeted audience. Consider the number of samples specific to your audience, to your publication format or category, and to your industry. One stellar sample that's suited to your needs might convince you that you've found your ideal writer.

Interview several candidates and ask specific situational questions. A professional writer will be well spoken, articulate, and straightforward. Don't base your selection just on his portfolio. Ask, for example, the involvement of an editor in a particular product. Try to gauge how much guidance the writer required and how close to final the first draft was. This is especially important if you're not an editor and will be reviewing the articles strictly from your audience's perspective—which, of course, is not to be underestimated.

Explain who your audience is, and try to get a feel for the writer's understanding of that audience. Give a few examples of the types of writing jobs you assign. Ask the writer what his approach would be to ensure that these assignments successfully call the readers to action.

Finally, in addition to the portfolio samples, request a client list and references, and then follow up. Ask specific questions: In general, how did the project go? How much guidance or hand-holding did the writer require from the client? How clean and on message was the first draft? How many drafts were needed to create finished copy? Would the client hire the candidate again?

Number of Relationships

Let's look at your freelance writing needs. Do you produce a single periodical—for example, a company newsletter? Perhaps its scope of stories can be satisfied by a single writer. Depending on his experience with your industry and his writing specialization, that same professional might be your first choice for other projects, too, such as an annual report and product brochures. Develop a relationship with another writer so you won't be in a jam if your favorite writer's calendar is full when you propose an assignment.

Consider whether your writing needs are more diverse, including, for instance, direct mail or advertising copy. Arrange interviews with writers skilled in these arenas in advance of projects so you won't be scrambling for a resource when work needs to begin. It's a good idea to establish a writer corral to call on for your various needs and for concurrent or overlapping assignments.

Relationship Tone

Think of the editor–writer relationship as a partnership. You're working together to exchange information and ideas, and to come up with the best communication solution for your readers. This relationship tone is suitable whether you're reviewing content from the reader's perspective alone or you're a skilled editor.

Sometimes it demands a great deal of diplomacy on your part to convince the writer that you genuinely want to be partners. A lot of creative talents have strong egos and might exercise them more than most. It can be difficult for anyone to hear criticism or handle rejection of work he's created. Be sensitive and encouraging to your writer, giving constructive criticism and supplying recommendations instead of tossing off a terse, "Fix it!" At the same time, be clear and firm in your direction to make sure you get the product you contracted the writer to provide.

At times, your need for a writer's particular talent, or at least his ability to complete your assignment, requires thick-skinned patience on your part. Such was the case with a freelancer assigned to me to write copy for an international hotel chain's promotional magazine. I had been chief copy editor at a city magazine for many years, and now was a publications manager at a marketing communications firm. But she was older and had more experience and from the start was bristly.

The first draft was in good shape, but I did have some queries for clarification and some style issues I wanted to discuss. Given that ours was a new relationship, I wanted to review them in person. I approached the meeting with friendliness and calm, beginning by complimenting her on fine work. Perhaps not surprisingly, this didn't go over so well considering my age at the time. But I pressed on, asking her to sit next to me in front of the monitor so we could line-edit.

Put It in Writing

Keep a checklist of written communications you should provide the writer or the writer should turn in to you. These include:

- Writer's notes
- Editorial style guide
- Organization literature
- Samples of relevant past publications
- Contract or letter of agreement
- Writer fact-checking
- Initialed writer signoff on final proof if required
- Hand-written thank-you note with samples

The writer's ego flared a few times at questions she thought were unfounded. I explained that if I didn't understand a passage, chances were that someone else might not. I just wanted this to be the most engaging and effective product possible, I emphasized. After holding my own—politely and patiently—and demonstrating my command of editorial style, she came around, actually admitting that the process hadn't gone quite as badly as she'd expected. Faint praise indeed.

Resource Education

Supplying your freelance writer with any existing literature from the client organization will give him an understanding of the mission and the audience. This will be important background on which to base a work of writing. It will help ensure that the piece is appropriate to the reader and accurately represents goals and objectives.

It's important to supplement this written information with personal discussion of the company overview and future direction, as well as the purpose of the publication, so the writer can ask you clarification questions. In addition to company literature, provide samples of previous publications to illustrate the type of tone you're after for the project at hand.

Writer's Notes

If your company contracts writers for several projects throughout the year, consider developing a document of company and procedural information for talent you hire and for freelancers contacting you for work. These writer's notes or writer's guidelines can be brief, yet they can save you time in reviewing the basics.

Writer's notes can include information about: (1) your editorial philosophy, (2) the coverage of your publications and descriptions of their audiences, (3) how the general draft-submission and editing process are set up, and (4) fact-checking responsibilities. If appropriate, also include interview protocols and how you wish your organization to be represented by the writer. If your freelancer will be talking with experts outside of your company, he'll be perceived as a company representative. Also cover your company's interview policy—for example, reviewing quotes before publication to ensure accuracy.

Interviews

If your writer will be conducting interviews, supply him with the subjects' written biographies, if available. At the least, tell the writer about each interviewee's organization role, relevance to the story, and areas of expertise. Include any personal observations that can guide your interviewer, such as how busy the individual is or whether it's likely to be a tough interview because the subject is shy or tends to barrel over people.

It can be difficult to coordinate two other persons' calendars, but if the interviewee is a challenging person to get hold of, consider taking on that responsibility. The subject might respond in a more timely way to your request than to that of a stranger. If your writer will be arranging the interview, make sure that the subject is informed of the writer's name and is aware that he will be calling to arrange a convenient time for an interview on a defined subject.

Sit down with the writer to compile important questions to cover in the interview. This will help him get the most value out of the interviewee and ensure that all of the relevant story details are captured.

Editorial Style Guide

Before the writer begins work, supply him with your organization's editorial style guide (e.g., see sidebar on page 104) if one exists. By following the guide, the writer can compose and format drafts according to your style, rules, tone, and formatting of heads, subheads, and other elements. This will save you time in the editing process.

Fee Considerations and Estimates

The writer's estimate will be an important criterion in making your freelancer selection. Although most writers have a set hourly rate, there might be room for negotiation depending on the simplicity of the project, for instance, or if you're managing a publication for a nonprofit organization.

Have your budget in mind when negotiating the project fee with the writer. After obtaining his hourly rates or ranges, consider sharing the budget you have available for the project instead of turning him down because of a fee that is too high. As small-businesspeople, some writers will try to find workable compromises rather than lose potential work. Request an estimate based on the project parameters you discussed. But be prepared—a writer might opt out at the estimating stage if your budget is too low to meet monetary needs.

Sometimes you can negotiate a higher fee with your client if you feel he is worth the bump in budget. A freelance writer, Susan, who always turned in a near-final first draft, was my first choice for a startup regional magazine's winery column. The publisher was prepared to pay $200 for 1,000 words. Susan was concerned that this would be a money-losing proposition considering her rate and asked my advice on how long I thought the project would take.

The column entailed researching two local wineries online, conducting a phone interview with each, and writing two drafts. I estimated an hour's research, an hour to complete the two interviews, two hours for the first draft, and an hour for the second, final draft if needed. Five hours at Susan's $75-per-hour fee nearly doubled the publisher's budget.

The Write Stuff

Consider the complexity of the writing project.

- Will independent research be required, or will you be able to provide completed research to the writer?
- Will interviews inside or outside the company be required?
- Will information need to be gathered over a long period of time—for example, over the course of an election campaign?
- What is the estimated word count?
- How many reviewers will be looking over the copy, perhaps adding to the number of changes?
- Will you coordinate the comments of multiple reviewers or leave that to the writer?
- How many drafts, two or three, say, will you feel comfortable with, given the nature of the project?
- Will you be requesting interaction between the writer and the designer—for example, to make cuts necessary to accommodate space?
- Will the writer do fact-checking?
- Will review of design and press proofs be part of the writer's responsibilities?

Although other writers were available, Susan had proven she was reliable, knew the material, and was a very good writer, so I recommended the publisher meet the additional $175 cost. I explained that any savings realized on a less expensive writer would be spent on additional editing time needed to bring the column up to Susan's quality. I further explained that I was convinced a high-quality writer was needed to establish credibility and ensure a well-read column. The publisher agreed, the fee was met, and Susan's column was excellent.

To establish your budget for a writing assignment, figure the number of hours you believe will be required for the job, then multiply that by the hourly fee.

Make sure you discuss the full project scope, length and number of drafts, and responsibilities with each candidate in advance to ensure that when all estimates are in, you can compare them item by item in writing. If you're requesting an estimate from a single writer with whom you've worked well before, an oral estimate would be fine as long as this is confirmed as the fee in a written contract.

Insist that you contract for a closed-ended project fee and not for per-hour payment. For instance, set the job at $712.50 rather than $75 per hour with the assumption that the writer's work will be contained to the 9.5 hours estimated (e.g., see sidebar on page 103). Specify instead that the project total is not to exceed $712.50. Different writers work at different speeds, and distractions can make a cut-and-dried project drag out for a writer; you'll be in danger of surpassing your budget—sometimes by a surprisingly high margin—if you leave the fee open-ended.

Contract and Terms

Some publications managers make the mistake of foregoing a contract or even a simple letter of agreement. Often the reason is something akin to "the writer is my friend" or "I've worked with this writer before, and there have been no problems." More obviously problematic is "This is a rush job, and I don't have time. I think we covered everything and are on the same page."

Even if you have a great relationship with the writer, are in a time jam, or think you were clear about the job description, fee, and rights, relying on an oral agreement and a handshake can strain a valuable relationship. Misunderstandings can easily occur on both your and the writer's parts. But because you are the one with the project need, you're likely to lose more. It only takes a few minutes to clarify the project in writing. Otherwise you'll risk alienating a valuable resource, end up with a writer who'll never want to write for you again—or who you'll never want to hire again—or find yourself in an argument over who owns what and how much payment is due. Save yourself hours of headache or unrecoverable situations down the road: Take the time to put it all in writing.

Learning this lesson too late cost me a great writing resource. After a freelancer's manuscript for a special new employee annual report was accepted, I was billed $2,000 as per our agreement—an oral agreement only. The amount reflected the full fee, and on the invoice she had described the job as "wrote employee annual report." Satisfied with her good work, I signed off and turned the bill over to the accounts payable department. The terms were net 30, and the writer was paid.

Estimate the Writing Job

This is a practical example of applying the two-step process of (1) establishing the number of hours required and (2) figuring the fee by multiplying the hours by the hourly rate. Here are the estimated hourly lineup and total tally:

Project review meeting	no charge
Review of company materials and samples	0.5 hour
Three interviews	1.5 hours
First draft, including fact-checking	3.0 hours
Second draft	2.0 hours
Communication with designer	1.0 hour
Proofing at three phases	1.5 hours
TOTAL	9.5 hours

9.5 hours at $75/hour = $712.50

A few months later I received a second invoice from the writer for an additional $1,000 for the same job. I called, and she explained that it was "just the balance of the bill." I replied that I had budgeted and approved $2,000 as per our agreement. I pointed out that there'd been no indication on the first bill that there would be a balance due and that the work was completed and accepted before the first invoice.

I further explained that I couldn't push this through even if I thought it was legitimate, that I couldn't turn in another invoice for the same work for the same project. I wouldn't pay the second invoice, I said. The call ended after the writer resorted to yelling. She was a talented writer whom I never called again. Had we signed a simple letter of agreement specifying the fees and terms, this situation would not have arisen.

What should you include in the letter of agreement? Here are several components to consider for a comprehensive document that not only serves you legally but also works as a project reference for all parties.

Start with a description of the project: the name or working title that identifies the piece, and a brief description of the content and scope.

Spell out the responsibilities of the writer—for example, interviewing, composing two drafts, fact-checking, and proofing design layouts and the blueline.

Specify the format in which the drafts should be sent, typically in Microsoft Word or in a text file via e-mail, and that they must conform to the company's editorial style guide, if provided.

Include the deadlines for the drafts and the writer's fee and fee schedule (net 30 from acceptance of the final draft, for example). Note in writing that failure to meet the deadlines might impact payment.

Include the publication date and how many samples you will be providing the writer.

Clarify who owns the rights to the story. Except in the case of a topical or opinion article with widespread appeal, it's unlikely that the writer will want or benefit from the right to publish a piece elsewhere in the future. Specify whether the job is "work for hire"; in other words, whether the writer is considered the employee on this project and the hiring company is the publisher and owner of the story's copyright.

Facts in the assignment might be of a proprietary nature. If necessary, include a statement that all information obtained during the course of research or interviews is to be kept confidential, and attach a nondisclosure agreement to the contract for added protection.

Make sure it's clear whether you'll be including a byline and/or author's blurb (a one- or two-line description of the author and his expertise or last work). If you're creating a corporate newsletter, such writer identification would rarely be relevant and could appear out of place.

Note that any issues arising during the project that may impact on-time delivery or the fee must be communicated to you immediately and before work continues.

You'll also want to proactively protect the writer's rights. Here are some examples: The writer performed the interviews and wrote the first draft, but the project was placed on hold indefinitely. You agreed to the writer's terms of payment, upon final draft acceptance. But there'll be no final draft.

Are you off the hook? No. To be fair and for your own public relations as a good client—and for your own ethical peace of mind—you must compensate the writer for the work performed. Or say you accepted the final draft the writer submitted, but the publication was subsequently abandoned. The terms were net 30 from publication. In fairness, you owe the writer payment in full. Specify the amount of a hold fee or kill fee in the contract.

On occasion I have paid writers for unacceptable work. I'd just begun a new position and was editing stories for a magazine contracted by my predecessor. One was submitted by a writer with a note that she was leaving for vacation that day and would be unreachable; there wouldn't be a chance for any questions from me or a redraft from her. Unusual, but I thought I'd make adjustments to smooth the tran-

---

The Editorial Style Guide

Many organizations rely on established references as their editorial style guides. Examples include the *Chicago Manual of Style*, *Words into Type*, and *Elements of Style* (e.g., see appendix B). Consider adding to and adapting your chosen reference to reflect your preferences regarding:

- Use of the company name and tagline, first and subsequent reference

- An explanation of company literature tone (for example, conversational vs. academic), mindful of company mission or positioning statement and audience or audiences

- Use of tense and person (for example, all writing in present tense with a second-person perspective)

- Use of parts of speech (For example, is "he" or "he or she" used? Are compound adjectives hyphenated? Are contractions accepted?)

- Use of gender-specific terms

- Treatment of heads, subheads, secondary subheads, sidebar heads, and so on

- Treatment of proper names of people and institutions

- Spelling rules

- Numbers versus numerals style

- Punctuation style (for example, italics vs. underlining, use of dashes and ellipses, serial comma use)

- Common errors, such as use of "which" versus "that"

sition. Unfortunately, the copy was dreadful and unsalvageable. New interviews and a total rewrite were in order, and I had to hire another freelancer to replace the traveling writer. Although the editor before me had no written agreement in place, I felt that the special circumstances—and my ignorance of any oral arrangements that may have been made—warranted the benefit of the doubt. I mailed a check for partial payment with a hand-written letter explaining that I was unable to use the draft.

Change in Scope

If there is a significant change in scope in the middle of a project, hold an in-person meeting with the writer to discuss the change, new research or interviews to be conducted, and if applicable, the new draft and final-copy deadlines. Depending on when during the process the change occurs, you might be responsible for paying the writer for work done to date or for renegotiating the total fee. An agreement addendum specifying the editorial change and the impact to payment and schedule—or a new contract—should be drafted and signed. If the deadline cannot be changed, you might need to pay rush charges to meet the original due date.

Project Direction and Meetings

As a publications manager, you need to go beyond making the writing assignment to the freelancer, simply hoping the project goes smoothly. You need to manage the writing process. In-person meetings at different phases, plus ongoing communication via phone and e-mail, will keep you apprised of progress and will keep the writer mindful of deadlines.

Typically you'll begin with an initial project sit-down meeting. This will allow for smoother, more in-depth discussion, giving the writer a chance to ask clarification questions about the project. It's advisable to prepare a detailed agenda, which will not only ensure that all of the necessary points are covered but set a tone of efficiency that won't hurt your management efforts.

For example, when overseeing a quarterly company newsletter, I would prepare a page of copy points and project parameters to review with the writer during our meeting. The meeting was always held in person so that I could turn over any reference materials.

Perhaps the most important communication between you and the writer will come unscheduled throughout the writing project. Make sure that you're available for questions when they arise; return e-mail and voicemail promptly to keep the project on schedule. Let the writer know in advance if you will be out of the office at any time during the writing assignment. If possible, provide a backup resource to answer questions.

A mid-project check-in will demonstrate your commitment to the best possible product and keep the writer mindful of deadlines. Check in by phone or e-mail at mid-draft and/or after critical interviews to see how they went. Find out whether the writer gained all of the necessary information or needs additional people with whom to speak.

A Writer Meeting Agenda

An agenda typically and simply could include:

- The issue's editorial lineup, with a description of each story
- Level of importance of each story, usually categorized as A, B, or C
- Approximate word count for each story
- Contact information for interviews, with key questions for the writer to cover
- A list of the company manuals or other related references provided for research, with the most important sections flagged in the books
- Deadlines for the first draft, my review, the second draft, and the publication date

If the writing assignment is especially complex or technical, consider setting up a first-draft meeting together after you've had a chance to review the copy. At this time you can give your comments in person and ask any clarification questions. You and the writer can brainstorm what still needs to be covered, corrected, or fleshed out, plus the approach to the second draft.

Call the writer after you've reviewed the second draft with any final follow-up questions or to give your approval. Any rewriting or corrections at this point should not be significant. Reiterate the final due date.

As you provide feedback to the writer, keep in mind that your editing might change the meaning of the writer's words and therefore could lead to reader misunderstanding. It's a good idea to involve the writer after editing to review the changes you've made. This will ensure that the original facts and meanings are maintained and clear.

Make sure that the writer has checked all facts and that the quotes are accurate. Have the writer turn in to you a record of fact-checking, for example, a printout of the article with checkmarks by facts—dates, name spellings, titles, program names, quotes, and so on—that have been verified. Keep this on file in case there are any questions after publication. In a company setting, it's a good idea for the writer or you to have the interviewees review the copy to ensure the quotes are correct and that the subjects' ideas and facts are presented accurately. You also might want to have the writer final-proof the copy before it goes on to the designer, as well as help with proofreading design and prepress proofs.

Special Considerations

Keep in mind that you are working with a person who is creating something for you. There often will be some degree of ego attached to the product, so don't overreact if the first draft is not what you had in mind. Keep your criticism timely and your comments constructive, and give specific recommendations for next steps to improve the copy. Remember, too, that your public relations and reputation as a client are at stake in any relationship with a freelancer, so act professionally and graciously. Provide samples of the publication as soon as available, and enclose a hand-written thank-you. Treat the contractor as you would wish to be treated.

EFFECTIVE RELATIONSHIPS WITH DESIGNERS

When I need to hire a freelance designer, my mind turns to Donna first. She is the dream designer. When met with any challenge, the first words out of Donna's mouth are, "Not a problem." The sing-song tone is actually comforting; I know she means it. Her attitude is straightforward, get it done, deliver on time, and when necessary, make changes—and more changes—to meet the client's needs. Donna treats every job, no matter how small, as the most important piece she's working on right now, and passes on her confidence to her client.

Even during a rush job, Donna exudes the can-do attitude that makes you know it's all going to work out. And she's able to grasp the business objectives of the job and work fast to invent a suitable solution. In the case of creating a new brand identity for two merging insurance companies, mindful of upper management's call for immediate action, she cranked out dozens of options in just a few days. Now "cranking out" design is, of course, not the ideal condition for superior work. But this designer's focus and ingenuity enabled her to explore enough versions to select from to meet the assignment. Donna's work answered both the company's need to maintain individual brand recognition and the audience's need for clear understanding of the new combined image.

Certainly, not every designer is a dream. Here are several considerations that will help you select the next best professional.

Selection Criteria

Begin by getting to know the work of the candidate by reviewing his portfolio—in person or online. By seeing what he has created over the course of his career, you'll be able to gauge whether his experience and specialization are appropriate for your assignment.

At a face-to-face meeting, it can be tiresome and irrelevant to go over every item a designer has ever worked on in a hefty collection of printed pieces. The removal and reinsertion of every single brochure and letterhead suite just makes the interview drag on that much longer. A designer should tailor his portfolio to the job at hand.

If the interview is simply more of a get-to-know-you session, the designer should show his range of talents but with each represented by only a few outstanding pieces. If this isn't the case, take the lead in the review and flip through to unearth only those projects that match the likely jobs for which you'll be tracking down the right designer. For example, for a corporate newsletter, make sure this type of work is one of the designer's specializations.

Throughout the review, ask questions about the designer's role in several projects and how he thought each through. How heavily directed was he by the art director? If you'll be judging the design and don't have experience as an art director, you should try to confirm that there was a light hand in direction. Ask how the designer arrived at the concept and how it answered the need or opportunity of the client's communication. Did a family of publications or a template for design already exist? Try to discern how much you can rely on the designer for original thought and invention.

Ask the designer about the steps taken to create, present, refine, and deliver the art. This will indicate how involved you will need to be in the process.

Your interview should reveal whether the designer is comfortable educating decision-makers and effective in building a rapport with them. This will be especially important for the publications manager who does not have much experience in evaluating design but who must place confidence in the designer—the hired expert—for guidance to the most effective solution.

The Designer's Experience

The following questions will help you evaluate the designer's experience and professionalism:

- Did the designer review information about or research the audience of the publication?

- How would the designer explain the problem that the publication was meant to solve? What special challenges might the client have been facing in solving the problem?

- What was the desired response to the publication? How would he explain the way his design answered the problem and those challenges?

- How many design solutions did the designer present to the client? Was he involved in a presentation to a larger group of decision-makers? What was his comfort level during that meeting?

- How did the designer feel about explaining and perhaps defending his design choices to ensure the best possible solution? For example, how did he express that a newsletter's three-column grid was easier to read than two columns? Why did a brochure's background color make the logo pop more? Or why should additional dollars be spent on sending a larger direct mail postcard, helping it stand out among piles of other unsolicited mail?

Printing Process Knowledge

Part of selecting an effective designer is assessing his familiarity with printers and with preparing art files for print shops. These aren't givens because not all designers have such familiarity.

Ask what printers the designer has relationships with. Is he knowledgeable about each printer's capabilities? He needs this information so he can create a piece with compatible specifications for the greatest time- and cost-effectiveness.

For example, say your newsletter is designed as an accordion-fold with five 5" panels, but the printer's folding machine cannot accommodate that length. Now you're looking at handwork that will cost time, money, and potentially precision, thus quality.

Equally important, does the designer know the software the printer uses? Even if a new program is becoming the design industry's standard, some printers might not have adopted it yet. The designer should know whether files created in his newer software can be used when the printer still uses the previous standard—at no conversion charge to you.

Finally, does the designer have all of the software and skills needed to complete the art without the printer's involvement in extensive prepress work? If photos are involved, for example, and silhouetting is required, can the designer fully prepare the artwork for the printer?

The designer's knowledge of the printing process and press checks will be particularly important to you if you're inexperienced in production and will need the designer to manage the process for you. Consider attending the press check with your designer to gain some education in the process—including the presses, what to look for, and what adjustments might need to be made to ensure accuracy and quality.

In addition to the designer's process knowledge, budget will be a prime consideration when selecting a designer for a job. Specialization, years of experience, and an award-winning portfolio will all play a part in the designer's hourly fee and bid for the job. Keep in mind what you can afford and what you truly need for the job.

Number of Relationships

As with other creative freelancers, the number of designers you work with regularly will depend on the volume and different types of projects you manage. It is essential to have a small group of reliable utility and specialized-design resources. A designer who creates your newsletter can handle other, similar design projects, such as product brochures. Another, who specializes and has solid experience dealing with a particular type of project—annual reports, direct mail campaigns—would be advisable for complex, high-cost projects. You'll want to forecast your possible design needs over the course of a year to determine the stable of designers you need to have available.

Plan ahead as much as possible, interviewing candidates far in advance of the project. Be sure to look closely at the projects that will require expert specialization, such as a new logo or brand. By projecting your design needs and approximate schedules for the year, you'll be able to consult the designers you want to work with early. This can eliminate the scramble for a designer as your deadline closes in.

For many projects, a designer with a corporate design background will cover your needs if you're managing publications for a company. Consider developing relationships with more than one designer even if your annual workload is not extensive. By dividing projects among a couple of freelancers, you'll double your available resources and ensure you have backup when one is booked and can't take on one of your projects.

Developing solid long-term relationships with a team of qualified designers is mutually beneficial. You'll have resources who know your system, understand your language, and provide a level of quality you can depend on—especially important when those rush jobs occur. The designers benefit from the prospect of steady work with a satisfied client.

Review the delivery dates and work together to establish design time frames to lock in the designer to projects. You'll need to make sure these dates are firm so your designer can block out time for you with confidence. This is a valuable exercise not only when contracting an external resource but also when working with a designer or design team inside your company. Enabling designers— and any creative pros—to reserve time for you will start the management of the publication off on the right track. Of course, early projected schedules aren't always reliable and should be planned as "windows" of time—the narrower, the better, but flexible. Asking any professional to remain committed through excessive project timing changes is frustrating and unfair, and new dates might not fit his schedule.

Relationship Tone

The degree to which your relationship with a designer is a partnership will depend on your design and art direction experience, and project responsibility. Approaching the relationship as a team makes for a comfortable and open exchange. If you don't have a design background, you'll be relying more on the artist's guidance about what works for your project. If this is the case, be sure you understand in lay terms why particular design choices are made.

Ask questions about use of color, line lengths, type size, or photo cropping. Try to look at all of the individual elements of the design and compare them with past literature deemed successful in your organization or by your client. How does each element that is changed or retained affect the impact, readability, or message clarity? Design choices aren't

---

Design Review Questions

- Is the logo or other branding elements positioned, sized, and color-broken correctly?

- Are company colors used throughout?

- Do various design and style elements appear to be consistent?

- Are the headlines, subheads, captions, and other editorial elements formatted correctly?

- Does the design present the client company in an appropriate, appealing light?

- Are the most important design elements treated in a manner that leads the eye to them first?

- Does the art or photography support the company image and the tone of the publication?

- Do the colors give the appropriate impression of the company— understated and businesslike, for example, or bold and casual?

- Is the copy easily read? Is the type size large enough? Are the lines of copy too long, making reading across the page cumbersome?

- Does the design serve to guide the reader through the publication's purpose?

- Is the physical format of the piece easy to handle?

- If a project contains several removable elements, such as separate fact sheets, is it easily reassembled?

---

arbitrary or magic; they are made to serve your project needs. And the more you are able to understand about those choices, the better you'll be able to explain them when they're questioned during the client review process. Like a precocious four-year-old, you'll want the question "why?" answered about everything.

Place yourself in the position of the end-user of your publication and ask questions that apply to the reader. Be sure to base your observations and assessment on the needs dictated by the specific project description and your target audience demographics.

Keep in mind, too, that all anomalies aren't mistakes. Exceptions might be purposeful and made with good cause. Before judging inconsistencies as sloppy work, ask your designer for their reasons.

It is important to present any questions and concerns diplomatically. By avoiding the dismissive critique and asking about improvement options instead, you'll be framing a solution rather than focusing on the problem. For instance, asking "Can the photos be made larger to give more prominence to the executives pictured?" will achieve the same change as the brusque "These photos just won't work. You haven't made them large enough!" while maintaining a partnership tone. The confrontational manner sets a negative tone, puts the designer on the defensive, and establishes a course on which neither one of you will want to continue. Remember that you're leading here, so it's up to you to shape the relationship in order to come up with the best product you can.

As team leader, you'll also manage the relationship between the designer and the client, whether you act as a go-between or bring the two together for an in-person design review. Treat your client as a team member, updating him on design progress as reasonable and appropriate. Keeping your client informed and reassured will encourage a positive, confident attitude toward the project.

The Graphic Standards Manual

A basic graphic standards manual should contain:

- The company's positioning statement or mission
- The brand logo or logos
- Registration mark and accompanying language
- Parent company and subsidiary logo use
- Position or positions of the logo or logos
- Acceptable logo sizes
- Primary company Pantone color or colors and complementary highlight colors and when to use them
- Background colors accepted for the brand mark
- Use of the brand in black-and-white publications
- Acceptable typeface or typefaces
- Reproduction specifications
- Company letterhead, personalized letterhead, memo, envelope, and label sizes, element sizes and spacing, and sample layouts
- Samples of other typical publications, such as brochures, to indicate sizes, grids, element positioning, and so on
- Photography examples, and desired tone and subject matter

Resource Education

You'll want your designer to review both general client materials and any established graphic standards guidelines, as well as materials specific to the project you are creating.

If your client has a graphic standards manual, be sure to obtain two copies: one for your office and one to lend to the designer for the duration of the assignment. Standardized manuals are terrific from a management perspective; they specify usage and placement for many of the graphic elements that should be included in each client publication. They typically cover logo specifications, color palette, acceptable fonts and sizes, and formats and grids for various types of publications, letterhead, and so on (e.g., see sidebar above).

You should also provide designers with a selection of existing client publications that illustrate the visual tone and design element treatments. This is especially important if a graphics manual does not exist. Materials that profile the client company history, mission, goals, and constituents are helpful, too, if available. These will help the designer create a graphic solution that's appropriate for the client's image and audience.

Fee Considerations and Estimates

Have a range in mind for design that fits within your budget before meeting with prospective designers. If you don't have a design background and need some understanding of design rates, refer to the *Graphic Artists Guild Handbook: Pricing & Ethical Guidelines.*

Ask each designer his hourly rate and the estimated number of hours for the job based on the project parameters. If you're working with a designer you've hired before, an oral estimate will suffice as long as it's confirmed in writing in the contract. If you're asking several designers to bid on a project, prepare a written description of basic parameters. Include the number and type of presentations, the approximate schedule, and any other information that allows them to make a tight estimate. Ask that they respond point by point, also in writing. Keeping your requests and responses consistent will allow for accurate cost comparisons.

In addition to the designer's rate, experience, and possibly the length of your relationship, other fee determinants include the scope, physical size, and time demands of the project. Project complexity extends beyond the obvious. For example, producing an annual report is a demanding design exercise often requiring solution plans that incorporate multiple treatments of text, photos, charts, and financials.

Recognize that the designer's responsibilities also can include a time-consuming range of ancillary responsibilities, adding long hours: preparing pre-photo-shoot layouts; art directing shoots; editing photography or selecting and purchasing stock photos; printer supervision and press checks; and so on. You need to determine all the project needs and be sure that your designer's expectations and estimate include all his responsibilities for your project.

One absolute: Do not agree to an open-ended assignment without a spending cap. Before beginning any fee work, you must come to an agreement with your vendor that specifies a description of the project and a maximum total. You need to know what the project will cost.

Contract and Terms

As with other creative and vendor relationships, allow work to begin on the design assignment only after the contract or letter of agreement is signed and dated by you and the designer. In addition to legal documentation of delivery date, fees, and payment terms, the contract can serve as a reference of tasks and interim deadlines during the assignment.

For example, describe the purpose and scope of the design project: "DESIGNER will provide roughs, color comps, box dummy, and final printer art for the JOB TITLE box and brochure." Include deadlines for each of these design phases. It will also be helpful to spell out the hours or the subtotal to be billed for each design phase. With this level of detail, work performed to date for an interrupted project can be paid accurately and agreeably.

In addition, include any approved out-of-pocket expenses to be reimbursed, such as purchasing a typeface for a headline or travel to a printer. Items such as travel and long-distance phone calls must be specified as reimbursable costs in advance for you to be obligated to pay them; otherwise you could legitimately construe that they are included in the design fee. Better to avoid any such ambiguity. This is not to say that you should avoid bringing up such topics to save a few dollars. It benefits your immediate relationship with the freelancer you hire as well as your reputation in the design community to watch out for the rights of the creative talent.

Be sure to ask about adjunct responsibilities, such as photo direction and press checks. And specify the designer's responsibility to deliver art in a format that's compatible with the printer's needs to avoid additional charges from the printer.

The Wrong Choice

Occasionally even a terrific, award-winning designer, one who's innovative and mindful of schedules and budgets, will end up simply being the wrong choice for a given project. Such were the qualifications of a designer I hired to create box packaging for a children's science product. We had worked on successful jobs together in the past. But his unsuitability to the project type made my choice a bad one.

Children's retail was new territory for this designer. When we sat down to discuss the needs of the project, the audience, the client, and the call to action—to buy the product—I felt confident that it would be a stride, but not a leap, for him to switch gears for this new audience. I provided him with several examples of the client's best-selling products' boxes and all the information he needed to proceed.

I was surprised and disappointed when the first-round design came in. It was off the mark. The graphics needed to appeal to the kids first. The audiences we'd discussed were children ages nine to twelve and their parents or other adults making the purchase. But the initial concept showed a dark front-face photo of a child emerging from shadows. The kid looked troubled, it wasn't fun or engaging, and it didn't even hint at the science activities inside.

Why had he departed from the successful samples? I wondered. Had he just ignored them? Perhaps he decided that a new direction would be more appropriate. After asking about his thinking, I concluded that the design just wasn't saleable and said that we'd need a second round.

Round two wasn't much of an improvement over the first. The colors were brighter, the child was somewhat less obscured, but overall, the serious, even dour look and tone of the design remained. When I reiterated my concerns, the designer balked, insisting that his drafts were on target and would sell the product. We just didn't seem to be communicating, and I came to realize that his corporate bent overshadowed this very different type of design. This was a project for children, and it needed to catch a kid's or parent's eye from among all of the other flashy products on the toy store shelf.

We had reached an impasse, and I had to move on. I explained that because he wasn't able to adapt to the project parameters and his two designs were so removed from the family of market-proven packaging, that his work was not satisfactory. Eventually he relented, accepting 50 percent of the total fee for the work he'd done to date. We parted ways, neither feeling completely satisfied.

This wasn't a good solution. Because I hadn't matched the designer's strengths to the needs of the project, I'd wasted time and money, and had caused a great deal of frustration for both of us.

Make sure the payment schedule is included in the contract. Example terms include (1) a third deposit, a third upon approval of comps, and a third upon delivery of final art and (2) net 30 from acceptance of satisfactory art. Note that the freelancer should provide an invoice detailing work performed and dates for your records.

Payment for design work executed should be based on your acceptance of work, either in total at the completion of design work, progress payments based on completion of design stages, or partial payments based on time frames throughout the project. Avoid scheduling any designer payment to coincide with the press or delivery date. Doing so links the designer's payment to events beyond his control. If this practice is a policy that cannot be changed, at least protect the artist by stipulating that the designer will be paid for all work performed in the event the project is canceled after work has been completed.

Also for the designer's protection, make a note that any change in scope for the project will necessitate a new contract or addendum, spelling out the assignment changes and the addition to the original fee.

Change in Scope

If the scope of the project changes radically after the contract has been signed or after work has begun, meet in person with the designer about the new assignment. Attach a signed and dated addendum to the original contract or draw up a new agreement.

Project Direction and Meetings

There isn't a fixed formula for the order or number of design presentations. This section is based on a typical design process: (1) concept comps, (2) full design layout, (3) second, corrected design stage, and (4) prepress proofs. On any project, these steps might be repeated, and additional presentations may be necessary to review photography, support materials, or other sub-elements.

Once the business of the relationship has been settled, meet with the designer before work begins. This will be your chance to review the scope of the job, the client's vision, the audience message, and possible initial specs or special elements to consider. It will also provide the designer a chance to ask you clarification questions before he prepares presentation comps or files for the client.

Discuss with your designer your presentation requirements (approximate number of concepts and, say, a cover, three spreads, and FPO [For Position Only] photos for each) and possible presentation methods (such as boards vs. laptop projection) (e.g., see chapter 3).

If the designer was not part of the team you consulted in developing the conceptual solutions, be sure that the two of you are in sync. The designer should be clear on the thought and reasoning behind the concepts and how they answer the client's communication need. With this understanding, your designer can explore freely and may be able to suggest imaginative alternatives or improvements that advance your publication's effectiveness.

Stay informed. Tell your designer upfront that you'd like to keep in touch throughout the process. You might suggest regular calls or e-mail updates from him. Ask how the designer would like to communicate his updates. By accommodating his preferred style, you'll allow him to concentrate on the creative work.

If you don't set these updates in advance, they might be difficult for you to get, or even seem threatening to the freelancer. I've worked a few times with a talented graphic designer assigned to me by a client. Although the designer is imaginative, creative, amiable, and an all-around nice guy, he frequently blows deadlines. And as each interim date approaches, he becomes uncommunicative. The impact is mitigated by the client's familiarity with his typical delays, but that doesn't make managing the situation any easier.

Photo Process: California College of the Arts Undergraduate Catalog

VANDERBYL DESIGN,
SAN FRANCISCO, CA

"When I'm shooting this type of catalog, I prefer to hire photographers who are more fashion photographers as opposed to annual report photographers," says Michael Vanderbyl, principal of Vanderbyl Design. "I find that they have a way of capturing people, and they're also used to shooting on the fly and going for mood more.

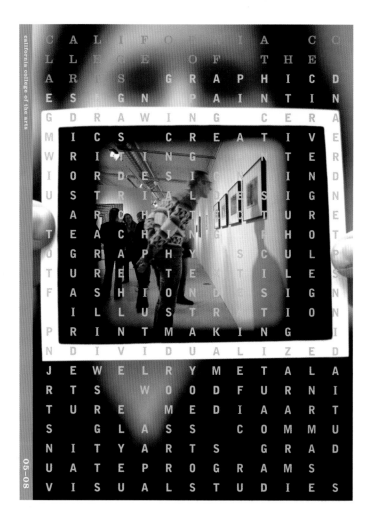

"Plus their daily work is people. With a catalog like this, you're really trying to show prospective students a little glimpse of what their reality would be day to day at the school and in the classrooms." Vanderbyl art-directed the photo shoot. He and photographer Karl Petzke "were able to set up the scenarios and actually did walkthroughs two or three times to get the shots.

"Even though they look like they're just sort of caught in the moment, they're not—at all. We always wanted motion around them, so we would 'cast' the people in the photos." Vanderbyl and Petzke then worked to create environments in which the subjects would relax, "because none of these are models. They're all students or faculty who hate having their photographs taken.

"It was also the crop. By coming in a little tighter on a lot of these instead of shooting back with a huge room, we were shooting quasi-portraits of them."

Vanderbyl uses an efficient, real-time technique to ensure he gets the shot when the photographer is in the moment of composing it. "I'll take an assistant with me, and we will have the design of the book in the computer already, the basic layout. We have a device that actually can scan Polaroids or work from digital. We download that into the layout to make sure that we're OK. The great thing about that is that we can actually design while we're shooting. We're able to adjust during the photo shoot."

The process has been perfected at Vanderbyl Design over the past six or seven years. "We take a 17-inch laptop with us, and there are these little hand-scanners that we use on the Polaroids.

"We've shocked a lot of photographers when we've done that; it's a lot of pressure on them, you know? But in a way, it actually takes pressure off of them, I tell them. It means that you're going to know if the shot's right immediately," so you don't have to recreate that scenario. "It's a little bit different technique than most people use."

Art director: **Michael Vanderbyl**
Creative director: **Michael Vanderbyl**
Designers: **Michael Vanderbyl,**
   Amanda Linder
Photographers: **Karl Petzke, Ed Kashi,**
   Douglas Sandberg
Writer: **Mind Power**

"As an artist, your job is to dismantle the world, then reinvent it."

Faculty **LARRY SULTAN**

PHOTOGRAPHY PROFESSOR

Larry Sultan's influence as an artist is felt worldwide. Larry's photographs have been exhibited in Dublin, Ireland; Florence, Italy; and Amsterdam, the Netherlands. He's received fellowships from the National Endowment for the Arts, a lectures grant from the U.S. State Department, and too many merit awards to count. He's been at California College of the Arts since 1988.

"I mine pop culture for my work. When you're looking at it, really closely, and turning it inside out—that's what being an artist is all about. I love dealing with the craziness of our culture and its poignancy. It's remarkable to be a teacher and an artist. I get to share my process of creativity and then witness theirs."

3rd year **RIKESH LAL**

GRAPHIC DESIGN

As one of the first members of e-Sputnik, the student web design team, Rikesh Lal designed and built Sitelines, an online publication for the MA Program in Visual Criticism, and Transmission, an online literary arts magazine for the MFA Program in Writing. Off campus, he had the opportunity to use his considerable skills at an internship at Esquire magazine.

"I worked side by side with Rhonda Rubenstein, Esquire's former art director. As my mentor, she worked with me to design a poster on intolerance and free speech for the Worldstudio Foundation. We met every week to work on the design concepts. Our work is now on exhibit in New York."

The first round is the time for asking questions; the next is for making the needed adjustments to answer those questions. The publications manager must ensure that any client corrections or changes are incorporated into the second-round and subsequent designs. This is where your management role is paramount. You'll want to avoid a drawn-out, back-and-forth, and possibly confused process that could cost time and require additional design work, and thus impact the schedule and budget negatively.

For a project of minimal to moderate complexity, corrections to the second round, if any, should be fairly minimal. Project management at this stage consists of communicating final, presumably minor corrections to the designer, incorporating them into a new layout, and getting signoff to proceed to final art. Proof the design carefully before it's sent to the printer to ensure that it's absolutely error free.

Your next review phase will be the prepress proofs, which should hold no surprises if close attention was paid to the final art. You and the designer might elect to review them together—this can be a time saver. You might review the proofs directly with the printing rep, depending on how involved in the production process you are. If you're a novice at this stage, reviewing the proofs with the designer and/or the rep will help educate you on what each is looking for and what you should be paying attention to. Your presence at the press check with the designer can serve the same learning purpose and can strengthen your relationship, showing your interest in understanding the artist's process and expertise.

Special Considerations

It can be easy for design to overtake editorial, making important information difficult for readers to understand and therefore rendering the publication ineffective. In other cases, the design might be breathtaking, perhaps award winning, but inappropriate for the audience.

Make sure the designer understands the audience so that he can put readers' needs first. And remember that the company identity must be made consistent throughout the project as well as from publication to publication. A designer might require a bit of reining in if his personal preferences overshadow serving the publication's purpose.

Remember, too, that you're working with a professional whose creativity is at the heart of his services. While ego shouldn't get in the way of the project, there will be times when special care is called for. Ask questions and offer recommendations positively and constructively, with the focus on the design, not the person.

Proactively supply several samples of the finished project with a hand-written note of thanks for a smooth process. Keep in mind that in every relationship you have with a freelancer, good public relations should play a part.

EFFECTIVE RELATIONSHIPS WITH PHOTOGRAPHERS

Your role with a photographer has the potential to be far more involved than with a writer or designer. In addition to being the contractor, scheduler, reviewer, and research resource, your responsibilities may include extensive coordination among the client, photo subjects, and photographer. You may choose (or win by default) duties as the on-site liaison and "handler," addressing the countless details of a complex assignment and keeping everyone calm and satisfied.

Ownership of art or photographs and establishing which specific reproduction rights are being purchased can impact your current project's budget as well as your long-term expenditures. Here's where your publications management skills really count. At the same time you're managing the development of the publication step by step, you're anticipating your client's future needs. By identifying those future needs, you'll be in a position to negotiate for those rights while structuring the assignment, thereby avoiding costly, often much more costly, renegotiations later. Educating yourself on the industry's terms and conditions also can mean the difference between a bill that reflects the estimate or one that carries an additional charge for a canceled shoot.

Your role will be easier if you can contract experienced artists who are able to handle a lot of the legwork and on-the-spot client care and communication. In some cases, the higher fees that these experienced professionals may charge will be offset by the time you save not micromanaging the entire experience.

Selection Criteria and Number of Relationships

Your client or client's company might have an inside person who typically takes photos of employees and events. As publications manager, you could even be responsible for this task. Many people think that a satisfactory photograph is no more than point-and-click. Try to convince your internal or external client otherwise, explaining that lackluster or technically inadequate photography can damage the overall quality and effectiveness of a publication. You absolutely need a pro.

A photographer's or illustrator's style and specialization are essential to your selection of the appropriate creative talent. A client company might have established relationships with one or more photographers who are responsible for, say, executive portraits and for covering company events. You might be required to use these resources. If, on the other hand, you'll be responsible for selecting a photographer, first look at internal and external publications—such as product brochures, annual reports, and newsletters—that include the type of photography you'll need for the project on the table. Find out who took the photographs (there might be photo credits).

If you need to locate a photographer in a specific geographic region, visit the American Society of Media Photographers Web site (*www.asmp.org*). Its member database is searchable by location and specialization. Results will give you full contact information, including an e-mail link, and in most cases sample photos.

Categorize the types of photography you anticipate needing before conducting your search. A photographer might be experienced in many different types of work, but the most accomplished typically focus on one area. If your particular project requires more than one area of expertise—such as portraits and industrial landscapes—try to contract more than one photographer. This may entail a slightly higher overall fee, but it usually pays off with consistently high-quality, appropriate work.

When you meet with a prospective photographer for the first time, you'll be evaluating his portfolio and professionalism. If he has a Web site, research it in advance. This will help you make an initial judgment about his suitability for your project. When setting a portfolio review, tell the photographer how much time you have to spend. This will help him edit his presentation to ensure you see the most relevant work.

Looking the Part: Evan's Life Foundation "One Girl" Brochure

SAMATAMASON, DUNDEE, IL

"It's important to look the part," says Pat Samata, principal of SamataMason.

"I received an annual report from a nonprofit organization and [the design, paper, and printing] had been donated. But still it was slick, it was beautiful," she remembers. "I thought, 'You know, this isn't sending the right message.'

"Because of that, all of the materials that Evan's Life Foundation has ever produced have been no more than two colors. We've always kept the photography black and white, and that obviously has been done by design. I think it tells the story in a better light."

Samata explains that Evan's Life Foundation has assisted children at risk since 1992. "From the very beginning we did, for lack of a better term, an annual report in which we would photograph several of our grant recipients and tell their stories. That's what we would send out to our donors.

"At one point I thought we're at a place now where we really need to get people in their gut, to make them realize that these children are really in a bad way—and it's not just one or two. I wanted to do something that had, I almost hate to say, shock value, but really that's what we were going for."

The point of *One Girl* was to walk through the life of Angela, whose "entire life was totally dysfunctional. She was literally thrown out of the house at the age of fourteen because her mother's boyfriend attempted to molest her. But to meet her, she was polite, articulate, she was a good student. . . . How many people would come out of this environment ending up the way she did?

"It was an interesting dichotomy. I thought we'd show a day in the life of Angela, and at some point we're going to really hit the reader with the reality of what her life is all about."

Samata's prime advice for photographer selection when it counts? "Hire a good photographer. Because there's one story. And the story is important to tell in the most succinct way possible. It should start at the beginning and end at the end, and I know that sounds very simplistic, but that's the best way to communicate any message.

"So often the story gets jumbled up. I guess maybe it's harder to make it simple. That's always the key that I think everybody struggles with when they try to communicate. To me, the simplicity is what it's all about."

Designers: Steve Kull, Pat Samata
Writer: Tura Cottingham
Creative director: Pat Samata
Photographer: Emma Rodewald
Client: Evan's Life Foundation

Criteria for evaluating image appropriateness isn't part of this book, but I will direct you back to the project outline and encourage you to rely on what you've gathered about the client. Response to photography is often immediate and emotional. Look for a tone and style that serves your established publication needs and reflects the company's or client's image.

Review the photographer's client list, ask for contact names, and call a few for references. You'll want to confirm that such basics as meeting deadlines, professionalism with subjects and clients, and adherence to the photos' subject matter as outlined were fulfilled.

Also inquire about how much behind-the-scenes coordination was required by the client and whether the photographer was able to follow the shoot plan as discussed. Establish how closely he follows or needs art direction. Most important, ask the contractor's opinion of the finished product and whether it supported the business objectives of the printed piece.

Finally, find out how the photographer prefers to work and what his standard operating procedures are, such as whether he uses assistants on location.

Relationship Tone

Depending on your creative background, you might approach your relationship with a photographer as a more formal client–vendor one or more as a partnership. Either way, you could be fulfilling the role of guide when it comes to the logistics of shoots, whether on location or in the studio. If this is the case, the photographer and his team will look to you to facilitate the introductions and arrangements to make the shoot go as smoothly as possible (see "Project Direction and Meetings" on page 123).

Resource Education

Provide client literature that explains the mission, objectives, and audience to the freelancer to educate him about your client's public image. Supply previous publications including design—and hopefully photography—that illustrate the style of that image.

If the new project will be taking a different direction in design and photography, consider supplying samples of outside publications or other artists' work that conveys the tone or mood and the style you're after. Try to provide the photographer with the written copy for the project to give a more in-depth look at the tone and message of the publication.

Estimate and Fee Considerations

If you have worked with the photographer in the past, an oral estimate is fine as long as it is followed in writing in the contract before any billable work begins. If you're collecting bids from several photographers, have them submitted in writing to ensure clarity and for your convenient reference. Although it might seem that the scope, photo sizes, and relative importance of the assignment would be the primary determinants of the project fee, the length of time required for the photography will nearly always determine what is charged.

The photographer's half-day and day rates—or creative fees—will depend on experience, renown, clients, and specialization. Some photographers offer hourly or per-shot fees. You might be able to negotiate a project fee instead of paying a day rate if, for example, several single shots, such as portraits, are to be taken over a series of days. If your company or client qualifies, ask whether the photographer offers a reduced scale for nonprofit organizations.

Good with People: Ransom Everglades School Capital Campaign Brochure

AND PARTNERS, NEW YORK CITY, NEW YORK, NY

David Schimmel's photographer-selection philosophy is straightforward: Make sure he's right for the job. "We tend to find photographers to work with who shoot in the style that we're looking for," says Schimmel, principal of And Partners, New York City. "We don't try to hire people who we have friendships with and ask them to shoot like somebody else. We hire people who have talent who we can let go out and do what they do best, and not try to be so heavy-handed that we [cramp] their style."

For Ransom Everglades School's capital campaign brochure, And Partners hired Dick Frank. Schimmel showed the client a beautiful Princeton piece Frank had shot in 1995, and the client said, "'That's it.' We didn't even have to bring his portfolio.

"Dick calls himself a dinosaur," Schimmel says. "He's so on the ball, though. He shoots medium format film. He didn't shoot digital; it's all film. And he came down to campus, and it was Dick and an assistant and me. And we went around and we saw the shots. We captured the moment that we were looking for."

There's more to it, of course. Schimmel points out that "you can't raise money without that emotional hook, the human side of the equation. One of the things that was a part of that [for the project] was photography.

"This is a hard thing to pull off because when you're shooting real people and not models, they get uncomfortable in front of a camera. So you need a good photographer who knows how to" relax them. Frank made the featured students, faculty, and alumni comfortable enough to truly come to life. The "Through Faculty Excellence" section of the book, for example, "is actually a simulation of a film strip," showing the teachers in motion "to try to make these people real."

And the capital campaign? "So far, so good," Schimmel reports on his alma mater. "They're more than three-quarters of the way to their goal. So yes, it's been hugely effective."

$5,000,000

through faculty excellence

EVERY STUDENT DESERVES to encounter at least one teacher who ignites a life-changing idea.

Ransom Everglades School has been fortunate to have leagues of such individuals throughout its history, beginning with Paul Ransom, a progressive educator who believed in teaching by asking challenging questions rather than imparting mere information. Today we are fortunate to have such a faculty to inspire our students' dreams.

Maintaining faculty excellence is a challenge today. Educational institutions in the United States are facing a faculty crisis of major proportions. 60 percent of the people now teaching will retire in the next five years. To recruit and retain the best teachers in their field, Ransom Everglades School needs to offer competitive salaries and benefits as well as opportunities for professional growth and development.

Just as the faculty is the foundation of the School, so is the endowment the foundation of the faculty. With an endowment that is currently one-third the level of other nationally recognized independent day schools, Ransom Everglades School faces serious challenges in addressing future faculty needs.

To sustain faculty excellence, we can defray spiraling tuition costs only by increasing revenues generated from a permanent endowment. One-half of our $10 million endowment increase goal will be dedicated to faculty recruitment, retention and development.

Top to bottom: Jennifer Nero, Social Studies Department; Christopher McGrath, English Department; Susan Feiz, Fine Arts Department; James Monk, Foreign Language Department; Virginia Onorati, Mathematics Department; and Jay Calkins, Science Department

Creative director: David Schimmel
Designers: Ashley Lindenauer, David Schimmel
Copywriter: Mary Anne Meyers
Photographer: Richard Frank
Printer: Hemlock Printers
Client: Ransom Everglades School

Other factors impacting the total charge will be the nonartistic responsibilities, including location scouting, research, equipment, setup, assistant fees, travel, and meals.

Determining Future Needs

Which usage rights you purchase may also impact your bill, but ultimately you will save money by negotiating wisely before work begins. Your use of the photography will play a major part in the fee you pay. Plan ahead to make the most efficient use of the photographer's time and the most economic use of your photography dollar. To avoid an additional half- or full-day rate and travel expenses, consider your needs—or possible needs—for future publications.

Say you've planned portraits of top executives. If there will be time left in the half or full day of photography scheduled, include shots of managers as well. This can save on coordination, setup and assistant fees, and an additional shoot. If you know your newsletter will cover stories on the IT and marketing departments in future issues, add those shots to the assignment for the current edition about R&D and the customer call center. If your photographer will be traveling to a client site across the country to shoot the headquarters for the annual report, think of all the possible publication or Web site uses for photos that might be taken at that location. Schedule them during that one shoot to save on travel and possibly on days as well.

In addition to predicting future photography needs and planning shoots accordingly, you'll want to consider the possible future uses for the primary shots planned. Remember that unless specified, you're purchasing just one-time use of each image. You or your client do not own the physical photograph and do not have the right to publish it except for the use or uses specified in the contract. By looking forward, you could determine, for example, that you'll want to include the CEO's portrait in multiple publications and on the Web site over the next several years. Negotiate with the photographer to purchase unlimited future use of the image.

If you know you'll want to include the school chapel on the cover of next summer's alumni magazine as well as in the student prospectus you're working on now, negotiate a slightly higher fee to use the image twice instead of repurchasing one-time use when the magazine project rolls around. If a shoot produced dozens of photos of facilities and employees at the corporate headquarters, consider what other company publications might need these images—even if they're not completely planned yet—and consider a buyout of the entire shoot so your art options will be open down the line.

Contract and Terms

Most photographers will provide their own contracts and documents of terms and conditions. Familiarize yourself with the fine print and negotiate changes as needed.

Put It in Writing

At minimum, any photography contract should cover the following:

- All fees and payment terms
- The allowed out-of-pocket markup, if any
- Deadlines
- The impact of late delivery on payment
- Future use rights
- Reshoots required for unacceptable work
- Weather dates and cancellation fees

Also provide the photographer with written project details including:

- All location information
- Client contact information
- A map of a multi-building site
- A schedule of shots taking place throughout a day's shoot
- A written shoot subject list
- Names and titles of all people to be photographed

A few additional points I suggest you address, although they aren't included in the standard contract: As appropriate, specify that no images taken in relation to your assignment may be sold to competitors or stock houses. This will save the embarrassment of your clients' finding themselves portrayed in a sales flier. Also, any proprietary information or property photographed should not be displayed in physical or online portfolios.

Depending on the complexity of the project, consider including with the contract a description of the scope of the photography assignment. This should cover the specific shots needed and description of the expected tone and style. Detailed information like this can be especially helpful to the photographer for a multiday shoot off site.

Project Direction and Meetings

During your assignment meeting, you will need to educate the photographer in detail about the people, places, and things to be shot. What is the temperament of the CEO, for example? Is he used to and comfortable with being photographed or likely to be a stiff clock-watcher? Will there be crowds of students hanging out around the campus quad around lunchtime, making that the best time to shoot the student recruitment piece? Will the photographer need to scout the offices and conference rooms of the company building in advance of the shoot to determine what lighting equipment will be needed, and will you be accompanying him? If the photographer will be shooting products in the studio, consider handing those items over in person instead of having them delivered. In person, the two of you can discuss what special features of each should be emphasized.

Consider whether this "advance art direction," details about people, places, and things given during the assignment meeting, will suffice to ensure the project goes smoothly. Alternatively, you, the designer, or your client might need to be in the studio or on location as art director, as the company representative, or as the logistics coordinator.

On a shoot for a large student-recruitment piece for a university in North Carolina, I accompanied the photographer on the three-day trip to help make sure everything ran according to plan. The photographer was responsible for shooting student and faculty portraits, classroom and outdoor student activity, campus buildings and scenery, and taking studio shots of campus icons and student paraphernalia to be used in multi-image collages in the publication. The schedule had little room for mishaps; portraits, for example, were scheduled to the half hour.

My presence helped guide the photographer and assistant to the appropriate buildings, introduce them to subjects and make the subjects feel at ease while the crew was setting up, make sure that all the props were used and that university identification was visible in the shots, and that all of the dozens of activities and campus locations on the checklist were covered. This enabled the photographer to concentrate on making good images, not trifling with logistics.

Except in cases of simple, limited, or straightforward assignments, you should be part of the photography review. Selection of appropriate photography relies on more than just aesthetics. Your familiarity with the project, the subjects, and other nonvisual considerations makes your input essential in early stages of selection.

You'll want to make sure the photographer is aware of any client political issues or special emphasis that needs be placed on any given subject. Often these considerations aren't fully understood until the shoot is underway or even completed. Once the creative team members are aware that they have to give special attention to a particular subject, they can make selections based on image quality of other design-specific criteria.

Written Communication

Specify that it is the photographer's responsibility to obtain signed releases for all subjects and review the release form to be used. Make sure that once completed, each release contains all of the information you might require, including the subject's name and title printed clearly, the signature (signature of parent or guardian if the subject is a minor), and date. Have the release specify use by the client company only; this will help ensure photos are strictly used as authorized.

As your final written communication, send the photographer several samples of the completed publication with a hand-written thank-you for a job completed to your satisfaction.

If photos are added or changed after the contract is signed or photography has begun, discuss with the photographer what additional time is needed and draw up a new contract or addendum.

Photography Recap

Select a photographer whose work demonstrates the ability to deliver a style and tone appropriate to the purpose of the publication and consistent with your client's image.

Coordinate the photos to be taken during a single shoot to maximize cost-effectiveness. Consider your future uses for the photos, and negotiate ownership accordingly.

You are working with a creative professional. Pride and ego can be part of the review process; voice comments constructively.

8

Testing the Publication

Hindsight is always 20/20.

—BILLY WILDER

Testing can be something as simple as feeding people pizza at lunch and having them talk about copies of the publication you bring to the table.

—ANGELA SINICKAS

Effective publications managers should test developing publications throughout the creative process. This is especially true when the content that needs to be disseminated is complex or contains critically important information. Testing should always be a part of the process when creating a communication that will need to hold its place in a competitive marketplace. It's the only way to reach beyond your own and the client's assumptions to the response of the target end-user audience.

Test the assumptions that form the framework of your publication concept. "If there are specific metrics that need to be achieved," says Kinimod principal Dominik D'Angelo, "I make sure I understand exactly what will be measured and how." In addition to conducting objective testing, bomb-proof the copy tone and design style, and how they work together. Every test needn't be an elaborate science project. Pop into a colleague's office to bounce some copy off him before the draft goes to the client. Even with this off-the-cuff, informal review, you'll have a better shot at being on target before your presentation.

Obtaining readers' input in advance will ultimately save time and money. Instead of mourning what might have been, test your communication to help ensure it's on message and encourages the audience response you're after. As Angela Sinickas, president of Sinickas Communications, Inc., says, "Clever people will always use their own judgment, but they'll find that their judgment becomes more finely honed if they actually hear from their audiences how they perceived those same things."

Initiating and coordinating testing is often handled by an account executive, the client, or in some cases by an internal market research department. But as discussed in chapter 1, many account executive duties can fall to the publications manager, and not all of your clients have a staff dedicated to gauging market perception. Further, the testing I recommend you make part of your regular process doesn't have to be a long, labor-intensive study. So although you might not be managing the testing, read on; it's an important phase in the publications process that impacts other phases for which you will be responsible.

In this chapter we'll explore how to plan a basic test session and various types of testing suited to your project, and available time and budget. You'll learn that even simple, fast, and cost-free reviews can increase your publication's effectiveness. And you'll see that the publications process isn't complete until you gauge the completed communication's effectiveness against the original goals set. Finally, the acid test: evaluation of the publications process itself.

PLAN ON TESTING

Time and available budget constraints can significantly limit the testing you can perform, but that's no reason to skip testing altogether. Include time in your schedule for testing and revising your publication—and if necessary, retesting. Don't assume that the review will go smoothly and that you won't have to dedicate additional time to making changes to improve the piece.

It needn't be a heavy investment. A meager budget doesn't have to rule out sound testing. Sinickas suggests those with small budgets visit local universities' psychology, social sciences, organizational development, or journalism departments to try to team with classes looking for projects. By understanding what professors see as good projects for their classes, you can plan accordingly. Sinickas says that very complex or involved projects could even end up being graduate students' thesis projects.

Your creative budget will need to allow for changes based on audience testing. It's important to include these additional hours and dollars to cover further rewriting or redesign if testing reveals that the communication is not delivering the message to the audience with the needed impact. Corrections, major corrections, even going all the way back to the drawing board at an early stage will be far less costly than late-process changes. Almost anything is better than having to recover and redo a publication after your untested but published one is found to be ineffective.

Of course, not all untested publications fail completely, but most of us have experienced a problem that simple testing could have avoided. Sinickas offers a perfect example of a publication that looked like the right solution but didn't function properly. "There are things that we do with the design of our publications that look really cool but might be a problem," she says. "One publication was dramatically gorgeous, award-winning. It was oversized, probably 12" × 18" or more. So, even when you folded it in half, it would not fit into any kind of standard envelope, which normally wouldn't have been a problem. However, the client was a consulting firm, with a lot of employees working off site at client locations, and needed the communications mailed to them. The result was that mailing the publications was often delayed while the mailroom staff looked for the right size envelopes. But it did look beautiful."

DETERMINE THE METHOD

The level of testing needed will vary based on your familiarity with the communication, market, and client. Testing can range from a fast eyeballing—sometimes literally grabbing some people in the hall and asking for a quick read for clarity—to elaborate focus groups coordinated, managed, and facilitated by an outside market research firm.

Your own experience will influence your method and resource selection—but scheduling and monetary restraints may affect your choice. For example, there might not be time or funding for several sessions with audience samples conducted by a professional consultant. In that case, you'll need to punt. But there are solutions.

Live with It: Sprint Logo
LIPPINCOTT MERCER, NEW YORK, NY

"When Sprint and Nextel launched their new identity as a merged company, in September 2006, the amount of exposure and promotion was phenomenal," says Rodney Abbot, Lippincott Mercer's senior partner on the project. "I believe Sprint CMO Mark Schweitzer stated this was the largest consumer brand launch in the US." Overnight, the new visual identity was everywhere, with advertising, banners, signage, and sporting events all boasting the fresh logo created by Lippincott.

From start to finish, from the first strategic brainstorming to the public unveiling of the Sprint logo on Day 1, "the timeline was roughly five months," Abbot says. He explains that "there were many points of connection with the clients, both Sprint and Nextel, to engage them in the process," plus time for "doing the research and time to digest the results of the research."

Part of this research was devoted to "identifying and measuring the personality traits of both Sprint and Nextel, and ensuring that the new identity brought forth the key visual equity elements of those brands," Abbot says. "The two companies possessed distinct brand attributes: Nextel represented an entrepreneurial, instant communications spirit while Sprint was more known for its long history of innovation."

The process of visually exploring a wide spectrum of ideas began with creating "hundreds of logo alternatives and several rounds of informal presentations with the combined work team of Sprint and Nextel," Abbot says.

"We then took a subset of a broad range of designs into consumer- and business-group research. This helped identify the most compelling ideas to develop further. We presented those to the most senior management and made a recommendation of three designs. Then we went back and did a very thorough logo exploratory around those designs."

After a few more rounds of review and feedback with the client team, the new logo candidates were narrowed down to two. "At that point (and this is pretty unusual in the design process)," Abbot says, "the decision was made to sit with the two designs and live with them for a while, not to say, 'OK, that's it, let's just run with it.'" Everyone recognized that they'd "be living with this for a long time, so they really wanted to be sure that they picked the right one."

The one they selected blends elements of Sprint's signature "pin drop"—representing clarity—and Nextel's straightforward, iconic palette of bold yellow and black colors.

In addition to the logo, Lippincott Mercer developed identity guidelines, including modules for use with sponsorships and business partnerships to ensure that the identity is used consistently in all formats and mediums. A full signage program for Sprint's retail environments and an environmental design package of banners and signs was developed to build employee awareness and excitement around the launch of the brand.

Senior partner and lead designer: Rodney Abbot
Design team: Adam Stringer, Ryan Kovalak, Alissa Tribelli
Client: Sprint
Copyright: © Sprint Nextel

Down and Dirty

Fast-turnaround bomb-proofing was the efficient and cost-effective testing method employed by a Fortune 500 banking institution in the midst of a merger. Sometimes it seemed that news broke hourly as management played musical chairs. The company created an internal newsletter to share knowledge with employees at all levels when job security—and the future of some major subsidiaries—was shaky.

As a necessity of time, the publication was a rather down-and-dirty one- to three-page publication laser-printed on masthead designed specifically for the project. Delivery was at least weekly, with extra editions distributed on an as-needed basis. The newsletter was blast-faxed to mid-level managers, who shared the information with their reports during Q&A sessions. (Blast-faxed? Antique-sounding I know, but this was the early nineties, and the testing principles are still sound.)

When the publication premiered, the process began with the communications department receiving updates on several topics from multiple senior execs. An internal writer would draft the issue, and the publications manager would preview it with the CEO and company spokesperson before incorporating their changes. The revised final edition was broadcast to hundreds of fax machines up and down the East Coast.

After a few issues, middle managers complained that the copy didn't speak to the typical employee. The information was directed too specifically to the managers and didn't address what exact impact the changes might have to individual departments and employees.

The solution? Add testing. The communications department pulled together a panel—in short order—to review each draft before it was sent to the top floor for signoff. The purpose was to ensure the copy reflected the needs of average employees, and used language and examples that related to them.

Putting together the panel was a challenge. The corporate population included a wide range of personnel: MBAs with decades of financial expertise; new managers just learning the human resources ropes—and therefore perhaps not yet adept at communicating some dire merger news; assistants with narrowly focused administrative responsibilities. The employee population also reflected a wide range of educational backgrounds.

Faced with this challenge, the communications department assembled about ten readers drawn from various subsidiaries who represented a range of occupations and reading levels. They were on call to read the newsletter on short notice. Their duty: Ask questions about anything that didn't make sense to them.

Some questions were easily answered by a different turn of phrase. Others required discussions to tease out what precisely needed clarification. Sometimes a back-and-forth with the spokesperson was necessary; the hurdle was to keep employees on board and motivated by supplying as much news as possible while also protecting proprietary interests of the company.

The new review process made for an extra-hectic day each week. No matter: The result was a publication with critical information that was more effective through audience testing.

Obtain Advance Buy-in

An important benefit of testing a communication involves buy-in to the idea. Identify the internal and external individuals who have some stake in the communication, and get their blessing before the real in-depth work begins. This can save time and lots of changes later on.

Typically executives and managers need to know about a new, forthcoming publication before the people who report to them do. Others might simply feel entitled to offer input—and many times you won't hear back from them; they just want to be asked their opinion. In any case, protect yourself and your publication. Give everyone who could possibly have a reason or need to be involved the opportunity to sign off on the project upfront.

Obtaining advance buy-in would have saved this publication: At the same bank mentioned above, the head of employee communications planned a postmerger "keeper" desktop publication, a sort of greeting card welcoming everyone to the new, settled organization. The assumption was that the thousands of now-secure employees would respond favorably to the welcome card, with its clever die-cut design that popped out when the piece was opened. Wouldn't it make a nice surprise? Not really.

No one involved in its development thought beyond the clever design and the well-meaning message to people's reactions. Especially impacted were the managers and senior executives with no advance knowledge of the piece; in that newly calmed office environment, surprise was not considered a positive. Managers were unprepared for any employee questions about the meaning or purpose of the publication. And most objectionable, the managers weren't consulted about the content: The subsidiaries were listed inside with brief descriptions of their missions—especially sensitive information in the postmerger company.

The fundamental mistake: failure to communicate plans for the communication beyond corporate headquarters and the primary subsidiary. Lessons learned: Get buy-in. Test every publication. Surprises aren't good when your audience's reaction is at stake.

Barry Nelson, of the Story Board, recounts a hard-learned lesson about the need to get buy-in: "Sometimes it's the things you couldn't anticipate that blow you out of the water. I remember doing an annual report once with an editorial section where the chairman wanted to call attention to the rising importance of employee participation—employees' being involved and contributing directly to the success of the company. So we themed the annual report on that topic. The chairman and I were on the same page with this. I did, and he approved, a big, magazine section that was a take-out on why it matters so much to have people fully engaged."

Nelson kept the chairman and other senior managers, presumably the ultimate decision-makers, in the loop at every stage as the report was developed. "We went through all the clearances, completed the book, and got it to the printer."

With mockups in hand, the chairman proudly presented the annual report to his board of directors. "Well, the board hadn't been consulted, hadn't been briefed, hadn't heard anything about the concept or gone through any of that buildup. The chairman presented it and had a riot on his hands. The board's position was: 'Your shareholders don't want to hear about this subject; it will scare them; it's a foolish expenditure of money. If you do it, it'll be the biggest mistake of your CEO tenure.'"

Nelson got the chairman's eleventh-hour call while he was at the printer. "We didn't want the fact that *we* loved the story to dictate our options. Our chairman had a problem on his hands, and we could solve it by chopping out a big piece of the story. So we did," he says. "The report went to press without its climactic center-piece essay. Journalistically, it really was a loss."

But Nelson has a positive spin on this tale: "The win was learning that everybody who's going to have a say in what finally gets published needs to be consulted along the planning phase."

Campus Keeper: George School Book

RUTKA WEADOCK DESIGN,
BALTIMORE, MD

"Our goal is always to elevate the form. We don't want the audience to see a book as just another piece of junk mail," says Rutka Weadock Design principal Tony Rutka of the George School project. "Since our quantity was small, we had the opportunity to package the message in a unique format."

The design firm, whose clients are nearly all nonprofits—schools and colleges, hospitals, foundations, arts organizations—tries to avoid standard formats like 8½" × 11". "It's too ordinary," Rutka says. "Any time you can deviate from the obvious, it makes the piece inherently more interesting. The physical attributes of a piece are an important part of the design."

Most of Rutka Weadock's institutional publications feature unusual, attention-grabbing formats. The concepts for these projects are "intuitive," he says. "I'm not a big believer in focus groups. It's one thing if you're selling soda pop in a grocery store, but it's totally different when you're trying to attract the attention of students who constantly are bombarded with publications. I've been designing long enough that I understand this audience, and they are really quite sophisticated visually. You should never underestimate your audience."

Because the job for George School called for a small quantity, Rutka says, "I knew that I could afford to do a hard-cover book. The text was printed in one color using halftones. We spent most of the budget on the binding, which is a smyth-sewn, case-bound book with a debossed area for a letter-pressed, tip-on label."

The content focuses on the game Four Square as played on the George School campus. The book takes a humorous look at the game, then segues into a description of what it takes to succeed at George School. The publication is used as a yield piece: It's sent to accepted students before they commit to come to the school. "It's a gift," Rutka explains. "It reminds students why they wanted to go to George School in the first place. This is a special school, which takes a special interest in the students who want to go there.

"It's been a huge success. Alumni have even asked to buy the piece. But the admissions office won't let anyone else have them. It's a carefully guarded publication.

"Visually, it's a keeper. No one will want to throw it away."

JUST A GAME?

**SURE.
AND GODZILLA
IS JUST A LIZARD.**

This is Four Square we're talking about. And, to borrow a phrase, "whoever would know the heart and mind of George School had better learn Four Square."

The George School version is not the garden variety Four Square you see played in schoolyards. Ours is much more evolved. Like those who play it, George School Four Square is joyful, artistic, cerebral, spontaneous, flexible, gregarious, imaginative,

THE
**DEFINITIVE
GUIDE**
[FOR NOW]
for Playing Four Square
at George School!

Design: Rutka Weadock Design
Writer: Will Schwartz
Photographer: Bruce Weller
Illustrator: Gregory Nemec
Printing: Teagle & Little
Binding: Advantage Bookbinding

Pretest with a New Audience

Audience testing is even more critical in cases where publications are being sent to readers who don't know the sender and might not even be expecting communication. For Queens College, a North Carolina women's college embarking on a campaign to reposition itself in the eighties, the hurdles were predictably high. And in this case, buy-in was the mission itself.

The marketing communications firm redesigning the recruitment materials faced a daunting challenge. Largely due to financial need, the school was going co-ed. The decision had little support from current students and alumnae. The name, Queens College, added to the challenge. Recruiting young men to matriculate at a former all-women school with a feminine name was a monumental task.

In some cases, research about the likes, dislikes, and behaviors of the target demographic might have been sufficient. However, heightened sensitivity dictated careful testing at every step.

The purpose of the testing was two-fold: (1) to help ensure the communications would call the audience of high school juniors and seniors to the desired action, which was contacting the college for more information—or better yet, beginning the application process—and (2) to help develop the school's stakeholders into ambassadors for a reinvented institution.

The first step was to obtain buy-in from the existing audiences. The creative team visiting the campus interviewed the president, deans, and a sampling of faculty, selected by the internal communications department. Most of the interviewees accepted that the decision to recruit men was the only viable solution to the dire financial situation facing the school, but they had disparate views on whether alumnae would continue their support of the institution.

The consensus was that the recruitment materials, advertising, and specially targeted appeals to previous classes would be the critical vehicles for announcing and building the school's new image.

Several publication themes were developed, and with design comps in hand, the creative team set up in a student lounge to convene informal focus groups of handfuls of students. They had been selected by the campus communications director. To make sure the group of hand-picked students didn't only represent the cream of the crop, the team also grabbed some students at random off the quad to ensure a good cross-section. The college already had a few young men beginning studies there, and they were included in the groups. In addition, the trip was planned to coincide with visits by prospective students to gain their fresh input on the publications' concepts and graphic directions.

An important point about efficient planning: Because the recruitment materials would include dozens of candid photos of the campus and student activities—regardless of the overarching concept selected—the shoot was scheduled to coincide with the trip to the campus for interviews and comps testing.

The test setting and the conversations were intended to be informal to make the students most comfortable. Each group was made up of only three or four participants to ensure everyone had a chance to voice opinions. The students were first asked about their reaction to the news that the college was turning co-ed (the reactions were mixed but trended positive).

The designs represented a wide range of approaches: from active pop-media-influenced graphics to much more traditional, academe solutions, one even featuring medieval-style etchings of knights with jousting lances. The results proved not only the value of testing but the importance of exploring all solutions as objectively as possible. At the outset no one involved could have predicted that the students, mostly young women, would overwhelmingly select a knight in shining armor as their school's symbol. Today Queens University of Charlotte (Queens College earned university status and changed its name in 2002) has a student population of 70 percent female and 30 percent male students.

Test Through Observation

There are some cases where your observation alone, with little or no guidance for the reader, can be most helpful.

This was the case when an international toy company tested collateral publications for children's educational activity kits. The goals were to gauge through observation the effectiveness of background and instruction materials, as well as the age-appropriateness of the activity, and the enjoyment and success quotient of the craft. Children were selected for informal focus groups through employee contacts and friends, keeping costs for the exercise low.

The youngsters, gathered in small groups at the company headquarters, were given kit materials and instruction mockups to follow. Volunteer parents and company employees in attendance included the instructions designer, writer, and illustrator. The adults walked around the tables or sat with crafting kids unobtrusively but at the ready to answer any questions. Quiet observation, with guidance only when needed, helped identify several elements that could make the publications more effective: some language simplification, design revisions that would guide the eye better, illustrations that showed more process detail, and publication resizing to be friendlier to small hands.

Changes made, based on observing those children, enabled the company to proceed with the assurance that the instructions would be understandable and engaging for most readers.

Online Testing

Online information-gathering is an effective and efficient way to pre- and posttest understanding of one or a few subjects. "A company can run a poll or quiz on the front page of its intranet every day," says Barry Nelson. For example, "we would ask a quiz-type question—true or false or multiple choice—about a topic we were getting ready to publish a story on. We would record that data, and then put the story out. A day or two later we'd post the same question, and then compare the results. Sometimes we'd see a double-digit percentage point gain in understanding of the topic.

"Look for opportunities to test whether a publication or story actually changes behavior or causes something to happen that wasn't happening before," Nelson advises. "Get a baseline, then publish, then measure and report the difference—it's very powerful."

Sophisticated—but easy—publication testing can be performed online with Web site or e-mail surveys. Software by companies such as Zoomerang and SurveyMonkey is simple, intuitive to use, and cost-effective. Programs tabulate and chart results, among other functions. This is more quantitative research you can do on your own.

But beware of some simple solutions: "There are certainly advantages" to online survey programs, Sinickas says, "because you can do some measurement fairly quickly and fairly inexpensively. The problem is that it's just a tool. It doesn't tell you what is a good question or a bad question.

"It's almost like the days when desktop publishing software became available" and anyone could create a newsletter, she says, but it wasn't necessarily a well-designed newsletter. With survey software, "everyone's a survey designer. But you still need to know what should you be asking about, how should you be asking about it, and then also important is how to interpret the numbers you get." Sinickas recommends recruiting a colleague or consultant in human resources or a person with organizational development background for help in designing an effective survey and interpreting it correctly.

PLAN YOUR TESTING SESSION

Regardless of your testing method, and the time and money involved in carrying out your research, make sure you prepare thoroughly for your session. Here are some pointers:

Define your goals. Establish what you need to learn. Here you're looking to qualify success, so refer to your original project overview to help develop questions that directly test your publication goals. For instance, if you needed a particular response, you'd ask whether the call to action was clear and acted upon.

Define your testers. Your audience will have one to several demographic characteristics in common. If there are subsets of your audience—for example, current students versus prospective students or people of varying education levels—group the testers in like categories for their greatest comfort level. This will increase the likelihood that they'll participate.

Define your testing environment. Your research method, determined in part by the available time and budget, will be the primary determinant of your testing environment: in person, in writing, online, on site, at a market research facility, and so on.

Define your test questions. Focus on as few and as straightforward questions as possible for the best and clearest results—and so you don't overwhelm your participants or tax their time. For an off-the-cuff bomb-proofing, you might have just one question: "Does this copy make sense?" The primary question for a concept-selection session will be, "Which concept do you like the best?" Next you'll want to delve into the details that answer the question *why*, such as, what colors attract their attention most, which font is easiest to read, and what words would they use to describe the company that mailed this publication?

Define how you'll conduct the testing. Will you be the facilitator? This might be necessary, depending on your resources, even if you don't have the research experience you'd like. Try to remain unbiased and nonjudgmental during the session. Ask follow-up questions if a comment isn't entirely clear or if you need more information, but don't question the actual content of the tester's response. There are no right or wrong answers.

Consider whether others should be present. An assistant for note-taking or for operating recording equipment? The client? The writer, designer, or illustrator? Your supervisor or members of management? The number of observers should not outnumber the testers—they might feel ganged up on. If there are people attending simply to observe, place them in an adjacent room with a two-way mirror, if available, or make sure that they understand they should not participate if present in the testing room.

Define the agenda. Limit the test session to a time that will be comfortable and enable participants to remain focused, typically no more than an hour to an hour and a half. Make a list of how the session will unfold: introductions, statement of purpose, overview of process, opportunity for testers to ask any questions, your questions and discussion, opportunity for any final tester questions, and wrap-up and thank-you.

Define how you'll analyze and respond to the results. Your research method will likely determine your analysis process. For example, you might simply be reviewing copy comments and inputting changes to resolve content issues. You might need to hold an update session with the creative team to explain which concept your focus group chose and why, and to discuss together what the next best steps should be. Or you might be using a survey software program that tabulates results on which you can base your follow-up actions. Revisions and additional testing might be required to gauge the effectiveness of new concepts.

TEST THE PRINTED PIECE

Annual industry awards and exhibits recognize superior artistic and creative achievement. Winning or being included usually garners you respect, is great for public relations, and may bring more work your way. But these awards aren't the true test of a publication's success.

Testing shouldn't stop when the communication is published. Those who don't test their publication's effectiveness can delude themselves into thinking it was successful, especially if the project "looked good." Relying on that measure is dangerous; it places the communication and clients' needs second to those who do test and are able to make adjustments and better communicate their message. Once the completed piece is in readers' hands, you need to evaluate it against your original objectives.

In the case of periodicals, you should check in with your readers on a regular basis.

There are cost-effective means for getting reader input and gauging satisfaction that you can conduct on your own. "Once the publication is out, you can take a dozen of them, mail them to a randomly selected group of people with a letter, a red pen, and an envelope," Sinickas suggests. Ask the recipients to read "this issue of the publication and scribble all over it, [marking] what they liked, what they didn't like, what appealed to them, what drew them away from reading it—just write notes right on the publication and then send it back. Very simple."

In the case of a health care association's monthly national journal to members, the publications division created a readers' panel to check in on a quarterly basis. The self-selected panel members committed to responding to the surveys and to returning them within a specified time frame. The vehicle was a simple, fast mail survey. The point of creating a panel instead of sending out a survey four times a year to the journal's 5,000 readers was three-fold: (1) save money in mailing, (2) save time in waiting for responses, and (3) guarantee response.

Identifying Existing Testers

Look around: Your "readers' panel" might already exist. A national insurance and financial services corporation called on its advisory council to test the sales and marketing department's communications. The council was composed of about fifteen geographically representative agency principals. At biannual meetings the executives were interviewed in groups about existing publications, and forthcoming projects were previewed before being developed into communications sent to thousands of agents. This testing was supplemented as needed by regular phone and e-mail contact and one-on-one visits throughout the year.

Topics for ongoing testing included:

- Editorial clarity
- Relevance of coverage
- Reception of letters from upper management (an additional testing step: letters were sent in advance to council members for comment on particularly sensitive material)
- Whether the issues were read by the agency principals and by their employees, who could also benefit from the news
- Future editorial ideas, including agency stories about marketing the insurance brand

Take a Bow:
Portland Center Stage Poster Series

SANDSTROM DESIGN,
PORTLAND, OR

Portland Center Stage was just getting established, "struggling to become the premier theatrical venue," says Sally Morrow, a creative director and principal at Sandstrom. In designing the company's poster series for the 2004–05 season, she says, "My direction was to add a consistent factor so that people came to expect a high-end look.

"The consistent poster design created a recognizable format to identify PCS throughout the season. It helped to differentiate the company among the other arts group postings around the city. And the clean aesthetic juxtaposes well with the intensity of the photographs."

Morrow took cues from PCS artistic director Chris Coleman and worked with photographer Mark Hooper—"a fantastic storyteller"—on the sophisticated theater profile. "The humor came through because that season, there were a lot of humorous productions. I wanted to pique playgoers' anticipation of the plays coming up."

In designing the poster for The Santaland Diaries, Morrow says, "to add the irony and pathos, that was a difficult one because they were offering two plays. The image refers to the David Sedaris one, and the other was a Truman Capote play. We felt that was the strongest image going forward." And the selection of images seems to have paid off: "Actually I think it affected their sponsorship," she says. The theater received support "from Adidas because of the funny quality and the beautiful look they established."

And "ticket sales were great that year; it was one of the highest participations. The subscription brochure and mini-postcard booklet that accompanied the posters were really great sales tools. Chris had said in particular that [the package] was so impactful that they were getting response across the country.

"We felt that not only the storytelling but the quality of the photography would go a long way, and I think it did."

Associate creative director: Sally Morrow
Designers: Sally Morrow, Shanin Andrew,
Kristy Adewumi
Project manager: Jim Morris
Photographer: Mark Hooper
Writers: Leslee Dillon, Mead Hunter
Printer: Graphic Arts Center
Client: Portland Center Stage
Copyright: © Sandstrom Design, Inc.

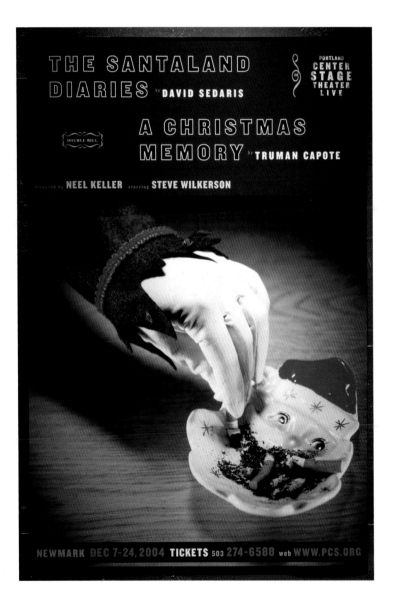

Panel participants were solicited through a card stitched into one issue of the magazine. It announced the new reader's panel and invited association members to join a group that would allow them to help improve the journal for all readers by offering their input. The perforated mail-in card requested basic membership and contact information. The three simple steps of receiving, completing, and returning the quarterly surveys were explained succinctly.

Survey questions covered everything from editorial preferences to photography, from advertising presence to whether the magazine was received on time and in good shape. Because panel members were surveyed every quarter, ongoing and closely timed feedback was gained. Each questionnaire could be limited to a few multiple-choice questions, with space for additional comments.

The time invested to develop the questionnaire, mail it to panelists, and receive and tally the responses wasn't more than a few hours four times a year, which meant that the small department wasn't taking on more than it could handle. The ongoing development of new journal features demonstrated that the association was listening and responsive to its membership. The readers' suggestions could be implemented in a manageable time frame, and features that received favorable response were touted in profiles of the journal as valuable benefits to new members.

EVALUATE THE PROCESS

Don't limit your evaluation to the success of the publication; also review how smoothly the publications management process went, and plan ways to improve it for future projects. The effectiveness of future versions will depend on honest evaluation of the initial project.

At the outset of the publications process, you defined the needs and opportunities for the communication. You identified what response you wanted from the audience. As stated in chapter 2, the more specific your goals for a publication—and your advance planning of how to measure achievement of those goals—the more you'll be able to evaluate the effectiveness of the communication.

When evaluating a publication's success with a creative professional, Dominik D'Angelo, principal of Kinimod, Inc., bases her critique on three factors: "The first is whether we believe the publication accomplishes the desired, previously set strategic objective in relationship to its audience. The second is the publication's visual appeal, both in relation to its readers and to the highest

---

Publication Postmortem

Address the following, and then brainstorm about what could be changed to facilitate a smoother publications process.

- Print quality
- Photo quality
- Size of type and images in accordance with audience
- Is the design in keeping with the graphic standards established for the company or client? If there was a divergence, was it justifiable?
- Were there any graphic errors—for example, widows or inconsistent treatment of common design elements, such as sidebars?
- Were there any typos?
- Were there any content inaccuracies?
- If there were inconsistencies or errors in design or text, who was responsible for proofing and how can the process be improved for future projects?
- Sufficient prominence and readability of branding
- Comparison with similar publications created by your competition: Does your piece stand up to and stand out among work by competitors?
- Cost-effectiveness of the creative work, the printing, and the shipping: Did anything during the publications process, such as corrections on press, cause the job to go over budget?
- Adherence to the schedule: What bottlenecks were there, and how can they be prevented next time?
- Individual responsibility: Did creative talent, clients, and reviewers fulfill their delivery and review obligations on time and in a hassle-free manner? Does anyone on the team need to be made aware of his adverse impact on the schedule, budget, or quality?

design standards. The third is how close we came to delivering what the client expected. After assessing the degree of the publication's success on each of these three points, my critique focuses on resolving any existing problems while respecting any strategy, production, or time constraints."

Learn from effective outcomes. Even if your communication met its objectives, a thorough evaluation will help define what made the publication a success. This will help you create other successful pieces and avoid mistakes in the future. For the annually updated project, turning back to the original product that delivered the message well can eliminate the need to create an all-new direction solely for the sake of change.

Yang Kim, principal of BBK Studio, cites this example of success: "Recently we designed a new brochure system for a client. The program has proven so successful, the client has gone through a year's supply of all five brochures in six weeks. Good news all around, except for the unexpected reprint costs."

Hold a postmortem analysis meeting, where you can report on any numerical measurements that enable you to define the communication's success. Your measurements

> ### *SEE*ing is Believing
>
> Clark Malcolm, editor of Herman Miller's *SEE* magazine, says the prime evidence of the periodical's success is management's support. "We put *SEE* out in October and May. It's not inexpensive, and it's quite a commitment on Herman Miller's part.
>
> "We publish *SEE* for customers and for salespeople and dealers who come in contact with architects and designers—also management types interested in architecture and design. We sell *SEE* through three or four bookstores, museum stores, and a couple of architecture bookstores. We give *SEE* away to design schools and design students. We have not a large, but a growing, mailing list of people who have contributed to the magazines and friends of Herman Miller.
>
> "The use so far has been pretty good, by which I mean we print 20,000 and we go through 10,000 pretty quick. We have no way of telling whether *SEE* sells X dollars of Herman Miller furniture. I'm sure it contributes. We do know that it's a favorite piece of literature for our sales force, particularly for the architect and design sales force. They participate in determining the contents, and they use it quite a bit. They tell us they can't live without it.
>
> "With all the good ideas at Herman Miller competing every year for budget dollars, the biggest proof for me—and a great motivation to do our best—is the fact that we get a budget."

might be more qualitative than quantitative. If your publication did not have a clearly measurable objective and you want to establish specifically what worked or needs improvement, conduct additional testing. You can begin planning viable types of publication testing, based on budget and resources, at your review meeting. Evaluating the publication's success can also help gauge the effectiveness of any preproduction testing methods you employed.

Review the publications process as part of your postmortem or a separate meeting. Include the creative team and depending on the complexity and outcome of the job, production vendors as well. "We typically measure success through project evaluation and/or client surveys at the end of a project," says Kim. "Success can be measured in various ways, and for us, many times that is client satisfaction, meeting goals, schedules, budgets, and most important, getting the next project."

Document the Evaluation

Create a samples file that includes the publication, its project overview and/or creative brief, the original schedule with any missed deadlines noted, the original estimates and the actual costs, the defined goals, and the publication results against those goals. Document your evaluation by including discussion notes you can refer to for revisions or similar projects.

In addition to keeping these in individual job jackets for reference when updating a publication, develop a central file or binder for samples of all your work by category—brochures, advertisements, direct mail, and so on—for reference when creating a new publication.

Employee Pride:
Crane Co. Branding Program

SALSGIVER COVENEY ASSOCIATES, INC.,
WESTPORT, CT

"There's no point in doing something this important halfway." Salsgiver Coveney principal Karen Salsgiver integrated the Crane Co. annual report, wall calendar, hard-bound and electronic versions of the company history, poster series, and new Crane 150 logo into an employee communications program to celebrate the organization's 150th year. A special anniversary Web site, a three-day celebration, a video, and the CEO's quarterly talks were also designed as integral parts of the strategic plan.

"I've been working with Crane Co. for a number of years, developing annual reports for the financial community," Salsgiver says. Crane is an "American manufacturing company with roots in the Industrial Revolution and a compelling story to tell. We thought, 'Wouldn't the 150th be a great opportunity to comprehensively integrate this story into communications for Crane's 10,000 worldwide employees, so that at the end of twelve months they would have a sense of shared pride, shared values, and shared history?'"

Salsgiver and her team developed the whole program from scratch, so she was able to ensure that all of the print and other media were cohesive and reinforced each other. "We had the opportunity to plan right from the beginning any venues for communication with employees that would further our message," she says.

"Crane makes everything from brake controls that safely stop a plane, to vending machines from which you select a snack when you land, to the valves through which fluids flow in the airport—their innovations can be found behind the scenes virtually everywhere, helping everyday life run efficiently. I researched many of these innovations and selected twelve to highlight in a 2005 calendar for employees." In addition, a series of posters inspired by the basic tenets of the founder's credo (honesty and fairness, dealing fairly with customers and competitors, being liberal and just toward employees, and putting one's whole mind upon the business) were printed in multiple languages and posted quarterly worldwide; these coincided with management-led presentations about those values in action today. "Employees in every location discussed how core values drive their business today and remain more relevant than ever."

The annual report stresses the shared values, shared tools, and shared disciplines that bring the company's people together as an integrated whole. The logo on the cover reflects that, too. It's a "mark that represents a company that possesses strength, transparency, and cohesion. The interlocking parts at the center of the logo form one vibrant and multifaceted whole, symbolizing the collective power of five business segments that come together to form a strategically linked, integrated operating company," Salsgiver says.

"This was really about making sure that as many people as we could possibly include were aware of Crane's culture and could take pride in shared core values and history. It was a dream project for great people—it's an enlightened group."

150 YEARS OF
CRANE Values

Continuous improvement.

Improving some of the time, in one or two areas, just won't cut it.
Our success is built on an accelerated stream of incremental and breakthrough
improvements in products, manufacturing, finance, distribution — the works.
We have to look for new ways to create value, and then translate those ideas
into advantages our customers will understand, appreciate, and act upon.

**Concept and design: Salsgiver Coveney
Associates, Inc.
Writers: Karen Salsgiver, Tony McDowell,
Susan Harris, Patricia Watson
Printer: Finlay Printing
Client: Crane Co.
Copyright: © 2005 Crane Co.**

WHAT THEY MEAN   The most important legacy of our founder, R.T. Crane,
is a set of core values that keep Crane Co. on the path of uncompromising integrity and
continuous improvement. As we observe our milestone anniversary, we celebrate the
strength of our values and their continued relevance at 150 years of age. Throughout all our
businesses, in every facility in every country, we are heralding 150 Years of Crane Values
with a series of posters. *The text from these posters is reproduced inside this fold-out spread.*
In addition, roundtable discussions are being held company-wide to highlight examples
from all our businesses that illustrate Crane Values in Action today.

shared values

WHY THEY MATTER   Optimum performance depends in part on employees'
knowing what needs to be done — and why. By internalizing the Company's values,
employees are able to set their own boundaries and act independently to achieve
Crane's goals. When employees understand what is guiding Crane Co., where they
fit in with the team, and what they can do to help drive success, they perform more
efficiently and make greater contributions to profitable growth.

On July 6, 1905, 16 trains of ten cars each carried the
Company's employees, their families, and their picnic
baskets to Northwestern Park (16 miles from Chicago
on the banks of the Des Plaines River) to celebrate the
Company's 50-Year Jubilee. Richard Teller Crane was
a man ahead of his time, who, that day, talked about the
values that bound them all together and about his
profound happiness at being there with his employees
to commemorate their company's 50 years of growth
since its founding as a one-man brass and bell foundry.

9

Determining Production Needs and Selecting Vendors

When you're out of quality, you're out of business.
—ANONYMOUS

Quality is remembered long after the price is forgotten.
—GUCCI FAMILY SLOGAN

In this chapter we'll discuss how matching your production vendors' capabilities and client requirements will help ensure a timely, cost-effective, and quality project. And you'll learn about the many factors that will aid your selection of the best production and printing professionals for the job.

EFFECTIVE RELATIONSHIPS WITH PRINTERS

As the publications manager and as the client, you might be the point person for the printing rep. In this role, you'll educate yourself on the capabilities of each prospective vendor, negotiate the contract and hire the appropriate printer, and manage the process for *your* client, including blueline or other prepress proof reviews and press checks.

SELECTION CRITERIA

"Quality of work, quality of account service, speed, and price." Those are Kinimod principal Dominik D'Angelo's top four considerations when selecting a printer. "On huge projects it is absolutely crucial to have a great relationship with your account rep and everyone in the print shop," she advises. "Unavoidably, problems occur during the printing process, and it is so much easier to resolve them when everyone is on the same team."

You should be able to gauge the level of service and professionalism during an interview with a print sales rep. He should not assume that you're familiar with industry jargon and should communicate with you accordingly. Ask questions about the typical job process to get a feel for what's comfortable for you and to understand how involved you'll be in the production phase. Ask for and follow up on client references; this information often is posted on the printer's Web site.

Historic Event: Clark Metal Products Co. 50th Anniversary Invitation

MIZRAHI DESIGN ASSOCIATES, INC., PITTSBURGH, PA

"Our goal was to create a historically engaging invitation that was evocative of Clark Metal's expertise," says Mizrahi Design creative director Kevin Kennedy of the unusual invitation folded into a stamped tin. The packaging and design of folds and die cuts reflects Clark's business: precision sheet metal fabrication.

"We actually die cut all those holes in the invitation and used the curved edges and the idea of the paper being bent in an accordion fold" to represent Clark's capabilities, Kennedy says. "The tin itself was a standard size; we designed the invitation to work within it."

In addition to the celebration invite, Mizrahi Design created an anniversary picture book and other collateral materials. "The book included a variety of specialty printing techniques and a unique hand-stitching," Kennedy says. "We wanted to create a history book that was more than a chronology of dates. We took a more retrospective approach and grouped information under six core headings: beginnings, ownership, facilities, equipment, products, and commitment. The text is light, readable, and full of reminiscences from the retiring company president."

Creative director/account manager: Kevin Kennedy
Designer: Brad Ireland
Writers: Todd Erkel (history book), Sue Cardillo (invitation and media kit)
Print/production: Alpha Screen Graphics (invitation tins), Consolidated Graphics (remaining items)
Client: Clark Metal Products Co.

For each of the project components, Mizrahi Design made extensive use of the company's archives of old personal photos and business correspondence that had been saved by generations of owners. The family had held onto all of this historical data since its founding, even the cancelled check used to purchase its first punch press.

The project team wanted to ensure that the captivating invitation wasn't lost in the shuffle when sent to the hundreds of employees, clients, prospects, media members, and dignitaries invited to the celebration. "We had to carefully consider how it was being mailed," Kennedy says. "This was coming to people from out of the blue, so we didn't want to lose the impact of the tin by hiding it in an envelope.

"We decided to just shrink-wrap the tin with a custom mailing label that included the special 50th anniversary logo. Recipients would know it came from Clark Metal and still be intrigued enough to open it.

"They got a tremendous response to the invitation, not only from their employees and existing clients but from people who were willing to take a second look—'This is something interesting I should check out.'"

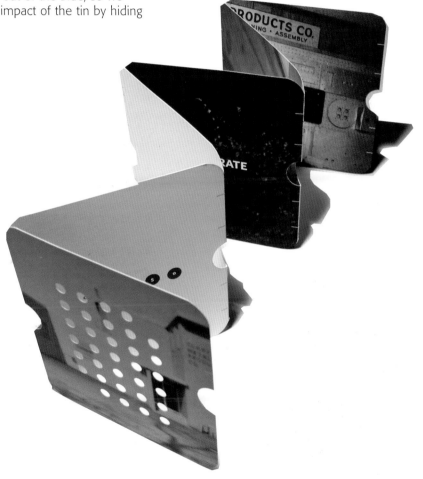

Consider touring the plant to become more familiar with the machinery and the services offered. Meeting the press workers can be an important first step toward starting a firm and amiable relationship with all of the shop's personnel. Your visit to the facility shows your interest and eagerness to learn from and work with the people running your job. Remember that many of these same workers probably will be seeing your face again when you attend the press check. Remember, too, that these individuals are experts in their industry. Ask questions and treat them with respect.

In addition to hiring a printer, you might be contracting other production vendors, such as paper houses, binders, and box and other packaging manufacturers. But your primary production relationship will be with the printer, who may also have these capabilities in-house.

If your designer is the key contact with production vendors, you'll still want to be involved to the extent of signing off on estimates, ensuring that scheduling jibes with your delivery date, and reviewing any client changes to the project after it's been released to the printer.

If considering working with a new printer, you or your designer should ask the printing rep for a capabilities brochure and representative samples of his company's work. You can check the printer's Web site for this information and then confirm that it's current.

It's important to educate yourself on the vendor's production capabilities plus such in-house services as handwork and binding. The fewer additional vendors involved in the production process, the more efficient and cost-effective it will be. Fewer hands on your project will decrease the variables that can cause confusion and unmet requirements.

Having the printer send a job out for binding, for example, will add to your budget if the printer marks up the bindery's fee. Think about whether you want to manage the relationship with another vendor by contracting with the bindery separately to avoid the markup. You might not have the time or feel that you have the technical knowledge or quality-control experience.

Better to hire a printer with the full capabilities needed for your project if possible. Better still to determine all of the production, finishing, handling, shipping, and storage needs for the job in advance. Then match your vendor to the project according not only to experience, estimate, and quality, but to capabilities to fulfill your job requirements.

Always request and review samples from the printing rep. Make sure the printer is experienced in jobs with the specifications you'll be requiring. Ask to see a family of publications or perhaps a series of a periodical. This will enable you to compare the printing consistency from piece to piece or issue to issue. Although they might be hard to obtain, a print job and its subsequent revision would offer an ideal comparison, showing consistency between an original publication and its reprint. If you don't have an experienced eye for evaluating print quality, ask your designer to review the samples.

In addition, you'll want to give a new printer samples of previous publications from your company, and discuss what you did and did not like. This is especially important if the vendor will be reprinting materials originated by another printer, adding pieces to a family of publications, or continuing a periodical originally printed by another shop.

ARRANGE VENDOR MEETINGS

Building a strong printer–designer relationship is critical, even when you're the point person. Besides your meeting with the printing company's rep, make sure your designer gets to know both the rep and the print-shop person who will be actually handling the art files. Remember that the designer will need to understand the printer's capabilities to ensure the job specifications do not exceed the vendor's capabilities.

Sound Economics:
Station Casinos Annual Report
KUHLMANN LEAVITT, INC., ST. LOUIS, MO

"We knew that the challenge would be to make an econ book interesting," says Kuhlmann Leavitt principal Deanna Kuhlmann-Leavitt. The Station Casinos annual report, a supply-and-demand presentation charmingly titled *Econ 101*, relies on stunning photography plus appealing, tactile specifications to enliven what typically is a desert-dry topic.

Kuhlmann-Leavitt says that first the team "identified what makes an econ book—text heavy with an abundance of charts and graphs. Rarely do econ books have photography, but we knew we needed to show Station's properties. Images were used throughout the report to support the econ data and liven up the content. One section was dedicated entirely to lush eye-candy photographs, giving readers' minds a break."

The firm used a variety of visual indicators to guide readers through the report for a more satisfying experience. "The book has five distinct sections: three econ chapters, one chapter dedicated to the shareholder letter, and the last 'chapter' is the requisite year-end financial data. In addition to typography, we used six different paper finishes and colors as well as printed color fields to signal the reader that a new section has begun. The result is a series of subtle tactile and visual cues that add a bit of quiet excitement while honoring the econ premise."

Econ 101 is an annual report that serves both the reader who wants to be entertained and those who need to absorb all the details.

Art director: Deanna Kuhlmann-Leavitt
Designers: Deanna Kuhlmann-Leavitt, Kerry Layton
Client: Station Casinos
Copyright: © 2004 Station Casinos, Inc.

Your designer should receive die lines or templates from the printer as necessary for creating the artwork and understand how to deliver art files to the printer. He should also confirm that the software programs he's using are the same as or compatible with the printer's. In a new relationship, the designer should sit down with the printing rep and develop a list of all preflight items that need to be completed and checked before art is sent to the printer.

It's important that each vendor prepare his portion of the project so that it dovetails with the next. The designer must work directly with print-shop personnel to assess the best and most efficient solution for getting a job produced. It's his responsibility to help avoid the need for the printer to perform additional work on the art files.

Often at the production end of the schedule, with the final deadline fast approaching, there is a tendency to pass along ragged or unfinished work to the next guy. Beware: Fear the words "They'll just clean that up in prepress." Any extra labor has budget implications, especially when the printer is holding art files and needs to move forward, and you're asked to approve big dollars to make the scheduled press time. The designer is responsible for investigating art preparation specifications that will work with the printer and stay within budget.

In addition to introducing your designer and printer, arrange for vendors working on different stages of the same product to meet—the printer and a box manufacturer, for example. This will give them the opportunity to learn each other's process, needs, and key contacts. Make sure you and all team members have names and contact information on file and understand who to call to resolve what type of problem or situation.

NUMBER OF RELATIONSHIPS

Depending on your needs, you might have relationships with several printers with different capabilities and specializations. For example, you'd want to use the same printer for a magazine, newsletter, or other periodical requiring consistent quality and color-matching. You should have several reliable printers for each level of capability you require.

If you're looking for printers in your area, contact your local chapter of the Printing Industries of America, affiliated with GAIN, the Graphic Arts Information Network (*www.gain.net*). Also obtain recommendations from designers and your counterparts at other firms or organizations.

ESTIMATES

Obtain a written estimate detailing all charges for printing, proofs, binding and other handling, and shipping/delivery. Make sure that the estimate, as well as the contract, clarifies everything that is included in the estimate. Be on the lookout for hidden or assumed costs, such as an additional charge for delivery to your or your client's site. Proofs, for another example, are not necessarily covered in the printing and handling costs; specify in advance the type and number of proofs you require, and be sure they're included in the estimate.

When obtaining estimates from more than one printer, it's especially important to check that the costs meet your specifications as precisely as possible. Due to the varying capabilities among printers, this might not be so easy. To ensure your ability to make accurate, apples-to-apples comparisons, ask that the estimates break down costs for various subcategories of work. Detailed information will enable you to make fair assessments.

For ongoing jobs, be sure that estimates are kept current. If you're contracting a printer for a periodical or for a job that will be reprinted on an annual basis, reestimate the job each year—before your budget cycle, if applicable—for two reasons: to reevaluate pricing and to rebudget if pricing increases.

Check on how long any estimate will remain in effect. Print industry standards specify that an estimate is good for thirty days. A job awarded to a printer six months after the initial bid should be reestimated so you're not surprised by the possibly higher bill. Also consider the potential for rising costs of ancillary services by other vendors contracted by the printer (if you've agreed to that arrangement). The price of paper stock and other materials also could increase if the job goes to press long after the original estimate.

Of course, estimates will play a big role in your vendor selection. You'll need to choose a printer whose estimate is in line with your budget, but if possible that should not be your sole selection criterion. In addition, base your selection of a printer for a specific job on the interview, samples, capabilities, references, recommendations, and your relationship history.

CONTRACT COMPONENTS

After you have compared estimates, evaluated all of the selection criteria for the bidding printers, and made your printer selection, put everything in writing. Some printers work with no contract, no initials on an estimate, nothing in writing. Others require an umbrella letter of agreement (e.g., see appendix A) and a purchase order from the client noting the project "as spec'ed" and the quantity.

Without thorough documentation, you might run into trouble. The following recommendations represent what might seem like a lot of paperwork, but preparing a comprehensive document will save you time, money, and misunderstanding in the long run. Depending on the project and your needs, consider including the following in the letter of agreement or contract:

A copy of the comprehensive estimate. All components of the estimate should be separate, with their individual charges specified. Double-check that all costs, including folding or other special handling, proofs, shipping, and so on, as well as tax, are included so there are no surprises when you receive the invoice.

The allowable difference between estimate and invoice. Be aware that the industry standard is 10 percent. If this will not fit your budget, negotiate the precise cost in advance of work.

The allowable underrun quantity. Say you require no fewer than 10,000 publications. To meet your amount, you might have to order a higher quantity. The industry allowance for underruns is 10 percent. Try to negotiate that there can be no underruns—at no additional charge to you. If this can't be arranged, you'll need to purchase a quantity that allows for the printer's underrun percentage.

The allowable overrun quantity. Planning for overruns is necessary for press and printing problems. The industry allowance is 10 percent. Try to negotiate that you'll pay no additional cost for overruns.

Client notification of increase. What happens if a press situation arises that will add to the original cost? Make sure the contract specifies that you'll be notified to OK continuance of the job. Depending on what time of day or night the job will run, you or your designer might need to be available around the clock to answer questions. Otherwise you'll hold up the print process and possibly miss your place in the job queue, adding time to your schedule.

Dates. Detail the dates for the delivery of art files to the printer, the press check (as closely as possible), and receipt of the finished publication by you or your client. In addition, include the date or dates on which you'll receive proofs. You'll need to make sure that you're available to turn the proof around as quickly as possible, especially if other reviewers, your client, and your designer will be sharing a single blueline and set of color proofs.

Maximum Coverage:
The Kennedy Center Press Sheet
THE KIRWAN COMPANY, INC., TOLUCA LAKE, CA

Ten printed pieces on a single press sheet? That was the novel cost-saving solution devised by Goetz Printing Co., in Springfield, Virginia, in collaboration with ArtsEdge, a program of the John F. Kennedy Center for the Performing Arts in Washington, D.C.

The project was a children's treasure hunt kit to accompany a play about Teddy Roosevelt's children on just such an adventure. The proposal was to create a treasure hunt for the audience, too, complete with an oversize map and individual clues. The problem was that the clues and other documents were contemporary or period, necessitating quite different specs and ideally different stocks—but the budget for paper, printing, and trimming so many pieces wasn't available.

The solution: (1) Assign the separate publications—from the treasure map of the White House to a set designer's letter, from an early-1900s-look postcard to a brochure about Roosevelt—a variety of background and font colors. (2) "Layer" elements such as fading and wrinkles to suggest aging and different stocks. (3) Scan and place paper clips, pieces of tape, and other 3D-look graphics to add even more dimension. (4) Size the pieces to fit patchwork style to run on one sheet to save on stock, printing, and trimming.

The greatest challenge for designer Steve Kirwan, principal of the Kirwan Company, was "creating and assembling heavily layered textures for the different backgrounds of each piece. Knowing we didn't have the budget for a variety of papers for this project meant that if each piece didn't feel old to the touch, it needed to look old and worn enough to create that illusion in the mind of our audience."

The result? Michael Warchol, the Kennedy Center's content coordinator, says, "We dreamed big on this piece to make it a special experience for our young theater-goers. We could not have pulled off such a monumental print piece without the significant cost savings of printing ten unique 'documents' on one sheet. We are still getting comments about the impact this study guide has made."

Coordinator: Michael Warchol
Editor and art director: Cathy Lips
Design: The Kirwan Company, Inc.
Writer: Theresa Sotto
Printer: Goetz Printing
Client: The John F. Kennedy Center for the Performing Arts
Copyright: © 2006 The John F. Kennedy Center for the Performing Arts
Images: Courtesy of ARTSEDGE, www.artsedge.kennedy-center.org

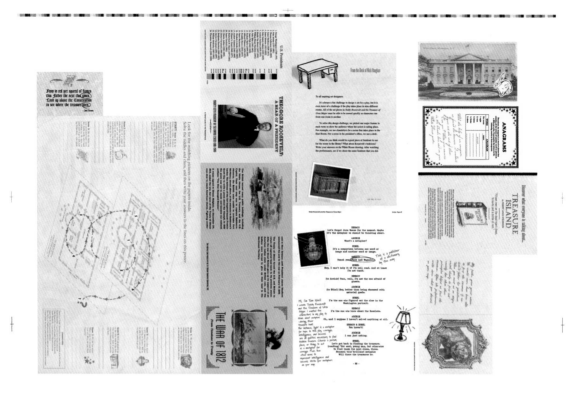

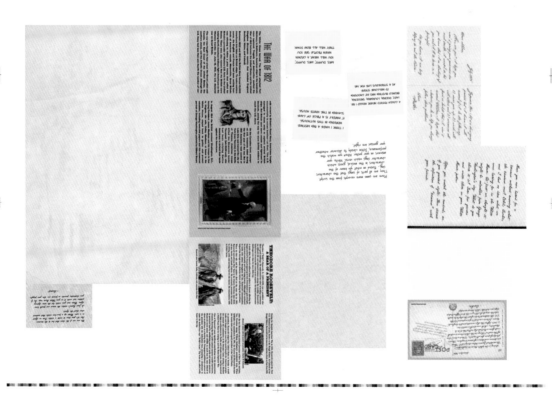

The impact of late delivery. Put in writing the repercussions for late delivery of the product by the printer. This can only be enacted if all of your schedule obligations have been met on time. Negotiation could range from cutting a percentage of the bill for throwing you off schedule to your not accepting a job that cannot be used due to lateness.

Try to allow several days for the unforeseen in your printing schedule. Too often there are rush print jobs, with delivery scheduled for the morning of a meeting, for example. This situation increases the margin for errors, it can compromise quality, and it raises the pressure point for you, the client, and the vendor.

The printer's markup. Spell out the printer's acceptable markup on the cost of stock and other materials, and on outside vendors such as folders and binders. It will be your decision whether to contract other resources yourself to avoid paying the markup or to turn the logistics and management of this extra responsibility over to the printer to save you time and headaches.

Accurate samples. Request a paper dummy of the job that fully reflects the stock, size, number of pages, stitching or other binding or folding, die cuts, pockets, and so on. This is especially important if the finished product will require gluing, tabs, or other elements that are to hold the piece together or enable it to function properly.

Printing industry standards state that such hand samples are not intended to reflect the performance of the actual finished product; however, you might need to negotiate otherwise when tab-fitting and gluing will determine the success and usability of the piece.

The press check. If possible, note when the press check will be and who from your team will attend.

The types and quantity of proofs. Specify whether you want a blueline, a color proof, or both, as well as how many of each you want. Remember that these are not necessarily contained in the printing cost.

Author's alteration costs versus printer alterations. Author's alterations are changes made by you or your client, and printer alterations are corrections that the printer needs to make to its own work. In the contract, note the hourly fee or range the printer will charge for your alterations made to proofs. Recognize that your changes at this phase, if substantial, can impact the press date and possibly bump you from the print queue.

Delivery or shipping. Include detailed instructions about how, where, and when your finished job will be delivered. This is especially important if shipping to a number of locations is involved or if an initial quantity will be delivered on one date, with the balance delivered later. Note the type of transportation and the receipt date or dates.

Storage. Only part of your job might be delivered initially. If you or your client doesn't have room at your facility to store the balance, you can ask to have the rest of the publications held at the printer. Specify your storage needs in the contract, including the time frame and the cost negotiated, frequently a charge per pallet per month.

Billing. Include the agreed-upon billing terms. Examples include payment due when the job is delivered and net 30 from delivery, perhaps with the option of a discount if payment is made net 10. Make sure you've followed the procedures for setting up a billing account with the vendor before work begins.

Terms and Conditions

Be aware of policies that might impact your job process, cost, and ownership of your project's components. Ask a printing rep for your state's or region's printing industry standards (e.g., see appendix A). Negotiate terms that meet your needs and expectations in advance of signing a contract or sending a

Premium Design: 10 Cane Launch Kit
WERNER DESIGN WERKS, ST. PAUL, MN

Make it "easy for the salespeople to carry around." That was the goal of designers Sarah Nelson and Sharon Werner as they created the launch kit for the introduction of 10 Cane Rum. Together they devised a format that allowed for customized presentations. It also helped to involve prospects in the handling of kit pieces that interested them, bringing them closer into contact with the brand.

"Normally they would have a binder. That was actually more expensive, to do a binder construction," says Nelson. "We simplified that part of it so we could use the money toward a paper-wrapped cover with a deboss and the applied label on it. That also keeps it looking like the bottle itself."

The partners wanted the launch portfolio to reflect the elegant, upscale bottle for the premium brand, Nelson says, "which is very textural with the embossed 'Rum' on the side of the bottle itself.

And the crest is screen-printed on the bottle so you can actually touch it. It's very tactile, so we wanted to carry that quality through to the kit."

They also wanted to make it "really easy, a book form," to facilitate customer meetings. With the pockets, salespeople "could pull out what they wanted to talk about with the client, if someone asked where did 10 Cane come from, what's the history of it, what will this do for sales for me? Each piece of information was on a separate sheet that they could take out to tailor it to how they wanted to present it.

"The notepad is the only thing in there that was really just filler. We needed to make the kit balanced, and we thought at least this will be something that's useful"—and free advertising on the customer's desk.

Creative director: Linus Karlsson, Mother NY
Art director: Sharon Werner
Designers: Sharon Werner, Sarah Nelson
Printer: Diversified Graphics
Client: Moet Hennessy, Mother NY

purchase order to your printer. Any deviations to the standard printer's contract should be expressed in writing as part of your hiring contract. Some examples include:

Quotations/Estimates

"A quotation not accepted within 30 days may be changed."

Make sure you're aware of this condition before preparing your final budget for a publication that has been held for more than a month.

Experimental Work

"Experimental or preliminary work performed at the customer's request will be charged to the customer at the provider's current rates. This work may not be used without the provider's written consent."

Time spent solving your packaging challenge or designing the die for a unique pocket folder might not be included in the job. Try to negotiate a cap on the design aspect of the job instead of allowing an open-ended hourly charge.

Creative Work

"Sketches, copy, dummies, and all other creative work developed or furnished by the provider are the provider's exclusive property. The provider must give written approval for all use of this work and for any derivation of ideas from it."

See "Experimental Work."

Electronic Manuscripts/Images

"It is the customer's responsibility to maintain a copy of the original file. The provider is not responsible for accidental damage to media supplied by the customer or for the accuracy of furnished input or final input."

It is reasonable that some discount be provided in the event the printer damages the files prepared and provided by your designer. It should at least be discussed that every precaution will be taken by the printer to safeguard the files provided. Your designer should maintain file copies to send to the printer again in the event of accidental damage.

Alterations/Corrections

"Customer alterations include all work performed in addition to the original specifications. All such work will be charged at the provider's current rates."

Make sure you understand the hourly rate or rates for different types of work that might need to be performed by the printer. When possible, have your designer make these corrections and send the corrected files to the printer. The designer might be able to make the corrections more quickly and less expensively than the printer.

Preparatory Material

"Artwork, type, plates, negatives, positives, tapes, disks, and other items supplied by the provider shall remain the provider's exclusive property."

Negotiate in advance that these materials will be your property; you are paying for their preparation and production. You will need these materials if you change printers for an ongoing job or for reprints; you will not want to pay for having the job recreated by a new printer.

Two for One: Canyon Amphitheater Concert Poster

f2design, LUBBOCK, TX

Dirk Fowler, principal of f2design, had a built-in audience for his Loretta Lynn concert poster: the musician's hordes of longtime fans. But he was charged with appealing to a second audience as well: the new, younger listeners who were just tuning into the unique sound of the Coal Miner's Daughter. As he considered the dual assignment, he says, "I wanted to capture something about her spirit. I felt like I could do that more with shape and color" than with a photograph.

As the graphic developed, Fowler says, "I had everything except the tuning pegs in her hair. It was lacking that extra little punch." When his wife, Carol, also a graphic designer, pointed out that Loretta's head looked like the shape of a guitar, "in my mind that final touch was perfect."

Fowler's hands-on production of the project added to the poster's universality. "The fact that I physically cut all the plates, I hand-inked everything, and then letterpress-printed it—that gives it a handmade quality that also seems to work with the Coal Miner's Daughter. I think that part of it appeals to a wide audience.

"There are people who have never seen a letterpress print. When a young person sees that, they're intrigued by the texture and can feel the printing—'what's that all about?' It's comfortable to an older audience, but at the same time it's comfortable to a young person because it feels good.

"I don't want my posters to be thrown away. I don't know that I necessarily sit down and think, 'Oh, I've got to make something that a seventeen-year-old would like.' It kind of happens that way."

Designer: Dirk Fowler
Client: Canyon Amphitheater

Press Proofs

"Press proofs will not be furnished unless they have been required in writing in the provider's quotation."

Make sure the types and quantities of proofs are included in your estimate request and in the contract. Don't assume you'll receive them automatically or that they are included in the printing estimate.

Color Proofing

"Because of differences in equipment, paper, inks, and other conditions between color proofing and production pressroom operations, a reasonable variation in color between color proofs and the completed job is to be expected. When a variation of this kind occurs, it will be considered acceptable performance."

Define "acceptable performance" with your print rep. You might need PMS colors matched precisely for your brand to comply with your client's strict graphics standards. For a periodical or family of publications, consistent color and ink coverage should be required. You can ensure precise matching and consistency by attending a press check.

Overruns/Underruns

"Overruns or underruns will not exceed 10 percent of the quantity ordered. The provider will bill for the actual quantity delivered within this tolerance. If the customer requires a guaranteed quantity, the percentage of tolerance must be stated at the time of quotation."

Make sure you understand the printer's "overs/unders" policy and either negotiate to meet your needs or order a quantity of your publication that will cover you.

Delivery

"Unless otherwise specified, the price quoted is for a single shipment, without storage, F.O.B. the provider's platform."

Check out the additional charges and time for your special shipping requirements. Include your arrangements in the contract.

Terms/Claims/Liens

"Payment is cash in advance or whatever has been agreed to between customer and provider. Claims for defects, damages, or shortages must be made by the customer in writing no later than ten calendar days after delivery."

Understand the payment terms and spell them out in the letter of agreement. Note the time limit on reporting product problems to the printer. If partial supply is being stored by the printer, require written and signed documentation of the quantity stored. Renegotiate the time allowance for reporting a shortage or defects/damage to be upon your receipt and examination of the stored product.

Liability

"The customer understands that all sketches, copy, dummies, and preparatory work shown to the customer are intended only to illustrate the general type and quality of the work. They are not intended to represent the actual work performed."

Consider whether you need handmade advance paper samples or other preparatory work to perform as, or as closely as possible to, the finished product.

Storage

"The provider will retain intermediate materials used until the related end product has been accepted by the customer. If requested by the customer, intermediate materials will be stored for an additional period at an additional charge. The provider is not liable for any loss or damage to stored material beyond what is recoverable by the provider's fire and extended insurance coverage."

Negotiate that art files, film, dies, and so on, be stored for an agreed-upon period at no additional charge by the printer; these will be required for reprints. Require that the printer be liable for replacement or reimbursement of any lost or damaged materials.

EIGHT PRODUCTION POINTS YOU NEED TO KNOW

What is a Hand Sample?

A hand sample, or dummy, shows the publication or packaging in its finished form without printing. Printing industry standards state that hand samples are not intended to reflect the performance of the actual finished product. There are some cases, however, when you'll want to impress upon your printer the need for performance accuracy.

For a hand sample of a paperboard box, for example, the end tabs needed to be glued. Because the adhesive was applied by hand and not machine, it was done liberally. The sample was held together firmly.

When the printed boxes went through the gluing machine, however, not enough glue was dispensed. The machine-glued job was delivered, and the boxes were prepped on the client's assembly line. As the boxes were folded, materials placed inside, and the boxes tucked closed, the glued tabs began popping open. Although the sight of dozens of boxes jumping out of line workers' hands was amusing, the situation was not. The materials were unusable.

The resulting letter of agreement (e.g., see appendix A) specified that hand samples had to demonstrate final product performance as closely as possible. Furthermore, steps performed by machine needed to be checked and the product tested before the run was completed.

What Happens If You Miss Your Art Delivery Date?

First, try to include several cushion days in your schedule to allow for unexpected delays at each phase of the publications process. Then make sure your designer understands that you need to be alerted to possible holdups as many days in advance as possible. If it looks as though you will miss your press date, contact your printer ASAP. See whether you can be reinstated in the print queue to avoid significant press date delay.

When Do You Need a Rush Job, and What Are the Cost Implications?

If you've taken on a fast-turnaround project for a client, explain to him the rush-charge implications. You might be charged more for night and weekend work or for being squeezed into a tight queue by your writer, designer, photographer, or printer. Get this information and report to your client for approval. If the decision is yours, evaluate the true need for rush delivery against the budget impact.

If an external client requests a rush job, remember that you have the option to turn it down. This might be advisable if you don't want to set a precedent for performing emergency work or you can't risk the timeliness and quality of other projects you're working on. You'll also want to consider the portfolio value of the job and its potential impact on your future relationship with a favored client.

As an alternative to rush charges, be creative with your printer and try to devise another plan. For example, if time is short but you don't need the entire job delivered all at once, consider splitting delivery of the job. Say you've ordered 10,000 new product brochures, and you'll be hosting 500 executives, prospective investors, and the press at a kick-off meeting. Explore with your printer whether the meeting deadline for 500 copies is feasible, with the balance of 9,500 supplied a week later.

What Proofs Are There, and Which Should You Request?

Each of the proofs "proves" different technical and qualitative accomplishments. The more closely you examine each level of progress, the less likely you are to face enormous charges associated with late alterations.

The blueline is the first prepress publication proof you're likely to review. One-color, folded, and bound, it demonstrates the quality of the negatives prepared by the printer. It shows whether sections of type and art are exposed, and will be included when printing plates are made. The blueline allows you to easily check all graphic and text elements, and their positioning within the context of the entire publication. Although a blueline includes no more detail than a last round of laser proofs provided by the designer, it should be read and reviewed extremely closely. Unfortunately, the mistakes that could have been corrected for little or no cost before submission to the printer now cost plenty. Most corrections at the blueline stage require new negatives to be made, and multiple rounds of negatives can be costly.

Color proofs are marketed under a variety of brand names. They all are essentially proofs of one-color or multicolor artwork or colored text. Color proofs are commonly requested for all black-and-white and color photographs and illustrations.

Press proofs or press sheets are actual printed pages of publications. This is the last chance to make corrections. An approved press sheet is the final "go" for printing. Corrections can still be made. However, because at this late stage—negatives burned, plates made, and the press running—any author's alterations made will be costly.

What Are Your Responsibilities for Proofing a Job?

Specify proofing responsibilities with your creative team and your client. This is a critical and repeated step throughout the publications process. Proofing at the press stage is the last—and most expensive and time-consuming—chance for corrections. Late changes can result in practically or completely redoing the entire job. Make sure all team members understand when changes can be made economically. Require written signoff by all reviewers who have proofed the job at different phases.

You might order multiple bluelines for multiple reviewers. On the other hand, although coordinating reviews on a single proof can be tricky from a logistical and scheduling standpoint, it can save time on compiling the corrections from several proofs onto one core copy for the printer.

Consider whether your client has the knowledge and publications process experience to be marking up that single proof. Even though you've explained that the proof stage is not the time for corrections other than typos and accuracy (both of which should have been finely checked before press time), some people can feel compelled to make their mark on the proof, as if to show they've read it. Or your client might not know standard proofing marks. This can lead to directions that are unclear or confusing to the printer; you then might need to cross through the client's markup and squeeze in clarifying instructions. If your client or another reviewer is inexperienced in the proofing phase, go over the proof with him if possible or at least request that recommended changes be made lightly in pencil or on sticky notes.

Remember to include signoff dates in your own schedule so all reviewers will be mindful of turning the proofs around promptly.

What Are Author's versus Printer's Alterations?

In terms of publications management, alterations made by the "author" are your biggest concern. Author's alterations refer to any changes requested by you or members of your team or the client to correct mistakes made by anyone other than the printer. As the author representative, you will be responsible for any costs incurred to make these types of changes or corrections.

Author's alterations typically involve content issues—for instance, misspellings or mistaken numbers that somehow made it through all the rounds of checks and proofs, or designs that need to be altered to accommodate some recent event. Of course, untimely changes requested by clients are often unavoidable, but you can minimize many costly changes at late stages by insisting that prepress design proofs be carefully reviewed for typos, factual errors, misplaced graphics, and so on, and released only after being initialed by each reviewer.

Printer's alterations are changes due to errors made by the printer during the preparation or printing of the job. Correcting these problems is the responsibility of the printer and should not add to your bill. Printer's alterations usually correct mechanical or physical mistakes that affect the print quality of the publication. Common printing errors that fall into this category include scratched or damaged film, stray fibers appearing as printed lines, and unwanted marks on the page; poor registration and photo reproduction quality; inaccurate color matching; and incorrect positioning of art or text sections.

Assigning responsibility for changes is important in terms of billing. You will be charged for author's alterations by the printer. Most changes or corrections made after a publication is turned over to a printer will result in additional costs. The only decision involved is who's responsible and who'll eat the cost.

Should You Attend a Press Check?

It's advisable that you and/or your designer attend a press check, especially for a complex job or a job with a new printer. The press workers need your guidance to determine acceptable variances from the proofs. You are not only an extra set of eyes but also the authority to suspend the press run to adjust color and to correct ink coverage for consistency throughout the job. As the team leader and surrogate client, it's your responsibility to ensure the print quality meets your specifications. Once you review and approve a press sheet, the printer will be responsible for maintaining a consistent level of quality throughout the press run.

What Happens if the Final Product Contains an Error or Is Not Up to Your Expectations?

Errors occur. Besides settling who is financially responsible for the errors and making acceptable corrections, it's important to understand how the flaw occurred. Determine whether it was an oversight or a process issue, then make adjustments to preclude the mistakes from recurring.

As cool-headed as that advice sounds, the ramifications of a mistake getting into print, or possibly even distributed, can make for a pretty hot moment. If you've kept original text and graphic proofs with reviewers' signoffs, you can usually track down the point during the process when the error sneaked through. This, however, doesn't solve the problem. As publications manager, you should establish what it will take to make the project "whole" again, as quickly as possible, and what the costs will be.

For example, an error may be explainable with an addendum to the publications. But perhaps the books will need to be recovered or even reprinted in total. To provide your frustrated/angry/panicked client with the broadest range of options, get estimates and schedules for all possible corrections promptly and have them ready for a client meeting. Explaining the cost and time advantages of each possible solution in person will go a long way in assuring your client that you've charted a course through this crisis.

You will have to address responsibility at this stage. If a client approves an expensive solution, assuming the error wasn't his own, he'll be much less likely to accept the costs no matter what the explanation later.

Although the printer is not responsible for copy-proofing or reviewing the quality or consistency of the designs, any inconsistency of the print quality throughout a press run is his responsibility. If the job is not usable, and if it's clear from the contract that the printer did not meet your written requirements, you have the right to not pay. If responsibility for the error is shared, often you can negotiate partial payment.

10

Ensuring Efficient Distribution

There is always room for those who can be relied upon to deliver the goods when they say they will.
—Napoleon Hill

"We need to pay as much attention to distribution processes as we do to the creation of the materials," says communications consultant Angela Sinickas. "If it does not literally get into people's hands, it cannot possibly get into their brains."

Delivering your communication to your readers on schedule can mean the difference between their action and inaction, their understanding and missing your message. If a potential audience receives invitations with too little time to make plans, you'll lose attendance. Miss delivery of the meeting agendas, and employees might not be able to prepare. Consistently mail your monthly journal late, and your readership will lose confidence in your ability to get them the news they need.

In this chapter we'll discuss how your audience's needs, your schedule, your budget, and your communication's format all are factors in identifying the appropriate distribution method. And you'll learn how to locate resources that can aid you in delivering your publication, plus the services those professionals offer to manage the process smoothly and take the burden off you.

PLANNING DISTRIBUTION IN ADVANCE

Three pieces of delivery information should be included in your publications planning phase: packaging needs and costs, mail preparation and delivery schedule, and shipping and budget.

Packaging Needs and Costs

With the initial design of the publication—or as early in the process as feasible—determine the type of packaging that will be required. You'll want to ensure safe and cost-effective delivery of the finished product.

Believe it or not, envelopes are often an overlooked publication component, left until the last minute. That means losing time and can mean going over budget. If your funds are tight, communicate to your designer that your publication should be developed to fit a standard-size envelope or other economical packaging solution. Also consider that some less-usual size envelopes, even if they are readily in stock and do not require special production, may need additional postage. Check the United States Postal Service site (*www.usps.gov*), which includes printable mail dimension charts for assessing cost efficiency.

Maximum Impact: TSUNAMI Awareness Book
de.MO, MILBROOK, NY

"Form followed content" for de.MO's nonprofit book *TSUNAMI* and its packaging, says editor and creative director Giorgio Baravalle. The large scale was "the best way to maximize the content. The size was dictated by the photography. The magnitude of the disaster was captured by many aerial shots." Published by the design firm, *TSUNAMI* was sold in bookstores to raise public awareness of the catastrophe. "We had a lot of discussion about how to package the project because the book was so oversized," Baravalle says. "The tube actually was only for a limited-edition book. The wholesalers couldn't haul around the tubes because they fell off of the forklifts. In the stores it sold in a flat cardboard box. It was a very successful solution."

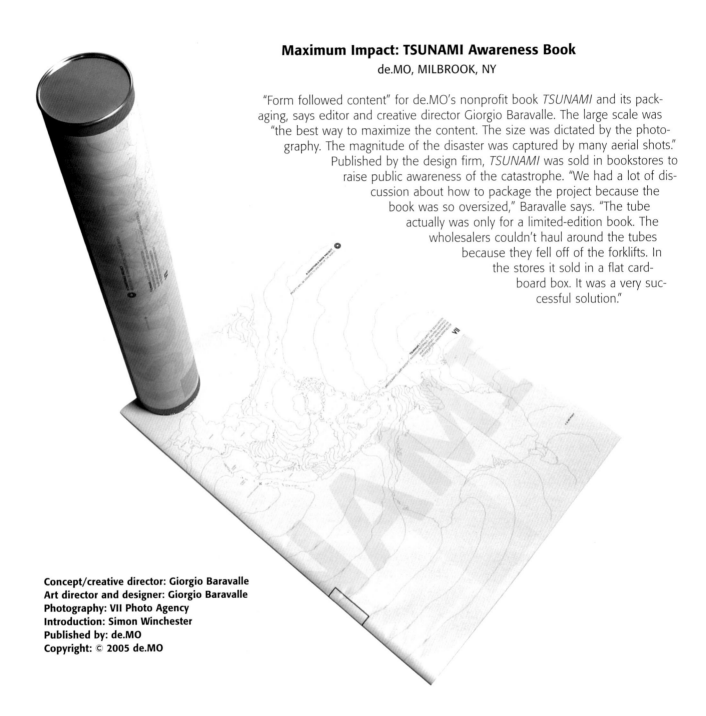

Concept/creative director: Giorgio Baravalle
Art director and designer: Giorgio Baravalle
Photography: VII Photo Agency
Introduction: Simon Winchester
Published by: de.MO
Copyright: © 2005 de.MO

Your budget might allow a custom envelope or package that accommodates original design specifications of the publication. Make sure your designer checks out in advance the stock availability, the production time, and the estimated weight that could be added to the piece, impacting the shipping cost. Envelopes or other packaging that will be printed or will require handwork or other special treatment need to have their additional production time figured into the schedule. Check with your printer or other appropriate vendor.

When developing your packaging plan for the publication, keep in mind the durability of the piece itself and how far it's traveling. This will determine how sturdy and protective the envelope or other packaging will need to be.

Even a hand-distributed report requires some protection to preserve it for presentation. For example, if you're distributing annual reports at a meeting, an envelope will help avoid bent corners and fingerprints.

Reader attention could influence your packaging selection. Consider envelope size, shape, and color. *Target Marketing* magazine cites several recent trends in envelope presentation meant to get the piece opened. Use out-of-the-ordinary paper stock to create upscale appeal, for example. Popular choices include linen and vellum, and high gloss for color designs.

Many companies mail materials in bright orange and yellow to grab the recipient. There are two schools of thought, though; others send mailings in official-looking envelopes so customers will think the contents are important and require their attention.

When budget allows, overnight shipment can add the element of importance necessary to draw attention to critical or timely communications. A widely used, far cheaper alternative, according to *Target Marketing,* is to design envelopes to look like they were mailed priority.

Perhaps in response to postal rates and rising paper prices, there has been a decrease in the use of custom envelopes and a return to standard sizes. The ubiquitous No. 10 continues to be the most prevalent, followed by the 6" × 9", 9" × 12", and Monarch sizes.

Beyond envelopes, special packaging—tubes, boxes, tins—can add significant cost in materials, production, assembly, and shipping, but the return on investment—strengthening the audience call to action—can justify the additional budget. You or your designer can consult with printers, box manufacturers, and corporate-gift representatives, as well as search online, to develop original or purchase ready-made attention-grabbing packaging options.

Mail Preparation and Delivery Schedule

Make sure you include mailing and delivery dates in your publication schedule. Too many timelines end with the press date or your receipt of the finished product from the printer. Include the mail date, the mailing time or time range, and the drop-dead reader receipt date.

Before you can define these dates accurately, you'll need to determine how long preparation of the mailing will take by consulting with your printer or other mail-prep and processing resources. Even the simple stuffing of a letter into an envelope will add some time, whether folding and insertion are performed by machine or by hand. Hand-folding of pieces that don't fit the capabilities of a printer's or mail house's machines will require additional time, especially because precision and extra care are called for. Multicomponent mailings typically require an assembly line of pieces to be ordered consistently; handling and collation of several communication pieces add time.

You can test the time required to complete assembly of pieces by using dummy publications and envelopes. This will help you estimate the hours your in-house team will need to finish the project. Build that time into your production schedule.

Your team might be members of your mailroom. Let the mailroom manager know your shipment date in advance so he can work with you to estimate the prep time required, work backward to a delivery date of all of the components, and then get on the facility's schedule. You also may be able to call on your printer to assemble and mail the communication. Depending on the size of the print shop, it might have full-time handworkers or resources available especially for the project. Make sure you discuss this option with your printing rep in advance to discern time and costs involved.

The cheapest, but perhaps not the most reliable, assembly option for an inside job will be your coordination of a team of volunteers. This might be charged to one or a few administrative assistants if that fits their job description. For mail-prep projects requiring several hours, you might need to recruit colleagues and make arrangements for a work area or conference room in advance; be ready to roll up your own sleeves and join in to maintain good fellowship.

Test Your Timing

When time is of the essence, test different types of delivery. You can mail hand-comps of your publication to individuals at your nearby office or to long-distance audience destinations, depending on where your readership is located. By taking this simple step while your piece is still in development, if possible, you'll be able to reasonably gauge which options best match your budget and timing needs.

Shipping and Budget

Remember to include shipping and related fees in your budget. You'll need to determine these costs early in the process to confirm or adjust what you've budgeted. If you're choosing a low-cost method with a lengthy delivery to save dollars, make sure you figure the additional time into your schedule.

Storage

As you determine your distribution plan, consider the possible need for storage of part of your publication quantity. You might be printing pieces to be mailed over a period of time or to be used on an as-needed basis. If you or your client doesn't have storage space, turn to other resources.

Discuss with your printer or mail house terms for storing the balance of your job. You may be able to negotiate free storage for a limited time, with a small cost per pallet per month beyond the initial time frame (e.g., see chapter 9).

SELECTING A DISTRIBUTION METHOD

The method of distribution will vary depending on several criteria. Three prime factors that will influence whether you can handle distribution on your own or need to contract the services of a mail processing company are: the size of your publication's readership, how geographically dispersed they are, and the timeliness of your message or publication content.

Considering delivery options at the outset of the publication process will give you the best range of distribution options. If your project has strayed from its original time frame, you could find yourself in the position of having to choose an expedited delivery method to be sure your readers receive your communication while it is still valid. Managing the publications process effectively throughout will help you avoid having to rely on last-minute, costly alternatives.

Easy to Digest: Monterey Bay Aquarium Fish Fact Cards

MONTEREY BAY AQUARIUM DESIGN DEPARTMENT, MONTEREY, CA

The Monterey Bay Aquarium Seafood Watch program is positioned as a positive conservation alternative for consumers. The five-year-old program began as a regional awareness campaign focusing on endangered fisheries and habitats within the Monterey area. From these humble beginnings, the aquarium now produces seven regional U.S. versions of the campaign.

The Seafood Watch Pocket Guide, a palm-size folding card, lists region-specific fish in three categories: Best Choices, Good Alternatives, and Avoid. The information helps consumers and businesses make purchasing choices that promote and sustain healthy ocean wildlife. Monterey Bay Aquarium has built partnerships with other institutions, as well as major corporate sponsors, to help distribute the guides. Approximately five million of them are produced each year.

For the sixteen different Fish Fact Cards to be effective with readers, aquarium design department director Jim Ales says, "we wanted to deliver one simple fact which quickly conveys the problem. It was not easy to convince our research staff of our strategy, so I conducted an informal focus group. I presented two different designs: one listing several issues, the other focusing on a single issue. The single-issue recall proved to be very effective. We designed the program to deliver the information as simply and as immediately as possible. The accompanying illustration helps make an important emotional connection with the animals."

Design director: Jim Ales
Senior designer: Mat Squillante
Graphic designer: Micah Kasman
Illustrator: Ann Caudle
Client: Monterey Bay Aquarium
Copyright: © Monterey Bay Aquarium

Rockfish

Quick Fact: Overfishing

Many rockfish populations have plummeted due to decades of heavy fishing. Even when the fishing stops, it may take 100 years or more for some species to recover.

Monterey Bay Aquarium **Seafood Watch**

Make Choices for Healthy Oceans

Issues
▶ Some rockfish live more than 100 years and don't breed until they're 7 to 20 years old. They can't reproduce quickly enough to keep up with demand.

▶ Fishermen catch most rockfish with bottom-trawls: dragging large nets along the seafloor. Trawling damages undersea habitats and accidentally catches other marine life that are dumped overboard, dead or dying, as bycatch.

Location
▶ Rockfish are found along the Pacific Coast, from Mexico to Alaska. More than 100 species worldwide live in kelp forests, among rocky outcrops and in canyons up to 2,625 feet (800 meters) deep.

Health Alert
▶ Environmental Defense has issued a consumption advisory for rockfish due to elevated levels of mercury. Visit www.oceansalive.org for more information.

Menu Alternatives
▶ Pacific halibut, U.S. farmed tilapia and black rockfish from California and Oregon are your best choices.

▶ Rockfish caught with hook and line from Alaska and British Columbia are good alternatives.

Other Common Names
▶ Pacific red snapper Rockcod

www.seafoodwatch.org

In-person Delivery

If you meet with your readers on a regular basis or are located at the same or a nearby site, your distribution method options obviously are the simplest. If available, a natural option is using your or the client company's internal mail system.

In some cases, you might employ a combination of methods. Publications could be handed out at a company's annual meeting, mailed to shareholders, and distributed to employees at the worksite either via the mailroom or at designated high-traffic locations for pickup. But will workers know to pick up the publications without clear instruction?

> ### Shipping Basics
>
> Factors that will figure into your shipping budget include:
>
> - Weight of publication and packaging
> - Size or format of custom or unusual envelopes or other packaging that might require additional postage or handling
> - Production schedule
> - Hand assembly of the package components by a team employed or specially hired by you or your client, your printer, or your mail house
> - Desired delivery dates
> - Method of USPS or other delivery
> - Contracting mail processing services

Beware of seemingly simple distribution means, so test for efficiency and effectiveness. "People spend a lot of time creating a publication, but they don't do enough to follow up to make sure the right people actually receive it," says Angela Sinickas. "Follow-up can be part of a survey, but you can also do it more observationally."

Sinickas cites a retail company with 100,000 employees. When she inquired about a printing bill that seemed quite low for that quantity of employee magazines, she was informed that just 30,000 were printed each month. Company management explained, "We send them to the break rooms of the stores and people share them." Sinickas asked whether management knew they were in fact sharing them.

After she investigated, Sinickas discovered that nobody knew they were supposed to share the publications. "The first people in there on Monday would take it, read it, and throw it away or take it to read on the bus home. The people who worked starting anytime Monday afternoon or later or Tuesday—especially in retail, where people work part-time schedules—never even knew there was a publication.

"This publication was [intended to teach] people in the stores how to sell more effectively and display merchandise more effectively; it was filled with lots of tips that could have helped the company make more money," says Sinickas. "But they were so 'efficient' by printing fewer copies that they lost revenue opportunities."

Self-help for Mailing Management

When a company delivery system is not available, turn to other resources. If you'll be managing mailings regularly and budget is a concern, check out software that supports your efficient, accurate hands-on coordination of distribution.

At Pitney Bowes's Web site (*www.pb.com*) you can explore time-saving mail management software, services, and hardware employed by more than two million businesses—from international corporations to home-based businesses. The company is the world's leading provider of "mailstream" solutions. Its products include programs that facilitate data quality and postal presorting, direct marketing and campaign management, document stream management, mail and package tracking, and security, among myriad other areas.

If you need less frequent or small-scale support, investigate economic services from nonprofit organizations, such as your local Association for Retarded Citizens or seniors groups. Frequently workers can be subcontracted to handle collating and materials assembly, bulk mailing, and related distribution tasks.

Your printer could be another viable resource. Ask your rep whether his company can oversee mail prep by machine, such as for folding, insertion, and sealing; or by hand, say, for collation of documents. Ask whether his company can ship your publications to several sites or mail them to individual readers.

Communications consultant Beth Swanson, former editor of *Wendy's Magazine,* employed separate printing and mailing vendors for the monthly, with a circulation of about 20,000. "Communication with our mailing house wasn't really effective, and we were having issues keeping the distribution list up to date," she says. Swanson and her production manager "looked at several different vendors and ended up doing two things: We took the magazine from being a typical film-executed, blueline-printed piece all the way to digital. At the same time, we switched to a printer that had in-house mailing capabilities," she says. "It was more advantageous to go digital because it was such a heavy-duty print job every month. And the mailing being 'in-house' was such an added plus for us."

The changes streamlined production and distribution, and alleviated the communication problem. In addition to its digital-printing capability, the new printer was "able to track much more precisely which of our magazines were not being delivered," says Swanson. "The new printer-mailer helped us set up a program where we tested the mailing list every year and adjusted it" to greatly reduce the number of returned magazines.

United States Postal Service

To ensure the most cost-effective and timely delivery of your publications, become acquainted with the policies and provisions of the USPS. Visit *www.usps.gov* for comprehensive information, services, and tools dedicated to efficient and economic business mailing.

Mailing Vendors

Mailing service companies can do your mailing for you. It's to your advantage to obtain estimates from several and ask that any costs quoted be detailed so that you can make fair comparisons.

A prime resource for locating vendors is the Mailing and Fulfillment Service Association (*www.mfsanet.org*). The MFSA recommends several considerations to help you choose a reliable company that's best suited to your project. For example, does the company serve organizations of your size and process similar types of mailings?

Free USPS Online Tools

- Direct mail campaign reference and tools
- Online ordering of the "Outsmart the Office" kit, including direct marketing results research, examples, and an ROI Estimator CD
- Letter and document mailing tools
- USPS standards for optimizing delivery time
- Postage rate tables and calculators
- Address verification for accurate mailing lists
- Online label and postage printing
- Online tracking and confirmation
- Online ordering of envelopes, boxes, forms, labels, scales, rubber stamps, stationery, and other supplies

Familiarize yourself with mailing industry trade customs. Read the fine print on the estimate or access the information on the MFSA's Web site. For example, be advised of this critical scheduling condition: "Mailer will make every reasonable effort to meet scheduled delivery and mailing date(s), but because of the many factors outside its control, accepts no liability for failure to meet scheduled date(s). In addition, mailers have no control over U.S. Postal Service, United Parcel Service or common carriers' delivery schedules and cannot guarantee when mail or shipments deposited with or released to these carriers will be delivered. The customer shall accept the date which mail or shipment were deposited with or released to these carriers as the date of delivery."

Also of note: If you choose to have a mail processing vendor maintain and update your distribution list for you, be sure to designate ownership of the data, restrict its use, and negotiate file access/transfer in the event you want to change vendors.

The Mail House Option

Typical mail house services include:

- Developing a mail list
- Data entry
- "Cleaning" your mail list—that is, editing entries for consistency and eliminating duplicate entries
- Processing your mail list with the USPS to get the lowest rate available for your particular mailing
- Giving you advice on your mailing options and helping you understand differences in price and delivery time
- Printing your mail pieces with automation barcodes and preparing them in presort order
- Providing an indicia, or permit imprint, that marks the mail as postage paid
- Creative/design
- Lettershop tasks, such as folding, tabbing (sealing with an adhesive wafer), inserting, labeling, metering, collating, sorting, addressing, and post office delivery
- Binding
- Warehousing
- List brokering
- Reports on ongoing/periodic mailings

Appendix A: Forms and Samples

Confidentiality and Nondisclosure Agreement

New Client Relationship Checklist

New Job Forms

Work Change Order Form

Schedule Time Frame Model

Schedule for a Rush Job

Newsletter Budget

Printing Bid Request and Estimate for Multiple Production Options

Printer Letter of Agreement

Printing Industries of Maryland Terms and Conditions

CONFIDENTIALITY AND NONDISCLOSURE AGREEMENT

WHEREAS, [YOUR NAME] agrees to furnish [NAME/BUSINESS] certain confidential information relating to ideas, inventions, or products for the purposes of determining an interest in developing, manufacturing, selling, and/or joint venturing.

WHEREAS, [NAME/BUSINESS] agrees to review, examine, inspect, or obtain such confidential information only for the purposes described above and to otherwise hold such information confidential pursuant to the terms of this agreement.

BE IT KNOWN that [YOUR NAME] has or shall furnish to [NAME/BUSINESS] certain confidential information and may further allow [NAME/BUSINESS] the right to discuss or interview representatives of [YOUR NAME] on the following conditions:

1. [NAME/BUSINESS] agrees to hold confidential or proprietary information or trade secrets ("confidential information") in trust and confidence and agrees that it shall be used only for the contemplated purposes, shall not be used for any other purpose, or disclosed to any third party.

2. No copies will be made or retained of any written information or prototypes supplied without the permission of [YOUR NAME].

3. At the conclusion of any discussions or upon demand by [YOUR NAME], all confidential information, including prototypes, photographs, sketches, models, memoranda, or written notes taken shall be returned to [YOUR NAME].

4. Confidential information shall not be disclosed to any employee, consultant, or third party unless they agree to execute and be bound by the terms of this agreement and have been approved by [YOUR NAME].

5. This agreement and its validity, construction, and effect shall be governed by the laws of [JURISDICTION].

AGREED AND ACCEPTED BY:

Date _____

By _____   Title _____

By _____   Title _____

Witness _____

NEW CLIENT RELATIONSHIP CHECKLIST

Work Scope
- Define scope of work to be produced under contract.

Presentations
- How many presentations are included in contract?

Project Team
- Who will be part of project team?
- How involved would client like to be in project?
  - _____ Very involved
  - _____ Somewhat involved
  - _____ Not involved
- How does client like to work and do business?
  - _____ By phone. When?
  - _____ In meetings. What are best days, times?
  - _____ By e-mail memo.

Decisions
- Who is the ultimate decision-maker?
  - _____ CEO/President _____
  - _____ Director of Marketing _____
  - _____ Other _____

Communication
- Open discussion critique and suggestions are necessary to ensure the best results for all parties.
- What is the desired level of record-keeping done by vendor?
  - _____ Phone update
  - _____ E-mail memo follow-up after each meeting

Proprietary Information
- Internal information and documents provided to vendor will be honored as confidential.
- Is a confidentiality/nondisclosure agreement required? _____

Financial
- Billing procedure: prompt payment; terms: 50 percent due to initiate work; balance upon delivery of completed work; 10 percent fee on expenses incurred by vendor; invoices occur on established dates.

- If work stops, vendor will invoice to date for work completed.
- Name of client's accounting representative _____
- Terms:
  - _____ Upon receipt of invoice
  - _____ Net 10, 30, 45
  - _____ PO required from client
  - _____ Finance charge will be applied to past-due invoices.

Change Orders
- Used for change in work scope.
- Change orders will be invoiced upon their occurrence and must be signed by client.
  - _____ Mailed
  - _____ Faxed
  - _____ E-mailed

Meetings
- Vendor will provide advance agendas.
- Location:
  - _____ On-site; travel time
  - _____ Conference call
  - _____ Video conference
- Meeting time charged by vendor.
- Additional cost for travel, long-distance phone and fax, express mail of meeting materials.

Schedules
- The first client meeting will be held on _____.
- Vendor will establish detailed schedules, including client review deadlines, with client input.
- Client failure to meet deadlines may impact timely delivery and cost; rush charges and overtime may apply.
- Change orders will require new schedule prepared by vendor, with client signature.
- Final proofing responsibility:
  - _____ Client
  - _____ Vendor

NEW JOB FORM ONE

Adapt this information intake form for your use. Include initial approximations of size, stock, colors, and other specifications, if known. This organization tool will help you outline the project needs and basic specs with your client. It also will keep important criteria in one place for easy reference.

Date _____   Working title _____

Department code _____   Original piece or revision _____

_____

Delivery date _____   Deliver to _____

_____

_____

Primary audience _____

Primary purpose _____

Secondary audience _____

Secondary purpose _____

Shelf-life _____

Other applications _____

Event-specific _____

Distribution method _____

Graphic precedence _____

Editorial precedence _____

Photography/illustration _____

Existing source or new assignment _____

Content sources _____

Interviews _____

Quantity _____   Initial/balance _____

Finished size _____   Flat size _____

Pages/panels _____   Folds/binding _____

Cover stock _____   Text stock _____

Printing _____   Separations _____

Packaging _____   Delivery method _____

M O N T E R E Y   B A Y   A Q U A R I U M M®

GRAPHIC DESIGN DEPARTMENT WORK ORDER

The Graphic Design Department creates and maintains a consistent brand identity across all departments and programs at the aquarium. The graphic design team will work closely with you to ensure all your project needs are met, while adhering to the established graphic standards and visual aesthetic of the aquarium.

PLEASE COMPLETE BOTH SIDES OF THIS WORK ORDER.

Project name: _____

Department: _____   Today's date: _____

Project coordinator/contact: _____   Phone extension: _____

Desired delivery date of printed pieces: _____   Quantity: _____

Bill to printing account #: ___ — ___ — ___ — ___   Budget: _____

Approvers: _____   Proofreaders: _____

_____   _____

_____   _____

DESCRIBE JOB: ○ New (please request launch meeting if applicable)   ○ Reprint with copy changes   ○ Reprint with no changes

What is the purpose of this piece? _____

_____

_____

_____

Who is the audience? _____

_____

_____

COMPONENTS

Is this part of a series? ○ Yes ○ No   Is this a package with multiple print pieces? ○ Yes ○ No

If so, please list all elements: _____

_____

Existing printed samples attached? ○ Yes ○ No   Will this piece be mailed? ○ Postcard ○ Envelope ○ Other

Is the text in MS Word file form? (Handwritten notes could result in typos or delays.)   ○ Yes   ○ No

Has the text been proofread and approved? (If not, changes will cause delays.)   ○ Yes   ○ No

Is final copy attached? (minor changes only after submitting to Graphic Design.)   ○ Yes   ○ No

....

DELIVERY INSTRUCTIONS

Name: _____   Phone: _____

Address: _____

....

WEB COMPONENT

Is all or part of this project going to be used on the aquarium's website?   ○ Yes*   ○ No

Please describe briefly how it will be used: _____

_____

* Web site use: If part of the project is going on the web site, contact the web team a minimum of 2 weeks in advance for existing projects and 4 weeks for new projects. You must license all photos and illustrations for web use in advance.

....

STEPS FOR SUCCESSFUL GRAPHIC DESIGN PROJECTS

1. Fill out the work order in full and submit a hard copy to the Graphic Design Department. (This form is also available on Tidepool under "Common Forms, Policies and Procedures.")

2. For new projects, schedule a launch meeting with the Art Director to be sure everyone understands the scope, budget, schedule and purpose of the new piece. This meeting is where you express to the design team what you're trying to achieve. The design team will share design options and ideas to ensure the printed piece will fit within the aquarium's established visual brand. Client input is welcome and encouraged, though decisions regarding graphic design are the final responsibility of the design team.

3. If the printed piece is part of an existing campaign or project, or is a revision or reprint, be sure to attach samples to the work order form. If there are any text changes, submit a proofed MS Word file.

4. Be sure all text is in MS Word and has been proofread and approved by the necessary approvers. Proofreading is your responsibility. Any text changes will result in delays or a missed deadline.

5. Use the sign-off sheet that accompanies each proof to be sure all the approvers sign off at every stage. Changes in copy and/or design late in the process can significantly delay a piece and affect the design process and its overall success.

6. To ensure your print pieces are completed and billed by year-end, be sure to submit your projects **no later than October 15.**

WORK CHANGE ORDER FORM

Work Change Order

Client _____ Date _____

Project _____ Project No. _____

Work Change Requested By _____

Stage of work

Sketches _____

Comps _____

Typesetting _____

Mechanicals _____

Prepress _____

Printing/Fabrication _____

Bluelines/Proofs _____

Other (explain) _____

_____

Content Change

Conceptual _____

Copy _____

Illustration _____

Photography _____

Specifications Change

Typography _____

Colors _____

Size _____

Pagination _____

Reproduction _____

Shipping _____

Other (explain) _____

Remarks _____

_____

_____

_____

_____

This is not an invoice. Revised specifications on work in progress represents information that is different from what the designer based the original project proposal. The following estimated charges in time and cost are approximate.

Estimated Additional Time _____

Estimated Additional Cost _____

Kindly sign and return a copy of this form. The information contained in this work change order is assumed to be correct and acceptable to the client unless the designer is otherwise notified in writing within _____ days of the date of this document.

Approved by _____ Date _____

SCHEDULE TIME FRAME MODEL

Here's a schedule model showing approximate time frames for process steps; some steps are conducted concurrently or within the same time frame. The publication has only a modest level of creative and production complexity. Specification and logistical points include:

- The piece is a new monthly newsletter for an external client: 8½" × 11" self-mailer, four-page self-cover, four-color.
- The writer is a freelancer who will conduct interviews.
- The designer is a freelancer.
- The freelance photographer is scheduled for a half-day, on-site shoot.
- The piece will be printed externally.
- The newsletter will be mailed from in-house to a national audience.

Initial client meeting . . . . 1 day

Proposal to client (overview of
design format, editorial, photos) . . . . . . 2 days

Client signoff . . . . 1 day

Assignment, schedule, and
meetings with writer, designer,
and photographer . . . . 1 week

Interviews and first draft,
first design template rough,
and photo shoot . . . . 1 week

Client creative signoff . . . . 2 days

Photo corrections; to designer . . . . 2 days

Second draft . . . . 3 days

Second draft review . . . . 1 day

Client signoff . . . . 2 days

Editorial to designer . . . . 1 day

First design layout . . . . 1 week

Layout review . . . . 1 day

Client signoff . . . . 2 days

Final design . . . . 2 days

Final design review . . . . 1 day

Client signoff . . . . 2 days

Final design changes; to printer . . . . . . 2 days

Printer proofs . . . . 3 days

Proofs review . . . . 1 day

Client signoff . . . . 1 day

Printing and delivery to client . . . . 1 week

SCHEDULE FOR A RUSH JOB

Less than two months were available for research, writing, design, production, and delivery of this theater program. The eight-page, full-color piece demanded heavy research and contained complex graphics and multiple photos, both provided by individuals and purchased from stock houses. This was definitely a rush job. Evening and weekend work was required from the start, and the schedule included some one-day and same-day deliveries.

This comprehensive schedule contains all of the creative and production process and review steps. Note that the document allows time for review of the schedule itself by the writer, designer, and client. Their input and approval helped ensure their commitment to turnaround times and therefore helped keep the challenging process on track.

One last point: Because the publications manager (PM), who served as editor, art director, and client liaison, worked on the East Coast and the freelancers operated in California, "A.M." and "P.M." (EST) were included for clarity of precise deadlines.

Project brief received from client	Wednesday, 2/22, A.M.
Proposal to client	Monday, 2/27, A.M.
Proposal approval by client	Thursday, 3/2, P.M.
Proposed schedule to writer and designer	Friday, 3/3, A.M.
Schedule response	Saturday, 3/4, P.M.
Schedule to client	Monday, 3/6, A.M.
Any schedule changes from client	Monday, 3/6, P.M.
First draft from writer	Friday, 3/10, A.M.
First draft comments from PM	Saturday, 3/11, A.M.
Second draft from writer	Tuesday, 3/14, A.M.
Draft with final PM comments to client and writer	Tuesday, 3/14, P.M.
Draft comments from client	Friday, 3/17, A.M.
Changes incorporated and draft to designer	Friday, 3/17, P.M.

First layout from designer	Wednesday, 3/22, A.M.
First layout comments from PM	Wednesday, 3/22, P.M.
Second layout from designer	Monday, 3/27, A.M.
Design with final PM comments to client and designer	Tuesday, 3/28, A.M.
Client design changes	Friday, 3/31, A.M.
Final design from designer	Monday, 4/3, A.M.
PM final design review and back to designer to prepare files and send to printer	Monday, 4/3, P.M.
Printer proofs to reviewers	Monday, 4/10, A.M.
Corrected proofs to printer	Tuesday, 4/11, A.M.
Programs to client	Monday, 4/17, A.M.

NEWSLETTER BUDGET

Here's a sample of a basic budget with a listing of individual tasks, personnel, hourly rates, times, and costs. This is a simple way of outlining and filling in your budget from scratch.

The job was a new quarterly newsletter for which a masthead and template needed to be designed. The size was 17" × 11" flat, four pages. An order form was printed separately and inserted into the self-mailer before folding and sealing with an adhesive wafer. The piece was printed in two colors.

TASK AND FEE	DESCRIPTION	TIME (total hours)	COST (total $)
Research, Publications Manager (PM) ($50/hour)	Meeting with client	1	50
Supervision (PM)	Designer, writer, printer	8	400
Client presentations (PM)	Two design meetings, one draft meeting	3	150
Design ($40/hour)	Masthead and grid	10	400
	3.5 pages at 2 hours per page	7	280
Writing ($40/hour)	3.5 pages at 2 hours per page	7	280
Proofing (PM)	Final proof and blueline	2	100
Printing (blueline included)	5M 2/2 newsletters		1,117
	5M 1/1 order forms		237
Handling	Trim, insert form, fold, attach wafer		465
		TOTAL	$3,479

PRINTING BID REQUEST AND ESTIMATE FOR MULTIPLE PRODUCTION OPTIONS

If you need a budget range for planning at an early phase of your project, you can save time for you and your printer's estimating department by exploring in advance all the possible quantities and print configurations on which you may ultimately decide.

Here's an example of a job for which the client had not decided on quantities or the number of publications that would need to print by the same deadline and that could be run together. By supplying all possible scenarios to the printer from the start, estimates for various production options could be prepared once. Because of the close and regular working relationship of the vendor and client, the estimates were simply hand-written at the bottom of the spec sheet and faxed back to the client.

DATE	11/17/05
TO	Lisa Brocato
FROM	Alexis Disipio
TOPIC	New Project Estimates

Hi, Lisa. Following are specs for three private-label projects that may be ready to run all together next month; at least one project will be. Please call me if you have any questions. Estimates by Monday, 11/27, would be appreciated.

Slug:	Product inserts (3 different projects)
Description:	4/C process bifold booklets to insert into clear acrylic hanging bags
Size:	Flat 6" × 5¾", finished 3" × 5¾"
Stock:	70# Springhill text white smooth
Printing:	4/2: 4/C process cover with approx. 2½" square separation; 2/C text inside
Quantity:	Please price an individual job, 2-up, and 3-up in these quantities: 2.5M, 6M, 12M, 14.5M
Handling:	Print, trim, and fold

(Printer's estimates supplied on bid request sheet.)

Individual		**2 booklets**		**3 booklets**	
2,500	$ 972	2,500 of 2	$1,145	2,500 of 3	$1,293
6,000	$1,062	6,000 of 2	$1,293	6,000 of 3	$1,561
12,000	$1,210	12,000 of 2	$1,596	12,000 of 3	$1,971
14,500	$1,279	14,5000 of 2	$1,722	14,500 of 3	$2,153

PRINTER LETTER OF AGREEMENT

If you have a long-term or multiproject relationship with a printer, you can draft a single umbrella letter of agreement that spells out conditions that apply to each job. Here's an example of an agreement prepared by a client for ongoing work with a printer-box maker. Note that it addresses the needs and interests of both parties and that several industry standards have been renegotiated.

Letter of Agreement

This document confirms in writing points about the professional relationship between Client and Vendor for work executed and delivered.

Reviews and Schedules

Client and Vendor will communicate frequently to agree on ongoing press proof review times and delivery dates of new and reprint Client packaging throughout the calendar year. Appropriate individuals will meet to design schedules, and to evaluate and improve communication and art-transfer processes as needed.

Quality of Product

Product design. Vendor will prepare box samples and prepress proofs with direction from Client. Box samples must exhibit all characteristics of finished pieces and perform as finished pieces as precisely as possible. Any potential divergence from samples to finished pieces and the impact (such as hand- versus machine-scoring, the potential for bowing, and placement of gluing) must be explained by Vendor and meet Client's needs before signoff. Opportunities for improvement will be communicated among appropriate parties as needed. Satisfactory samples and proofs will be dated and signed by Client and will constitute acceptance for production.

Cracking and other material-related problems. Recognizing that variation in materials is natural and some minor cracking may occur, Vendor will check product frequently, including test-folding, during the production process and will notify Client if significant problems occur before proceeding. Client will not accept product that does not meet basic quality standards agreed upon, whether due to a production problem, improper packing, or improper storage by Vendor. Client reserves the right to reject unsatisfactory product regardless of when the unacceptable items are discovered (e.g., in the case of the initial partial delivery of a job and the subsequent delivery of the balance of the job). Vendor will be responsible for reproducing unacceptable and/or damaged goods in their entirety when needed by Client (see "Delivery and Storage").

Color. Recognizing that because variation in materials and processes is natural, some variation in color may occur. Vendor will check product frequently during printing to ensure color accuracy, to minimize uneven color coverage due to the nature of the materials, and to maintain consistent color throughout a printing run as much as possible. Vendor will notify Client if significant problems occur before proceeding. Client will be available for press checks as much as possible for new jobs and only as needed for reprints.

Delivery and Storage

Vendor will deliver the agreed-upon amount of Client packaging product on the agreed-upon date. Payment for the entire quantity will be due according to terms (see "Payment") after initial partial delivery. Freight will be F.O.B.

Baltimore. Vendor will store the balance amount. Client will call with balance delivery dates as needed. Client will not be charged for storage for six months or less after initial partial delivery. After that the rate will be $5.50 per pallet per month. Total delivered and stored packaging for each product must meet the quantity ordered; no unders can be allowed. To ensure this, Client will accept and pay for up to a 6% overrun on Client product and will accept and pay for up to a 3% overrun on private-label product at the quoted unit cost. If a delivery is short, the quantity not delivered must be produced when needed by Client at the original total quantity's unit cost. Client will make every effort to coordinate any makeup printing to Vendor's scheduling and cost benefit, but this may not always be possible. Vendor will supply an inventory report upon request. Because the age of the stock affects its properties, Vendor cannot guarantee that product will not crack after one year from date of initial partial delivery.

Prices

Vendor will hold prices quoted (attached) through the end of the calendar year except for stock. Costs for stock may fluctuate depending on suppliers. Vendor will make efforts to minimize or avoid cost increases as possible and will notify Client of stock price increases approximately 60 (sixty) days in advance and of stock price decreases. Client will pay for stock at the new price. Quarterly, Client and Vendor will meet to discuss forthcoming jobs and projections for paperboard needs.

Payment

Client will pay in full for packaging delivered and stored according to net 30 terms. Client has the option to pay net 10 for a 2% discount on a case-by-case basis. Vendor will alert Client to any costs beyond the attached prices before work is done for each printing job.

Ownership

Client will own all dies, film, and other materials associated with the printing of ordered packaging. If necessary at any time, Vendor will deliver these materials to Client undamaged, clearly organized and labeled, and in their entirety.

Review

Each fourth quarter Client will review service, communication, delivery, and product produced by Vendor. Each year a new letter of agreement will be developed.

_____   _____
Client Representative   Date

_____   _____
Vendor Representative   Date

General Terms & Conditions of Sale

1. Quotations/Estimates

A quotation not accepted within 30 days may be changed.

2. Orders

Acceptance of orders is subject to credit approval and contingencies such as fire, water, strikes, theft, vandalism, act of God, and other causes beyond the provider's control. Canceled orders require compensation for incurred costs and related obligations.

3. Experimental Work

Experimental or preliminary work performed at the customer's request will be charged to the customer at the provider's current rates. This work may not be used without the provider's written consent.

4. Creative Work

Sketches, copy, dummies, and all other creative work developed or furnished by the provider are the provider's exclusive property. The provider must give written approval for all use of this work and for any derivation of ideas from it.

5. Accuracy of Specifications

Quotations are based on the accuracy of the specifications provided. The provider can requote a job at the time of submission if copy, film, tapes, disks, or other input materials do not conform to the information on which the original quotation was based.

6. Venue

In the event of suit regarding this contract, then venue and jurisdiction therefore shall be in either the Superior or Municipal Court, as appropriate, of the County of (*insert name*), Maryland (*or other state*). The parties agree and stipulate that the essential terms of this contract are to be performed in said County.

7. Electronic Manuscripts/Images

It is the customer's responsibility to maintain a copy of the original file. The provider is not responsible for accidental damage to media supplied by the customer or for the accuracy of furnished input or final input. Until digital input can be evaluated by the provider, no claims or promises are made about the provider's ability to work with jobs submitted in digital format, and no liability is assumed for problems that may arise. Any additional translating, editing, or programming needed to utilize customer-supplied files will be charged at prevailing rates.

8. Alterations/Corrections

Customer alterations include all work performed in addition to the original specifications. All such work will be charged at the provider's current rates.

9. Preparatory Material

Artwork, type, plates, negatives, positives, tapes, disks, and other items supplied by the provider shall remain the provider's exclusive property.

10. Prepress Proofs

The provider will submit prepress proofs along with original copy for the customer's review and approval. Corrections will be returned to the provider on a "master set" marked "O.K.," "O.K. With Corrections" or "Revised Proof Required" and signed by the customer. Until the master set is received, no additional work will be performed. The provider will not be responsible for undetected production errors if:
• Proofs are not required by the customer
• The work is printed per the customer's OK
• Requests for changes are communicated verbally

11. Press Proofs

Press proofs will not be furnished unless they have been required in writing in the provider's quotation. A press sheet can be submitted for the customer's approval as long as the customer is present at the press during make-ready. Any press time lost or alterations/corrections made because of the customer's delay or change of mind will be charged at the provider's current rates.

12. Color Proofing

Because of differences in equipment, paper, inks, and other conditions between color proofing and production pressroom operations, a reasonable variation in color between color proofs and the completed job is to be expected. When a variation of this kind occurs, it will be considered acceptable performance.

13. Overruns/Underruns

Overruns or underruns will not exceed 10% of the quantity ordered. The provider will bill for the actual quantity delivered within this tolerance. If the customer requires a guaranteed quantity, the percentage of tolerance must be stated at the time of quotation.

14. Customer's Property

The provider will only maintain fire and extended coverage on property belonging to the customer while the property is in the provider's possession. The provider's liability for such property will not exceed the amount recoverable from the insurance. Additional insurance coverage may be obtained if it is requested in writing and if the premium is paid to the provider.

15. Delivery

Unless otherwise specified, the price quoted is for a single shipment, without storage, F.O.B. the provider's platform. Proposals are based on continuous and uninterrupted delivery of the complete order. If the specifications state otherwise, the provider will charge accordingly at current rates. Charges for delivery of materials and supplies from the customer to the provider or from the customer's supplier to the provider are not included in quotations unless specified. Title for finished work passes to the customer upon delivery to the carrier at the shipping point or upon mailing of invoices for the finished work or a portion thereof, whichever occurs first.

16. Production Schedules

Production schedules will be established and followed by both the customer and the provider. There will be no liability or penalty for delays due to a state of war, riot, civil disorder, fire, strikes, accidents, action of government or civil authority, acts of God, or other cases beyond the control of the provider. In such cases, schedules will be extended by an amount of time equal to the delay incurred.

17. Customer-Furnished Materials

Materials furnished by customers or their suppliers are verified by delivery tickets. The provider bears no responsibility for discrepancies between delivery tickets and actual counts. Customer supplied paper must be delivered according to specifications furnished by the provider. These specifications will include correct weight, thickness, pick resistance, and other technical requirements. Artwork, film, color separations, special dies, tapes, disks, or other materials furnished by the customer must be usable by the provider without alteration or repair. Items not meeting this requirement will be repaired by the customer or by the provider at the provider's current rates.

18. Outside Purchases

Unless otherwise agreed in writing, all outside purchases as requested or authorized by the customer, are chargeable.

19. Terms/Claims/Liens

Payment is cash in advance or whatever has been agreed to between customer and provider. Claims for defects, damages, or shortages must be made by the customer in writing no later than 10 calendar days after delivery. If no such claim is made, the provider and the customer will understand that the job has been accepted. By accepting the job, the customer acknowledges that the provider's performance has fully satisfied all terms, conditions, and specifications.

The provider's liability will be limited to the quoted selling price of defective goods without additional charge for special or consequential damages. As security for payment of any sum due under the terms of an agreement, the provider has the right to hold and place a lien on all customer property in the provider's possession. This right applies even if credit has been extended, notes have been accepted, trade acceptances have been made, or payment has been guaranteed. If payment is not made, the customer is liable for all collection costs incurred.

20. Liability

(1) Disclaimer of Express Warranties. The provider warrants that the work is as described in the purchase order. The customer understands that all sketches, copy, dummies, and preparatory work shown to the customer are intended only to illustrate the general type and quality of the work. They are not intended to represent the actual work performed.

(2) Disclaimer of Implied Warranties. The Provider warrants only that the work will conform to the description contained in the purchase order. The provider's maximum liability, whether by negligence, contract, or otherwise, will not exceed the return of the amount invoiced for the work in the dispute. Under no circumstances will the provider be liable for specific, individual, or consequential damages.

21. Indemnification

The customer agrees to protect the provider from economic loss and any other harmful consequences that might arise in connection with the work. This means the customer will hold the provider harmless and save, indemnify, and otherwise defend the provider against claims, demands, actions, and proceedings on any and all grounds.

(1) Copyrights. The customer also warrants that the subject matter to be printed is not copyrighted by a third party. The customer also recognizes that because subject matter does not have to bear a copyright notice to be protected by copyright law, absence of such notice does not necessarily assure a right to reproduce. The customer further warrants that no copyright notice has been removed from any material used in preparing the subject matter for reproduction. To support these warranties, the customer agrees to indemnify and hold the provider harmless for all liability, damages, and attorney fees that may be incurred in any legal action connected with copyright infringement involving the work produced or provided.

(2) Personal or Economic Rights. The customer also warrants that the work does not contain anything that is libelous or scandalous or anything that threatens anyone's right to privacy or other personal or economic rights. The customer will, at the customer's sole expense, promptly and thoroughly defend the provider in all legal actions on these grounds as long as the provider:
• Promptly notifies the customer of legal action.
• Gives the customer reasonable time to undertake and conduct a defense. The provider reserves the right to use its sole discretion in refusing to print anything the provider deems libelous, scandalous, improper, or infringing on copyright law.

22. Storage

The provider will retain intermediate materials used until the related end product has been accepted by the customer. If requested by the customer, intermediate materials will be stored for an additional period at an additional charge. The provider is not liable for any loss or damage to stored material beyond what is recoverable by the provider's fire and extended insurance coverage.

23. Taxes

All taxes and assessments levied by any governmental authority are the responsibility of the customer. All amounts due for taxes and assessments will be added to the customer's invoice. No tax exemption will be granted unless the customer's "Exemption Certificate" (or other official proof of exemption) accompanies the purchase order. If, after the customer has paid the invoice, it is determined that more tax is due, then the customer must promptly remit the required taxes to the taxing authority or immediately reimburse the provider for any additional taxes paid.

24. Telecommunications

Unless otherwise agreed, the customer will pay for all transmission charges. The provider is not responsible for any errors, omissions, or extra costs resulting from faults in transmission.

2045 York Road, Timonium, Maryland 21093 • 800-560-3306 • pim@printmd.com • www.printmd.com

Appendix B: Professional and Educational Resources

COMMUNICATIONS, MARKETING, AND MEDIA

American Marketing Association, *www.marketingpower.com*

Association for Women in Communications, *www.womcom.org*

Business Marketing Association, *www.marketing.org*

Corporate Communication Institute, *www.corporatecomm.org*

Insurance Marketing Communication Association, *www.imcanet.org*

International Association of Business Communicators, *www.iabc.com*

Media Bistro, *www.mediabistro.com*

National Investor Relations Institute, *www.niri.org*

Public Relations Society of America, *www.prsa.org*

Publishers Marketplace, *www.publishersmarketplace.com*

Sinickas Communications, *www.sinicom.com*, an international consulting firm specializing in measuring the effectiveness of organizational communication

The Story Board, *www.thestoryboard-llc.com*, a provider of editorial content to employee communication programs, with an international network of business journalists and graphic artists

Swanson Communications Consulting, *www.swansoncomm.com*, a corporate communications and public relations consulting firm specializing in change management

Target Marketing, *www.targetmarketingmag.com*

DESIGN

American Institute for Graphic Arts (AIGA), *www.aiga.org*

Association of Professional Design Firms, *www.apdf.org*

Business and Legal Forms for Graphic Designers, Tad Crawford and Eva Doman Bruck, Allworth Press

Communication Arts, *www.commarts, com*

Creative Business™, *www.creativebusiness.com*

Design Management Institute (DMI), *www.dmi.org*

Emily Ruth Cohen, *www.emilycohen.com*, consultant to creative firms and in-house creative departments, specializing in implementing effective staff, project and studio management, client and vendor relationships, client surveys, and proposals and contracts

Folio, www.foliomag.com

Graphic Artists Guild, *www.gag.org*

The Graphic Artists Guild Handbook: Pricing and Ethical Guidelines, Graphic Artists Guild

Graphic Arts Monthly, www.gammag.com

The Graphic Design Business Book, Tad Crawford with the Graphic Artists Guild, Allworth Press

The Graphic Professionals Resource Network, *www.iaphc.org*

Graphis, www.graphis.com

HOW, www.howdesign.com

I.D., The International Design Magazine, idonline.com

InSource, *www.in-source.org*, an association of in-house corporate creatives

The Society of Publication Designers, *www.spd.org*

FEATURED DESIGN FIRMS

50,000feet, Inc., *www.50000feet.com*

And Partners, New York City, *www.andpartnersny.com*

BBK Studio, *www.bbkstudio.com*

Cahan & Associates, *www.cahanassociates.com*

Commercial Artisan, *www.commercialartisan.com*

de.MO, *www.de-mo.org*

Evins Design, *www.evinsdesign.com*

f2design, *www.f2-design.com*

Hambly & Woolley, Inc., *www.hamblywoolley.com*

HENDERSONBROMSTEADART, *www.hendersonbromsteadart.com*

Hornall Anderson Design, *www.hadw.com*

Howry Design Associates, *www.howry.com*

Kinimod, Inc., *www.kinimodinc.com*

The Kirwan Company, Inc., 818-985-2265

Kuhlmann Leavitt, Inc., *www.kuhlmannleavitt.com*

Lippincott Mercer, *www.lippincottmercer.com*

Mizrahi Design Associates, *www.mizrahidesign.com*

Monterey Bay Aquarium Graphic Design Department, *www.mbayaq.org*

nFusion Group, *www.nfusion.com*

Pentagram Design, *www.pentagram.com*

Ph.D, *www.phdla.com*

Rutka Weadock Design, *www.rutkaweadock.com*

Salsgiver Coveney Associates, *www.salsgivercoveney.com*

SamataMason, Inc., *www.samatamason.com*

Sandstrom Design, Inc., *www.sandstromdesign.com*

Vanderbyl Design, *www.vanderbyl.com*

Werner Design Werks, Inc., *www.wdw.com*

Widgets & Stone, *www.widgetsandstone.com*

Wink Design, *winkdesign.com*

zig, www.*zigideas.com*

WRITING AND PUBLISHING

American Society of Journalists and Authors, *www.asja.org*

The Authors Guild, *www.authorsguild.org*

Business and Legal Forms for Authors and Self-Publishers, Tad Crawford, Allworth Press

The Chicago Manual of Style: The Essential Guide for Writers, Editors, and Publishers, University of Chicago Press Staff

The Copyright Guide: A Friendly Handbook to Protecting and Profiting from Copyrights, Lee Wilson, Allworth Press

Editorial Freelancers Association, *www.the-efa.org*

The Elements of Style, William Strunk Jr., E.B. White, and Roger Angell, Allyn & Bacon

Fair Use, Free Use, and Use by Permission: How to Handle Copyrights in All Media, Lee Wilson, Allworth Press

Freelance Writers' Guide, National Writers Union

National Writers Union, *www.nwu.org*

The Oxford Guide to Style, R.M. Ritter, Oxford University Press

Words into Type, Marjorie E. Skillin and Robert Malcolm Gay, Pearson P T R

The Writer's Legal Guide: An Authors Guild Desk Reference, Tad Crawford and Kay Murray, Allworth Press

PHOTOGRAPHY AND ILLUSTRATION

American Society of Media Photographers (ASMP), *www.asmp.org*

ASMP Professional Business Practices in Photography, American Society of Media Photographers

Business and Legal Forms for Photographers, Tad Crawford, Allworth Press

Business and Legal Forms for Illustrators, Tad Crawford, Allworth Press

folioplanet.com, *www.folioplanet.com,* including illustration ArtistFinder™ and StockFinder™

The I Spot, *www.theispot.com,* illustration portfolio database

PhotoGraphicLibraries, *www.photographiclibraries.com,* directory of stock, photographers, agencies, archives, free art, and more

Pricing Photography: The Complete Guide to Assignment and Stock Prices, Michal Heron and David MacTavish, Allworth Press

Society of Illustrators, *www.societyillustrators.org*

PRINTING AND DISTRIBUTION

American Printer magazine, *www.americanprinter.com*

Digital Imaging magazine, *www.digitalimagingmag.com*

Goetz Printing Co., *www.goetzprinting.com*

Mailing and Fulfillment Service Association, *www.mfsanet.org*

Print, www.printmag.com

Printing Industries of America and local chapters, see Graphic Arts Information Network, *www.gain.net*

Index

Books from Allworth Press

Allworth Press is an imprint of Allworth Communications, Inc. Selected titles are listed below.

The Elements of Graphic Design: Space, Unity, Page Architecture, and Type
by Alex W. White (paperback, 6⅛ × 9¼, 160 pages, $24.95)

Designing Effective Communications: Creating Contexts for Clarity and Meaning
edited by Jorge Frascara (paperback, 6 × 9, 304 pages, $24.95)

Communication Design: Principles, Methods, and Practices
by Jorge Frascara (paperback, 6 × 9, 240 pages, $24.95)

Editing by Design, Third Edition
by Jan V. White (paperback, 8½ × 11, 256 pages, $29.95)

Graphic Idea Notebook: A Treasury of Solutions to Visual Problems, Third Edition
by Jan V. White (paperback, 8½ × 11, 176 pages, $24.95)

The Graphic Designer's Guide to Clients: How to Make Clients Happy and Do Great Work
by Ellen Shapiro (paperback, 6 × 9, 256 pages, $19.95)

Design Management: Using Design to Build Brand Value and Corporate Innovation
by Brigitte Borja de Mozota (paperback, 6 × 9, 288 pages, $24.95)

Business and Legal Forms for Graphic Designers, Third Edition
by Tad Crawford and Eva Doman Bruck (paperback, with CD-ROM, 8½ × 11, 160 pages, $29.95)

The Graphic Designer's Guide to Better Business Writing
by Barbara Janoff and Ruth Cash-Smith (paperback, 6 × 9, 288 pages, $19.95)

The Graphic Design Business Book
by Tad Crawford (paperback, 6 × 9, 256 pages, $24.95)

Inside the Business of Graphic Design: 60 Leaders Share Their Secrets of Success
by Catharine Fishel (paperback, 6 × 9, 288 pages, $19.95)

To request a free catalog or order books by credit card, call 1-800-491-2808. To see our complete catalog on the World Wide Web, or to order online for a 20 percent discount, you can find us at ***www.allworth.com***.